THE COSTS OF WELFARE

The Costs of Welfare

Edited by
NICHOLAS DEAKIN
ROBERT PAGE

Avebury

Aldershot · Brookfield USA · Hong Kong · Singapore · Sydney

Published by
Avebury
Ashgate Publishing Limited
Gower House
Croft Road
Aldershot
Hants GU11 3HR
England

Ashgate Publishing Company
Old Post Road
Brookfield
Vermont 05036
USA

British Library Cataloguing in Publication Data
Costs of Welfare
    I. Deakin, Nicholas II. Page, Robert
    361.941

Reprinted 1994

Typeset by
Jo Clark
School of Social Studies
University of Nottingham

ISBN 1 85628 513 8

Printed and Bound in Great Britain by
Athenaeum Press Ltd, Gateshead, Tyne & Wear.

Contents

Social Policy Association

The Social Policy Association was founded in 1967 as the Social Administration Association. It brings together teachers, researchers, practitioners and students of social policy and administration. Its members include academics and students in universities, colleges and schools, as well as other practitioners of social policy. Its object is to encourage teaching, research and scholarship in social policy and administration.

Publications

The Journal of Social Policy

The SPA's major intellectual activity is the publication, with the Cambridge University Press, of the Journal of Social Policy. It is a leading international journal with a world wide circulation and the most authoritative journal on the subject in the United Kingdom. The Journal of Social Policy is published quarterly and full members of the SPA receive copies free. An elected editorial board is responsible for the Journal's content.

Social Policy Review

Since 1992 the Association has also assumed full responsibility for the commissioning, publication and distribution of the Social Policy Review (formerly published by Routledge and Longmans under the title of the Year book of Social Policy. The most recent issues are N.Manning and R.Page (Eds) (1992) *Social Policy Review 4* (ISBN 0-9518895-0-8) and R.Page and J.Baldock (Eds) (1993), *Social Policy Review 5 : The Evolving State of Welfare* (ISBN 0-9518895-1-6). Copies of the Review can be obtained from Denyse Menne, Social Policy Office, Darwin College, University of Kent, Canterbury, Kent CT2 7NY.

Newsletter

The SPA also publishes a Newsletter three times a year to keep members in touch with current events such as lectures, seminars and conferences.

Membership

Membership of the Social Policy Association is open to both individuals and organisations. Full details can be obtained from the Membership Secretary, Francis McGlone, Family Policy Studies Centre, 231 Baker Street, London NW1 6XE.

Contributors

John Clarke   Senior Lecturer in Social Policy, The Open University.

Gary Craig   Senior Lecturer in Social Policy, University of Humberside.

Bleddyn Davies   Director, Personal Social Services Research Unit (PSSRU), University of Kent.

Nicholas Deakin   Professor of Social Policy & Administration, University of Birmingham.

John Ditch   Assistant Director, Social Policy Research Unit (SPRU), University of York.

Monica Dowling   Lecturer in Social Policy, University of Sheffield.

Caroline Glendinning   Senior Research Fellow, Department of Social Policy and Social Work, University of Manchester.

Howard Glennerster   Professor of Social Administration, London School of Economics.

Rachel Lart

Research Associate, School for Advanced Urban Studies (SAUS), University of Bristol.

Julian Le Grand

Richard Titmuss Professor of Health Policy, London School of Economics.

Robin Means

Senior Lecturer, School for Advanced Urban Studies (SAUS), University of Bristol.

Janet Newman

Lecturer in Strategy and Public Policy, Institute of Local Government Studies (INLOGOV), University of Birmingham.

Robert Page

Lecturer in Social Policy and Administration, University of Nottingham.

Richard Parry

Lecturer in Social Policy, University of Edinburgh.

Roland Petchey

Lecturer, Department of General Practice, University of Nottingham.

Clare Ungerson

Professor of Social Policy, University of Southampton.

Tables and diagrams

TABLES

DIAGRAMS

Acknowledgements

The editors would like to thank a number of people for their assistance with this publication in direct and indirect ways.

Jo Clark for producing the camera ready copy manuscript in her usual immaculate fashion despite having to deal with countless corrections and alterations.

Angus Erskine, whose enthusiasm and support during his period of office as Secretary of the SPA was instrumental in redirecting the publishing strategy of the Association.

Jo Gooderham of Ashgate Publishing for her support and encouragement with this venture.

Pat Marks of Ashgate Publishing for help and advice with a steady stream of editorial queries.

Jude Warrior, Karen Harrison and all other helpers at the 26th Social Policy Association Annual Conference at the University of Nottingham, July 1992.

The editors and publishers wish to thank the following who have kindly given permission to use copyright material:

Her Majesty's Stationary Office for Tables 5.1 and 5.2.

Office for Official Publications of the European Communities for Table 2.1.

Preface

Since its inception in 1967 The Social Policy Association has held an annual conference. Recent conference themes have included **Theory and Social Policy** (1981), **Social Security and Insecurity** (1985), and **New Agendas for Social Policy: From the 1980s to the 1990s** (1990). The papers presented at SPA conferences have not tended to be published in collected form. However, a selection of the papers presented at the 1990 Conference were published by SAUS in 1991 under the editorship of Graham Room (*Towards a European Welfare State?*). Following the success of that book it was decided to explore the possibility of publishing a selection of the papers presented at the 26th Annual conference at Nottingham in 1992, which was on the topical theme of **Paying for Welfare**. Jo Gooderham at Ashgate publishing responded favourably to an outline proposal and this volume is the end product.

The social policy community has always taken a keen interest in the 'costs' of welfare though it would be fair to conclude that for much of the post 1945 period there was a tendency to assume that increased expenditure was inherently 'progressive'. As Wilding (1992) notes, 'With all the wisdom of hindsight it is odd how seldom basic questions were asked about welfare programmes in the 1950s, 1960s and 1970s - What is the precise aim of the programme? What is it costing? What are the outcomes? State welfare was thought to be self evidently good. There was no attempt to develop appropriate definitions of efficiency and effectiveness.' (pp.12-13). The failure to give detailed consideration to the question of whether prevailing practices and procedures were delivering 'value for money' can be explained in part by the fact that a sustained period of economic growth limited the need to make painful choices about welfare expenditure. The faltering performance of the British economy in the 1970s ended the golden era of state welfare expansion. Since the mid 1970s more emphasis has been given to questions of preserving, or even paring back, existing services. In such a climate it is not surprising to find that the 'two E's' (effectiveness and efficiency) have come to the top of the policy making agenda - a position they are likely to retain even if the economic outlook were to improve dramatically. This is due in part to the resurgence of anti-collectivist ideas in the 1970s and 80s. The portrayal of the welfare state as an inefficient, producer driven institution which failed to meet the needs of citizens gained a degree of acceptance which served to undermine the collectivist case. Moreover, advocates of anti-collectivism found that their erstwhile opponents (i.e. dyed in the wool unitarists) were not only more circumspect (the persistence of poverty and homelessness and the continuation of class, race and gender inequalities had been a chastening experience) but also thinner on the ground (many had defected to the welfare pluralist camp).

The old welfare consensus (which may in any event have been much less pronounced than is commonly assumed - Raison (1990) no longer operates with the result that fundamental questioning about the role and purpose of state welfare is more commonplace as are discussions about legitimate needs, priorities, regulation and service delivery. These are just the sorts of questions that those engaged in the study of social policy and administration are best able to answer - as the contributors to the collection amply demonstrate. However, it can no longer be assumed that the answers put forward will be underpinned by an explicit or implicit form of Fabianism (Beilharz, 1992). As Pinker (1993) has argued elsewhere, there now exist a far more diverse set of value positions within the field. Indeed, some have attempted to avoid the charge of partisanship by assuming the mantle of disinterested policy analyst. The growth of the latter may be welcomed by some on the grounds it demonstrates a commendable degree of professional detachment and open mindedness. However, it should be noted that if too many of those engaged in the study of social policy and administration opt for the role of charting and analysing welfare developments rather than championing the interests of the disadvantaged then the subject will have lost something of incalculable worth.

Robert Page

Introduction: The costs of welfare – An overview

Nicholas Deakin and Robert Page

Current notions about the cost of welfare - more particularly, the cost of procuring, delivering, receiving and purchasing welfare - come freighted with the burden of innumerable past debates. This is especially true at a time, like the present, of such rapid change. In the melee of ideas thrown up recently there can be found the relics of Victorian concepts of accountability and control of public finances - and the means employed to that end (regulation and inspection); and the pale lingering ghost of the division between cash and care whose maintenance once seemed of such fundamental importance. By contrast, the divisions of welfare first charted by Richard Titmuss (1958) thirty years ago loom steadily larger as factors determining the distribution of costs and benefits.

The changing economic context of welfare policy also brings more reminders of past assumptions: the concept of a 'dividend of growth' which would painlessly fund increases in expenditure on welfare, so long taken heedlessly for granted; and its successor and polar opposite, the presumed 'burden' of welfare spending, latterly seen as an equally inevitable phenomenon. Some of yesterday's short cuts to solutions survive, though their form is strangely changed: vouchers for one, but without the simplicity they possessed when they took pride of place on the Institute of Economic Affairs' policy agenda. Charging for welfare (another IEA favourite) is another. Faced with all these tangled strands, the temptation is to pass a hasty verdict on current developments in terms often attributed to Gramsci but more elegantly expressed by Matthew Arnold many years before him: that in social policy we are 'wandering between two worlds, one dead, the other powerless to be born' (Quoted in Collini (1993 p. 243).

But there is every sign that the new world is already upon us; it is even possible to date with some precision the moment of accouchement. As Howard Glennerster argues in this collection (and elsewhere) the Conservative Government's social legislation of 1988/9 marks a watershed. Not just in terms of its content; the changes made in the structure of services and style of delivery in health, education and social services link with a broader agenda about the purpose and functioning of the public sector as a whole. The working through of this agenda began with the introduction of the Financial Management Initiative (FMI) in central government and the creation of the Audit Commission as a device to impose parallel changes in the operating culture of local authorities. The process gathered speed with the creation of the Next Steps Agencies and the division that this has created within Whitehall between policy making and implementation. This can now be seen in full flower with the putting in place of what John Stewart (1993) has christened the 'new magistracy'; a layer of all-purpose, non-elected government appointed and (generously) funded by and directly accountable to Ministers.

In the circumstances, it is hardly surprising that Ministers should have celebrated the tenth anniversary of Audit Commission with such gusto or that William Waldegrave should talk about a 'revolution' in government: the face of public administration in Britain will certainly never be the same - especially given the marked absence of any disposition on the part of the Opposition to reverse the process. Only the very centre remains untouched by it: so far from the Cabinet contemplating any devolution of responsibility, the process of gathering in of power and authority (though rarely accountability for its exercise) has continued unchecked over the past decade in all policy areas. And in the economic sphere the Treasury, that fat old spider lurking with undiminished appetite at the centre of the public policy web, adamantly declines, as a recent Chancellor has put it, to place any of its responsibilities in public finance 'in commission' (Lawson, 1992). Conflict between the devolved managerialism of the new style of governance, with its splitting up and passing down of the executive functions of public agencies, often outside the public sector altogether and the Treasury's persistent claim to exercise continued close control over the totality (as well as the detail) of expenditure seems inevitable. At the least, it will be a central feature of policy debates over the next few years. The urgency of that debate is bound to be sharpened by the impact of the longest recession of the postwar period, which has already provoked the present Chief Secretary, Michael Portillo, into announcing a no-holds-barred review of public expenditure across the whole range of Government activity.

Meanwhile, what we have in social policy, in particular, is a patchwork. Progress into the new operating environment has been more rapid in some areas than others; the new culture has taken hold in many of the mainstream areas but has left spaces: patches of resistance where an older culture of public service is still holding out in social policy Tobruks; others where professional providers still call the shots. However, their territory too is shrinking: in a telling image, Rudolf Klein observes that the secret garden of the medical profession has shrunk to the size of a window box (and as Roland Petchey, who quotes it, observes, one that's open to the elements). By the same token, recent (and current) legislation in education has left teachers with barely a potplant to call their own. Other sectors - institutional care, for one - are being deserted through withdrawal of the public sector: this has provided opportunities for what Bleddyn Davies calls 'late twentieth century Schumpeterian capitalism' to colonise. Or, in plainer English, there are plenty of opportunities for making a quick buck - or losing it.

Amid all this diversity, judgments about the implications of these changes are difficult to make. In particular, answering the core questions about who is benefiting and who is bearing the costs of change and how well equipped they are to do so poses formidable problems of analysis. It involves leaving the largely imaginary universe of Ministerial claims, set out in glossy pamphlets at taxpayers' expense and validated - if at all - in off the peg consultants' reports, and entering the real world of confusing and often contradictory developments with uneven and constantly shifting impact. Nevertheless the outlines of a picture are beginning to emerge: this collection is devoted to an attempt to establish its broad features. The first section sets out the basic policy structure within which these changes are taking place; the declared objectives of the present Administration, structural changes in machinery of Government and the cultural shifts which these changes are intended to promote. The second section is devoted to the processes of change and the impact of their introduction in selected policy areas; and the third to outcomes, linked to identification of some ways in which developments that are already emerging can be adjusted or adapted so that benefits spread more equitably and costs fall more evenly.

In outlining the issues for the nineties, Howard Glennerster stresses the importance of recognising the demise of 'the social administration paradigm of the 1940s.' He argues that the continuing demands for

3

welfare expenditure resulting from demographic change (the impact of which should not be exaggerated), technological advance, labour market shifts (the persistence of mass unemployment and increased casualisation) and higher consumer expectations will not in future be met by an automatic expansion of traditional forms of public welfare. Instead the response will be of a more pluralistic kind - a development which Glennerster is not averse to. Like a number of leading commentators on social policy - Hadley & Hatch (1981), Klein and O'Higgins (eds.) (1985), Judge (1987) and Knapp, (1989) Glennerster accepts that state provided welfare services have been unduly bureaucratic, inefficient, ineffective and unaccountable to consumers. However, he is keen to pinpoint potential weaknesses of the drift away from the public sphere (the unwillingness or inability of the private, voluntary and informal services to provide a satisfactory level of coverage: the difficulty in subjecting 'contractors' to appropriate forms of financial and political control: the assault on the public service ethic: the undermining of local government: the retreat from modest commitments to equity and the reinforcing of gender inequalities.

The need for further research to chart the contours of new welfare developments is emphasised by Glennerster. However, as Deakin and Parry's contribution to this volume (an examination of Treasury 'social policy') reminds us, it is equally important to continue to explore those spheres which have proved, historically, rather impenetrable. On the basis of the limited data available (political memoirs: policy statements official records and a small number of academic studies) the authors conclude that Treasury activity in this sphere was based on a narrowly focused financial control and regulation role underpinned by a 'crude social philosophy'; a preference for uncontroversial policies with fixed budgetary limits and a disdain for competing decision making bodies. The authors are confident that the increasing flow of information about Treasury activity will provide the basis for more rigorous academic assessments which will go well beyond more traditional forms of 'Treasury' bashing.'

The need for further research is also underlined by Clarke and Newman in their timely assessment of the impact of managerialism in the public sector. As the authors demonstrate, the demand for managerialism was stimulated in part by the vehement attacks that were mounted on the welfare state not only by new right or anti-collectivist adherents but also by left of centre, feminist and anti-racist commentators. One of the consequences of this onslaught has been the undermining of what Clarke and Newman term 'bureau-professional regimes', whose alleged commitment to a public service ethic,

4

professional disinterest and high quality universal provision has been 'exposed' as little more than a fraudulent cover for ineffective, producer driven working practices. The transposing of private sector managerial practices to the public welfare sphere has been heralded as one way to counter these alleged shortcomings. Although this transformation has been far from unproblematic (the tension between managerial responsibilities and professional loyalties: the defining of appropriate corporate objectives; the clash between efficiency and equity and the tension between competition and co-operation) it cannot be dismissed as yet another fashionable trend. As Deakin (1993) has noted elsewhere those who have 'tasted the delights of managing are not likely to give them up.' (p. 25) Indeed, it seems probable that, in the absence of any concerted opposition to this development, those public sector workers who prove unwilling to embrace the tenets of 'newspeak' will be marginalised and, if necessary, dispatched overboard.

Some of the more progressive elements of 'managerialism' as they affect both staff and 'customers' are addressed in John Ditch's chapter which focuses on the major restructuring which has taken place in the Department of Social Security. He draws attention, for instance, to the way in which the Benefits Agency has sought to become not only more client orientated (the adoption of a customer Charter which sets out the standard of service which claimants can expect to receive - e.g. speedy processing of claims; courteous treatment by staff) but also more sensitive to the needs of its employees (greater commitment to flexible working practices; adhering more firmly to equal opportunities policies; improved training opportunities and a greater commitment to employee participation). However, one is forced to conclude that although some of these developments are to be welcomed (particularly if they help to restore the reputation of the public services as a role model for private sector emulation) they appear to be driven in the main by cost cutting (efficiency saving targets) and cosmetic (uniforms, badges and a cheery disposition) considerations. As Ditch reminds us, it is no use adopting such user friendly practices if the product (such as pitifully low Income Support allowances) remains unappealing.

In turning to the second part of this volume Julian Le Grand takes up the question of the funder/provider issue addressed by Glennerster. Like Glennerster and others (Green & Lucas 1992: Lowe, 1993), Le Grand concludes that the welfare state proved highly resilient to change in the period from 1979 to 1987 - a verdict which becomes less easy to sustain if one considers broader indices such as the abandonment of full employment policies, the undermining of universalism and the growth of poverty as opposed to public expenditure trends and developments in mainstream education, health and social security programmes (Mishra, 1990.)

For Le Grand the changes since the late 1980s (most notably the introduction of quasi-markets) are far more significant and merit detailed examination. As he contends, the introduction of quasi markets might give rise to outcomes which accord with the goals of 'traditionalists'. For example, increased competition might lead providers of services to take a keener interest in consumers with resulting enhancement of both quality and choice. Equally, though, the outcome could be more 'negative'. Greater competition amongst providers can lead to an increase in costs (higher salary payments: increased advertising budgets); monitoring difficulties (checking the quality of services provided by a diverse range of suppliers may prove difficult) and questionable eligibility procedures (vulnerable citizens may be left without adequate services as providers concentrate their efforts on more 'profitable' clients.)

Of the contributors to the second part, Julian Le Grand has gone furthest in his willingness to put forward conclusions, though his verdicts are strictly provisional. By the criteria that he sets out - efficiency, responsiveness, choice and equity - recent reforms in social services and in the health service at DHA level have not promoted efficiency, as compared with changes in education and the GP practice element of the health service; but have not adversely affected equity, as the latter show signs of doing. His discussion of the ways in which new systems are functioning and the risks attached to their introduction provides a valuable check list for future evaluations.

The thorny issue of charging social service users has also returned to prominence in recent years as a result of the unrelenting attack on the principle of universalism. As Lart and Means demonstrate, charging (at least of a nominal kind) has been a common feature of the welfare state and can be defended even by traditionalists on the grounds that it confers 'consumer' status on the poor (who thus gain a 'legitimate' right to voice their dissatisfaction with current service provision.) However, once charging passes the nominal threshold a whole array of policy dilemmas emerge. Lart and Means consider whether the current shift towards a more pluralistic welfare model and the concurrent development of more diverse charging arrangements might help to empower social service users. They conclude that those authorities which embrace a carefully targeted charging policy might, given favourable local supply conditions which can stimulate a commitment to quality, empower some groups of users whereas those councils who spurn such income generating opportunities will, in consequence of

6

being forced to ration or dilute services, merely undermine the position of those in need. Given that one of the central features of empowerment - exit - is only likely to be available to a minority of those in need, the authors are at pains to stress the continued importance of ensuring that mechanisms are developed which ensure that the needs and wishes of those dependent on non-substitutable care packages are adhered to by planners, assessors and care managers.

The impact of the restructuring of the welfare state is highlighted in Dowling's spirited account of the experiences of social service users in Sheffield which calls into question the 'resilient welfare state' thesis. Social Security reforms (most notably the introduction of the Social Fund) and the demise of affordable housing have clearly intensified the hardships experienced by the disadvantaged. The continuing fragility of working class living standards is well documented by Dowling. As she notes, unemployment, illness, the loss of a partner or some other misfortune can all too speedily lead to debt, eviction and despair. The establishment of the post 1945 welfare state was an attempt (albeit flawed) to provide some basic protection against such contingencies. Although the solidaristic underpinning of this form of collectivism may have always been more apparent than real it still retains far greater credibility as a protector of minimal standards than alternative welfare strategies.

Discussion in the third section juxtaposes developments in two contrasting policy areas - health and community care. Both are crucial to any evaluation, however tentative, of the impact of recent reforms in terms of cost and equity. The constant political exposure given to the NHS and the continued high level of public esteem that it enjoys as a totality (though not in the detail of some specific services) has made it a crux case for the present Government - and one to be approached with intense caution. The first time the question of fundamental reform reached the policy agenda, before the 1983 General Election, the then Prime Minister backed off at once; and when such reform did come, it was planned and set in motion strictly behind closed doors. Implementation of the new system (including its funding) has, as Petchey shows, been strongly influenced by these two characteristics.

Community care is a crux of a different kind. Provision of care stands at a whole series of intersections - not just structurally but conceptually. Implementation of a new framework has involved a series of complex trade offs between health, social security and social services. These are problematic enough in themselves; but the situation is further complicated by the interaction between the private and the public spheres, which is of fundamental significance in terms of the nature,

7

extent and quality of the resources that can be mobilised.

Moreover, as the implementation of the new system proceeds, the structural gulf is widening rather than closing. The three systems are moving away from each other as the internal reforms within each of them takes hold: the benefits system operating under devolved agency status as an independent public corporation, or quango nineties-style; the mixed economy of the health service with its developing internal market and strong technocratic overlay contrasting with a more traditional approach to caring by local government in social services. The community care sector is also one of few where reforms have left some space for local democratic institutions and hence for traditional systems of accountability. Bleddyn Davies is not the only critic to have expressed concern about the likely compatibility of these widely (and increasingly) different structures and styles.

But ultimately the conceptual gap between the objectives as seen by Government at one end of the caring processes (where planning and funding takes place) and the carers and those for whom they care at the other end (where it is actually delivered) may prove to be the more important. Clare Ungerson exposes the risks attached to present policies that may affect not just the supply of informal care but also its quality; she shows how assumptions made by policy makers fail to take full account of the interaction between the private and public domains. That the present exploitation of the claims of kinship and the impulse to altruism cannot continue indefinitely is becoming generally recognised; but the devices by which they can be supplemented may also end by supplanting them. Professionalisation of care and payment for caring at economic rather than exploitative rates raise all sorts of questions about the proper value attached to caring as an activity. Caroline Glendinning and Gary Craig explore some of the financial implications of these developments in further detail: channelling resources direct to users rather than through intermediaries and the provision of information to enable informed choices to be made are obvious examples of possible changes; the introduction of additional charges would be more problematic.

Roland Petchey's review of the changes in the NHS does not set out to provide conclusions - it is necessarily a work in progress. He writes after the furore over the reforms during the 1992 General Election but before the renewed debate over rationing of health care precipitated by weaknesses exposed by the lack of provision for urgent cases towards the end of the 1992/3 financial year, when contracts had frequently been exhausted. But his emphasis on the political dimension in the reforms and the consequences of the perceived need to manage the newly introduced market in order to achieve 'smooth take off' gains further force from subsequent developments. In particular the emphasis in the pre-Election period on clearing the backlog of waiting lists and the reckless degree of freedom given to grant-holding general practices stored up trouble for the future which is now arriving on cue. More generally, the tension between decentralisation to local managers - one of the popular features of reforms in all sectors, at least among managers themselves - and the ever-increasing centralisation of control is once again evident: Petchey quotes another critic (Paton 1992) as observing that 'the Government has been forced to centralise ruthlessly in order to decentralise'.

This theme of central direction is among several picked up by Bleddyn Davies in his review of community care programmes and their outcomes. Although the analysis that he and his Kent colleagues provide of the detail of these programmes reaches some positive conclusions, Davies' expressed concern about the implications of continued tinkering to meet technocratic objectives leads him to enter a heartfelt plea for longer term thinking that might achieve a breakthrough to a new and stable universe. The reinstatement of local government as a major player, if necessary in drastically reformed guise, is one of the options that he urges on policy makers.

To have more than an eye to the far horizon, as Davies suggests, is clearly right - especially when sailing, as too often seems to be the case during the present period of drastic reform, without an up to date map or reliable compass. The sacred simplicities about the inevitable benefits of the introduction of market values into the public sector are still in circulation, as in the text of John Major's *Citizen's Charter*. But apart from that diminishingly credible document, dogmatic certainty is gradually being replaced by an appreciation of the complexities of processes of reform and the need to take account of special features in particular service areas. The introduction of businessmen (sic) and business values are no longer seen as sovereign remedies, especially now that their reputation is tarnished by recent experience in the health service. The constant light dusting of management slogans continues: incantation of terms like 'total quality' or ten-minute messages from the latest management guru carried to the benighted by ever-eager consultants. But real problems, exposed by the impact of prolonged recession after the blip of the Lawson boom, require more fundamental solutions.

That value change in the public sector of welfare - perhaps even more than structural reform - had to come is undeniable. But as contributors to the present collection and other analyses have shown, the costs of change have so far been borne unevenly and the benefits unfairly concentrated on those whose needs are at best questionable (tax breaks in health care is only one in a string of examples). Welfare provision for the middle class continues to flourish at the expense of their less fortunate fellow-citizens. The processes of change has also created a new provider oligarchy more powerful and even less accountable than the old one - and far more highly rewarded. Throwing out the dirty bathwater of excessive bureaucracy has put at risk that never very robust child, public service. The dilemma is how to capture what's rewarding (in every sense) about the changes that are taking place - sharper sense of direction, increased responsibility for those delivering welfare; sensitivity to costs, improved access and (crucially) availability of information for users - while preserving what was valuable in the older tradition. Present tensions are well captured in the phrase quoted by Newman and Clarke: recent changes have meant 'teaching managers to be bilingual'. It would be good to think that before too long circumstances might change to allow them to say what they mean and mean what they say, both within and outside the system.

Section One
THE POLICY DIMENSION

1 Paying for welfare: Issues for the nineties

Howard Glennerster

Themes

Three issues will, I believe, dominate the nineties. Some have been with us in an acute form since the economic crisis of the seventies, others began in the eighties.

First, there is the perennial question, how much of any society's resources can and should be collectively allocated for social purposes?

Second, how far should the public **finance** of social purposes imply public **provision**? Is a complete separation possible? How far should contracting go in public policy? What is the scope for quasi-markets and the balance sheet of advantages and disadvantages?

Third, where should the boundary line between public and private responsibilities lie, for example, in the case of informal and family care and social support but more widely than that? Is the presumption of dominant market exchange compatible with that of greater familial and communal responsibility?

Avowed social purposes

To a remarkable extent, it seems to me, avowed social purposes changed only slowly in the 1980s. Certainly, in the UK and the US there was an explicit abandonment of any claim to be seeking equality of incomes or outcomes. Indeed the virtues of **inequality** were proclaimed by both Mrs Thatcher and President Reagan, but it is doubtful how central that goal had ever really been in most politicians' idea of social policy, as opposed, that is to say, to some academics' aspirations.

In the 1980s politicians were careful to present their arguments for change while at the same time reiterating support for the basic purposes of social policy. Much the same is true in Western Europe and Scandinavia. Take, for example, the opening claim made in the White Paper that presented the case for radical change in the National Health Service in England.

> The principles that have guided it (the NHS) for the last
> forty years will continue to guide it into the twenty-first
> century. (*Working for Patients* 1989a, para 1.2)

Avowed social policy ends often survived even if the resources to achieve them were constrained and the priorities accorded them down graded.

It was beliefs about the best **means** of achieving those ends that changed. The British social administration paradigm of the 1940s was shaken to the core and will never reappear. Can that, in the end, leave our social purposes unaffected?

Let me deal with each of these themes in turn.

How much collective action can we afford?

In the 1970s a broad consensus emerged, shared by traditional economists and political scientists and Marxists alike (O'Connor, 1973; Bacon and Eltis, 1976; Rose and Peters, 1978). The pace of growth in social spending in western capitalist nations was unsustainable. The predicted resolution of this fiscal crisis differed but the diagnosis was in many ways shared between these ideological contestants.

What actually happened was not a cataclysm or a collapse or even a major shift to the market, but a pause, a ceiling placed on the share of welfare spending in western economies (see Table 2.1). You can see that very clearly if you look at the UK figures for social spending or indeed at almost any other OECD or European nation (Glennerster, 1992).

How was this achieved? Largely by a series of measures that cannot be sustained indefinitely.

Charges or co-payments for health care have been either introduced and/or increased in many countries. There is a limit to the extent to which you can extend this solution if you wish to exclude the poor from paying. Prescription charges are now 80% reimbursed. The figure used to be 60 odd per cent.

Table 2.1
European social protection expenditure as a percentage of gross domestic product at market prices: 1981, 1985, 1988

County	1981	1985	1988[*]
Belgium	-	29.0	28.7
Denmark	29.3	27.8	28.5
West Germany	29.5	28.1	28.1
Spain	-	18.0	17.7
France	27.2	28.8	28.3
Ireland	-	24.0	22.6
Italy	24.7	22.5	22.9
Luxemborg	-	25.4	26.6
Netherlands	31.7	31.1	30.7
Portugal	-	16.1	17.0
UK	23.5	24.5	23.6
Norway	-	-	26.4
Sweden	-	33.3	35.2
Finland	-	24.6	25.9

[*] or nearest year

Source: EEC, Eurostat, *Basic Statistics of the Community 1990*, Luxembourg, 1991.

The level of social security benefits has been squeezed. In this country they have been pegged to prices not to the incomes of the wider population. So the gap between earnings and pensions grows year by year (Barr and Coulter, 1990). More patients have been pushed through the same facilities. There is a limit to the extent to which that can go on except at the margins. But gains could only be reaped for a relatively short period. Strategic policy shifts will be needed. Avowed ends will no longer match means in a way that even politicians can cover up.

Then, there is the question of incomes in the public sector. You may recall that Baumol (1967) first pointed to the phenomenon Her

Majesty's Treasury came to call 'the relative price effect'. Productivity gains in the private sector generated real increases in wages that passed into the public personal service sector through competitive trade union bargaining. The relative price of social services thus continually rose. One answer, of course, was to hold down public sector pay and as Chris Trinder (1990) has shown the Government in the UK has been remarkably successful at doing that for much of the eighties.

It is not a permanent solution. It implies a continuous relative decline in the quality of staff employed in the public services and therefore in the quality of those services.

In short, the measures that squared the circle in the 1980s will not last out the 1990s. More than that, the scale of the contradictions, conflicts, call them what you will, will grow. New elements have been added by the transformation of the economy in the 1980s.

The demand side

First, the familiar demand side factors, demography, ageing, innovation, price changes, medical advance, will all continue to have their familiar effect. The NHS probably needs a growth of 2% per annum in real volume terms to survive at its present overstretched level in the 1990s (Robinson, 1991b). Personal social services require about 2.5% (Hulme, 1991). Education will need a rise of 0.5 to 1% of the GDP to get its post-school provision in line with Europe (Glennerster and Low, 1990b).

In many ways the UK is better placed demographically than most of its economic competitors (OECD, 1988). Japan will have to face a 40% increase in its social spending per employed person simply to sustain its services and benefits by the year 2020. The 1970s, 1980s and 1990s ought to have brought considerable fiscal relief to the UK in this respect. In the UK the number of people over the age of 65 is more or less stable even if the older age groups are growing. Out-weighing both that and the oil revenue, has been our complete failure to find any other way of controlling inflation except by high and **rising** levels of unemployment. Like any drug, it requires a more powerful dose in each successive economic cycle. We look like having three million unemployed for most of this decade.

Yet, added to these familiar pressures the nineties will bring others. The most important will be the frustrated tide of expectations built up as the general standard of service in the public sector falls farther behind the increasingly glossy, carpeted and consumer conscious private sector. The eighties have seen a seismic change in the structure of the labour markets in the west and most of all in the UK and the USA.

Temporary part time and low paid jobs at one end have been matched by higher earnings at the other. **Real** weekly earnings of the lowest decile in the US **fell** by 15% between 1970 and 1987. Unionisation prevented such a sharp effect in the UK but may not in the nineties. In both economies earnings at the top end have risen faster. The returns to skill, to higher education and to sustained labour market experience, in both the US and the UK, have risen sharply (Schmitt, 1992). Since 1982 the rate of return on a university education has increased by nearly half. But the return on labour market experience, being in a continuous job has increased even more.

This has two effects: the cost of labour market insecurity grows, it shows up in the social security budget and elsewhere. The other quite different effect is that the demands for quality service from the highest income groups grow disproportionately fast. They diverge more and more from what they actually find in the state schools and hospitals. Faced with static or declining service standards these groups leave the state services. The Institute for Fiscal Studies produced evidence of this for education using the Family Expenditure Survey (Pearson, Smith and Watson, 1988), for example. Their preferences are increasingly at variance with what the median voter is prepared to pay for. More of that later.

The supply side

The demands for human services and income security are likely to grow even faster in the nineties than they did in the sixties and those demands will bifurcate - the rich will demand even better services, the poor taxpayers will resist.

Taxes - being positive

Let me first be positive. It could be that the climate of ideas about taxation will change in the nineties.

Those of you who are familiar with the economic literature of the past decade or more will be struck by the paradox that as the market philosophy gained ascendancy, so our understanding of market failure deepened. To the theoretical contributions of the 1950s and 1960s, public or social goods, externalities and free rider problems, was added the concept of information failure in particular markets, notably health and insurance. Uncertainty and inequalities of information between supplier and demander produce inefficient results, adverse selection and cream skimming. This work has been admirably summarised by a colleague Nick Barr (1992) in the *Journal of Economic Literature*. As one marketing director of an American health insurer put it to me "Let's face it, competition in health care is all about making damn sure you do not end up with sick people on your books". The economics of the environment is bringing home to people, rather as the public health movement did in the nineteenth century, that individuals' health and welfare may be destroyed by unrestricted individual action. It is also teaching us that taxation can be used to produce efficient economic allocations. Taxing carbon emissions, cars in cities, energy are but some examples. Taxation can bring welfare gains - a conclusion that flows from the purist form of welfare economics. At the moment welfare economists are producing more arguments **for** social policy than against it!

Could we see a turning of the intellectual tide as the public and politicians catch up with these insights? Perhaps. Or again taxes could be made more user friendly. Taxes for specific purposes do seem to excite more support. Education at the last election may be a pointer. Specific social security taxes have risen in most countries in the last decade even when income taxes fell.

Abolishing most of the income tax allowances we have would enable us to lower the standard or basic rate of tax by broadening its base. Ordinary people would experience a lower headline rate of tax. Unfortunately many middle and marginal voters would lose. Mortgage tax relief is now targeted on average earners. A fairly careful exercise would be needed to get this electorally right. The best accessible review of the possibilities for tax reform is still Hills (1988).

The results of public attitude surveys show that in the 1980s there was a strong swing of opinion towards spending more on social services (Taylor-Gooby, 1991). More people in Britain also expressed themselves in favour of government services than those in any other country except Italy (Taylor-Gooby and Smith, 1989)! What weight to put on such surveys is another matter. The last election must make us treat them with considerable scepticism. The lesson may be that people are prepared to spend more on health and education but they are not sure that they are getting value for money for their tax take.

Certainly the public spending settlements in the pre-election round were more generous than in some past years but there is nothing new in that. Prospects for the current round and subsequent ones up to 1996 do not look good.

Will there be more people in the labour force to pay taxes? Yes, not least women. If it had not been for the rapid increase in female participation rates in the past two decades the welfare state as we know it would not have survived. To a large extent it has been paid for by the new women workers. That again may be a wasting asset. The really big change has already happened.

The pessimistic case

Now for the negative side. The supply side tax constraints seem to me to be daunting.

First, the international economy. The international movement of human and physical capital is now so easy that the comparative advantage a country can gain from low marginal tax rates is considerable. This becomes more important in the light of my earlier evidence about the rising marginal productivity of the most educated. It now matters less and less where you locate for physical reasons, like cotton needing a wet Manchester climate, but it does matter where you get your best human capital. If that is in low tax countries that is where you will locate.

Money capital is now largely uncontrollable. There is little hope of retaining capital under a harsh tax regime. We now face a potential if not actual Dutch auction in tax levels internationally.

Second, the real economy. Social policy writers have always been deeply sceptical of the economic costs of high levels of taxation and high marginal rates of tax. Economists have not had much, if any, positive proof to the contrary. Now colleagues at the LSE have undertaken a complex international econometric study (Newell and Symons, 1991) which suggests that productivity gains were greatest in the 1980s precisely in those countries that cut their marginal tax rates most. Indeed, they claim that lowering tax rates on the average worker was the most important factor associated with differential economic success. The UK, by the way, did **not** manage to reduce the overall direct tax burden on the average worker in the Thatcher period.

In short, there may be good economic reasons not to increase the tax take on the average worker.

Third, there are the life cycle effects. As my colleagues John Hills, Jane Falkingham and Carli Lessof (Hills, 1992; Falkingham, Hills and Lessof, 1992) have shown, over half the income redistribution that the welfare state achieves, and it is massive, is a transfer of resources from one part of people's lifetime to another. From the middle of life to the two ends, but overwhelmingly to the end! The costs of dependency at each end of the life cycle have grown and for men the length of the working life has shortened dramatically in the past few decades. The net tax burden concentrated in middle life has grown sharply, cohort by cohort, since 1910. Yet middle age is when people are at their most politically active and influential and there are more such people in the electorate. Being young is very tough these days. One of the reasons economists use to justify compulsory state pensions, or contributions to pension schemes is myopia. Old age is a long way off and the nursing home will never happen to me. This is a particular example of what Galbraith (1992) calls 'the short term view' that seems to affect modern societies. But if individuals can be myopic about their own old age provision why should they not be when it comes to social provision, especially when life is tough.

Fourth, and here I return to Galbraith (1992), there is the broader 'Culture of Contentment' that he describes.

> The comfortable monopolise or largely monopolise the
> political franchise; the uncomfortable and the distressed
> of the urban and rural slums ... do not have candidates
> who represent their needs and so they do not vote.
> (p.155)

This process can be seen at work in many western societies. What is peculiarly British is our voting system. After all at the 1992 election the majority of the electorate did vote for parties pledged to put up taxes but that did not translate into a Government pledged to do so. What we have is a **political** market failure that cannot translate voter preferences into effective demand. That is probably not going to change.

Finally, it may be that the middle class will be prepared to pay for good schools and health care but only on condition that they reap the benefits without them leaking to the undeserving or, indeed, just to others than themselves. That is one way to read the flight to the suburbs in the States where it is possible to enjoy good schools and public services, to pay taxes for them and to be sure that the poor and the blacks in the inner core city will not benefit. That is one way to interpret opting-out schools, Trusts and GP fundholding in this country. These institutional changes are really about capturing even more effectively than in the past not just most, but all the taxes the middle class pay, in services received.

Other systems of welfare

So far I have confined myself to tax financed welfare. But as we all know that is but a part of the total picture.

Those of us who study social policy are in the broadest sense, concerned with the allocation of those goods and services that are necessary to human well being, food, shelter, care and support, health, access to human capital and, as Rawls (1972) added to his list of primary goods, self respect. The way we can secure these things are many. Titmuss (1958) saw three systems of welfare. It is now clear that he had merely lifted the corner of a curtain on a star lit night. There were galaxies beyond. There is unregulated, regulated and enforced occupational welfare; capped and uncapped fiscal welfare; enforced or spontaneous loving informal care, supported or not out of public funds; all kinds of tax assisted charity; legal welfare through the courts and above all sophisticated market mechanisms for shifting resources through time, insurance based, capital based, so one may go on. All carry a price, all have to be paid for. During the Thatcher years we did **not** see the decline in state intervention in society, but its extension in more complex ways. Portable private pensions were given substantial tax advantages; charitable donations by companies and individuals were given tax subsidies; local councils were compelled to put services out to tender, to sell estates to housing associations who were subject to even closer scrutiny than councils had been. All put burdens on the Exchequer.

How far will non-tax forms of finance be able to step in and meet the shortfall I have suggested will arise?

What about charity? During the 1980s the Conservative government in the UK gave significant tax breaks to charitable giving in the hope that this would call forth a more than equivalent of private giving. Yet, a recent study (Jones and Posnett, 1990), has suggested that this has not happened. There has been very little change in giving when other factors were included in the equation. More recent American work they quote suggests much the same. Companies are another source also encouraged by tax changes. But the level of company support was low even before the recession. The top 400 companies give about 0.6% of their profits to charity - a fairly static figure. The top donors gave £150 million to education and welfare in 1990, a fairly trivial sum compared to the NHS's cost of £25 billion (Charities Aid Foundation, 1990).

For some the market will undoubtedly provide. Long term care of the elderly will attract more insurance and capital schemes. New schemes are being marketed, even if they are small scale as yet. It is already true that private pension income out paces state pension income (Barr and Coulter, 1990). Housing is now primarily privately financed. Private schooling expenditure as a share of all school expenditure rose in the 1980s for the first time this century (Glennerster and Low, 1990a). But in a society that can employ only perhaps half its population more or less continuously through their lives, occupational and private welfare will be fragile for very many people. It is not that in aggregate private finance will not grow but that a large part of the population will be excluded from it that poses the dilemma for the nineties.

Can we call the family back to meet the gap? It seems even less well structured to bear the strain than it was. Later contributors will be discussing this in more depth so I will leave it at that.

Conclusion

My conclusion has to be that by the end of the nineties no institution will have paid the price. Private purchases will meet the rising expectations of many people. Welfare will have returned to its residual role but it will be a very large residuum. That does not mean that Titmuss (1968) was wrong in his original complaints about residual services. The primary good we shall fail to buy may well be the self-respect of the poor.

If I am right, as social scientists, we should be seeking to devise ways of designing the most humane system of residual welfare we can, not nostalgically recalling the days of our lost universalist youth and innocence. For which services is it most important to retain a universalist framework? I would argue - health and schools. Housing never was universally provided and social care never was either. We should be examining social security closely to see what to do with a system that is neither good at being universal or at providing a residual minimum at the present. The present system will not survive the nineties.

To provide or not to provide?

If fiscal crisis will be one theme of the nineties, an old tune with a new twist, there is a second theme that is new in kind and significance. Nothing is really new in social policy, of course, and this debate would be immediately recognised by Victorian political economists. The seminal collection of ideas was Milton Friedman's book *Capitalism and Freedom* (1962) and Savas' book *Privatising the Public Sector* (1982).

Even when we accept that a social purpose exists and ought to be financed out of taxation, should that function also be performed by the state in some guise, local or national?

The great transformation of the eighties was that that question has been taken seriously and legislation put in place that will, in the nineties, largely divest the local state of its capacity to **provide** services. We are moving to a contract and voucher state. Does that matter?

It certainly breaks the social administration paradigm of the 1940s and the principles that underlay the legislation of that time. The really decisive debates in the eighties have been about social administration not about social policy.

There seem to me to be three parts to that old social administration paradigm.

The first was the presumption that in most cases services should be administered and provided by organs of the state that were also financially responsible for raising the revenue.

That had not been the case in the Victorian period or the early twentieth century. State involvement in education in the nineteenth century had been largely through the finance of voluntary and private organisations to educate children to a standard defined by Her Majesty's Inspectors of Schools. Housing subsidies had gone to both private and public builders originally. Voluntary agencies had predominated in the social care field. Approved societies did the same in social security. In each case the state came to fuse provision and finance. Why?

First, there was the question of accountability. Profiteering by private builders with the post First World War subsidies lead the Treasury to favour bodies over which it had close control. The same story is repeated elsewhere. All the tight principles of loan sanction, ultra vires, audit were attached to statuary bodies. Inspection and quality control proved difficult to sustain in anything but a crude fashion over private bodies.

Moreover politicians, facing the task of raising taxes, wanted to be seen to be providing the benefits.

Those who provide services should also raise a significant part of the revenue. For that not to be the case provokes unrealistic demands for money from service providers. That was the Treasury's view in its evidence to the Geddes Committee (1922) and the principle was reiterated by the Layfield Committee (1976).

The legislators of the 1940s and our predecessors learned from this experience and went for the fusion of provision and finance as the most effective way of achieving financial and political accountability. That was not an uncontested view of course; the approved societies and the voluntary hospitals protested strongly. Yet, it prevailed and so did a similar trend in private industry for reasons that at least overlap (Williamson, 1975).

However, this fusion of provision and finance had costs as well as benefits. The costs grew through the sixties and the seventies. Social service organisations grew in scale and in centralisation. Anne Power has traced this in the history of local housing departments (Power, 1987). Responsiveness, humanity and efficiency all declined. With scale went local monopoly power and with that went monopoly rent drawn by those who run and provide the service, from caretakers to hospital consultants. Having observed negotiations between local GPs and some hospital doctors in the past two years, the scale of this unresponsiveness and professional arrogance is only too evident.

Given the changes to the private market and the impact of the fiscal crisis on public services, the ground was fertile for a reassessment. Public choice theory provided a convenient intellectual framework. Public administrators' and service professionals' behaviour could not be understood in terms of duties, responsibilities and ethical standards but as interested action, professional power unconstrained by consumers' power of exit. Niskanen's (1971), Leibenstein's (1966) and Hirschman's (1970) ideas come together to form a powerful combination. If traditional social administrative forms of accountability and control had failed, market competition, the power of exit and financial incentives had to be reintroduced to replace them.

Shall we relearn in the nineties the problems our predecessors discovered about accountability and control in a mixed economy of welfare? Certainly the Americans have.

So much for the first leg of the old social administration paradigm. What of the second? The division of labour between central and local government in the delivery and responsibility for local services. In the eighties, here too, there has been a decisive shift in the constitutional assumptions of a century or more. A smaller share of tax revenue is raised locally in the UK now, 5%, than in any other major, or indeed minor democratic state. We are in the midst of a process that is systematically stripping local government of its power to run or even regulate local services. Local housing estates, schools, Trust hospitals are floating off into a world of semi-obscure accountability. Opted-out schools, for example, are run by a small largely self-perpetuating group with power to determine the educational opportunities of local unrepresented children. If rows break out between governors and the head teacher the only people who have the power to resolve the issue are the Secretary of State and the Courts. When there are 27,000 such free floating schools the Secretary of State will have his or her hands full.

Elsewhere, some colleagues (Glennerster, Power and Travers, 1991) called this the problem of the excluded middle in British politics. Weak and peripheral bodies will be unable to resist central government directives. This accumulation of central power and financial responsibility may make sense as a prelude to complete privatisation. It could make sense if housing estates, for example, had been democratised and if a clear local responsibility for access and equality of opportunity were kept by LEAs, for example, but none of this exists.

So what could a truly decentralised but democratic system of finance and accountability look like, for schools and hospitals and housing estates, given the opting out likely in the next decade? That is another theme worthy of a lot of detailed thought. These new structures could generate the political constituency for better services more effectively managed.

The third element to this old social administration paradigm was the belief in rational planned allocations, in collaboration not competition, in professional responsibility and public service as organisational motives not financial incentives and competition.

While I accept that the original paradigm was naive in many respects, its successor is also misleadingly crude. Personal financial gain and the size of a department's budget are not the only things that motivate individuals. What this economic analysis of public bureaucracies has failed to do is to apply any sociological or organisational understanding to the issues. Patrick Dunleavy's (1991) critique of the public choice analysis is the best yet:

> Downs's and Niskanen's uncritical adoption of a line bureaucracy paradigm; their use of fuzzy and soft-edged accounts of bureaucrats utility functions; their inability to come up with methodologically legitimate supply-side variations in bureaucratic behaviour; and their use of crude generalisations ... are a fundamental trait of public choice models ... the (central) principle *nobody spends someone else's money as carefully as he spends his own* is simply anti-organisational rather than distinctly relevant to ... the public sector. (p. 173)

It applies to government financed vouchers, too, by the way.

The ethic of service is more evident in the National Health Service than the ethic of the golf course. But that may not last. It is true from our experience that GPs are very resistant to the idea of turning expensive patients away, forty years of socialisation into NHS and professional norms help. But it may not take long for them to erode and the US experience is a dreadful warning (Glennerster, Owens and Matsaganis, 1992). If you transform professional understandings by enforcing contracts what effect do you have on the professional supply side? Do you limit the readiness to go the extra mile or stay to help with the extra curricula pastoral problem?

Nor are we are only talking about public sector organisations. One of the most striking things that has happened in the last decade is that public sector cash has become the dominant source of income for many voluntary organisations. This altered their organisational culture and contracting will do so again. They are not the same organisations and may indeed take on many of the same characteristics as public bureaucracies. Their governance and accountability regimes may be less well adapted than the despised public sector organisations they have replaced. The latter have had a century or more of post Gladstonian rules to hone their accountability.

In short, there will be complex gains **and** losses in organisational effectiveness as a result of the changes we can expect in the nineties. How best can we study them? My own preference is a mix of methods from close observation to more formal outcome studies. We shall have plenty to do.

The separation of finance and provision makes the task of allocating funds to semi-autonomous institutions in an equitable way even more important. We can, of course, abandon equity as a criterion altogether, the Government is showing every sign of doing so, but our traditions as an Association should make us resist that. If schools are to be formula funded, how should that formula reflect the different scale of task different schools face. On the ILEA we went some way to answering that question, open to criticism certainly, but an advance (Sammons, Kysel and Mortimore, 1983). Now the scope for including social factors in the formula has been restricted (Lee, 1991). It is an important issue we should not neglect. Work is in progress at Bath and the LSE on this. If parents are to be given a fair and informed choice of school, if the conditions necessary for a market to work are to exist, schools need equity in resources and parents need unbiased information on schools' performance. That requires value added measures to use the economic jargon, not just exam results. We are a long way from being able to do that well on a regular basis (Goldstein, 1991).

Exactly the same problems arise in deciding how much money fundholding GPs should get to neutralise their incentives not to take potentially costly patients; we are working on that too! How much should a care manager be allocated, a district health authority? How are districts to measure health needs? There is more social planning to do here not less.

Public and private spheres of action

Finally the past decade and more has seen the re-examination of a question that much exercised Victorian and Edwardian women of social conscience, where do the boundaries of social and personal action lie (Lewis, 1991)? Now women have rightly extended the question to men! Implicit and indeed explicit in much of the new radical right ideas has been the reassertion of family values and the caring role of women. Feminists have laid open the assumptions and the shift of costs implicit in such arguments. Caroline Glendenning (1992a) has recently shown again how important these costs are. The enforced, uncompensated care of a loved one, caused by a neglectful state is conceptually no different from a tax levied on women in some situations and not on other members of the community. Because it is a hidden tax it is also taxation without representation. What is or should be men's role in all this and the wider community? What of the finance of child care in an economy demanding more and more from women in the formal paid market place? How do we finance the growing insecurity of family relationships?

The complexity of human interdependency will grow in the nineties. The scale of lifetime income redistribution we shall all need will grow.

Conclusion

It is clear that in the 1990s we could see even greater changes to social provision and its finance than in the 1980s. The direction of change is far from clear.

My own ten point agenda would be:

1.   Sustaining the general tax based finance for health and schooling as an absolute priority.

2.   Abandon the present separate contributory system for basic social security benefits. It is gender biased, incompatible with the new world of fluctuating labour force participation and with unpaid work.

3. Fuse the tax and benefit system to create a basic entitlement income with matching obligations. No person has the right to expect others to support them without good cause.

4. Require contributions by those in paid employment to secure adequate levels of income and care in retirement giving choice as to the means by which this is achieved - personal insurance, occupational or state administered schemes.

5. Make free post-eighteen education dependent on a matching obligation to pay a higher base rate of tax.

6. Reverse the disastrous drift to central finance and control of local authority services by adding to a reformed property tax a local income tax. Make it possible for local citizens to add a voluntary contribution to a named local charity or service.

7. Phase out mortgage tax relief and concentrate all relief on the poorest in all tenures.

8. Progress very cautiously with quasi-markets but accept that choice and exit are powerful weapons for consumers if the information is good and if incentives against cream-skimming can be countered.

9. Concentrate Child Benefit on the early years of life when the opportunity cost of children is greatest and extend the principle of payment for care at any age.

10. Finally, shift the balance of taxation from taxing those on lower income and impose taxes instead on energy consumption, environment damaging activities, especially those indulged in by the rich. Charge motorists for the inconvenience they impose on others by driving into crowded cities. That way you would improve equity and efficiency at the same time - a positive sum game.

2 Does the Treasury have a social policy?

Nicholas Deakin and Richard Parry

It is strange how literally everyone 'hates' the Treasury -
including sometimes Treasury ministers (Barnett 1982
p. 58)

...the role of Philip Guedella's 'inverted Micawber, waiting
for something to turn down' (Bruce-Gardyne 1986 p. 173)

This chapter attempts a preliminary analysis of a suppressed theme in
British public policy - the role of the Treasury in framing and promoting
various emphases in the management of social policy as an extension of
its functions of economic management and public expenditure control,
and the changes (or in many cases distortions) that result from its
interventions. The oft proclaimed Treasury folklore is that it alone
stands between economic stability and financial irresponsibility,
expressed most potently in transfers to individuals and institutions
beyond what the country can 'afford'. Our proposition is that the
management of social expenditure implies, however crudely, an implicit
social policy - that is, criteria for judging the desirable means and ends
of government intervention in personal behaviour and life choices which
go far beyond the simple control of expenditure, either by individual
programmes or in aggregate. In short, we suggest that the institutional
memory of the Treasury and its operating culture is bound to comprise
such a social policy even if it denies having one. We also suggest that
the unrecognised persistence of such strong cultural values goes
unacknowledged and the Treasury continues to justify its interventions
by proclaiming value-neutrality between different spending proposals.

This is dangerous because:

1.   legislation and practice give the Treasury rights of intervention in quite small matters of expenditure in a control system separate from aggregate control of the planning total of expenditure;

2.   relatively junior Treasury officials represent its interests to spending departments, and it tends to host sub Cabinet interdepartmental gatherings: 'the Treasury, always encircled by predatory spenders, believes strongly and perhaps with justice that the host on these occasions starts with an edge over the guests' (Bruce-Gardyne 1986 p. 30);

3.   policy continues to emphasise the interconnection between economic and social policy and the contraction of the autonomous sphere in which social ends can be pursued as desirable on their own.

We organise the chapter, intended as a staking-out of the field and a stimulus to further research, in six parts. Firstly, we ask how we might find data about the Treasury's social policy. Secondly, we examine 'official' Treasury prose (especially that generated by the public expenditure survey system) in an attempt to detect outward manifestations of internal debates and changes of course. Thirdly, we consider more speculatively the relationship between Treasury organisation, Treasury attitudes and the policy process in Whitehall. The fourth section is a briefer discussion of budgeting outside Whitehall, where the Treasury has devolved some discretion to the territorial departments in Scotland, Wales and Northern Ireland. Fifthly, we suggest a number of long running themes which in our view amount to a 'social policy of the Treasury', but one which is implicit and derivative, and stems from their preoccupation with retaining rights of control and from their sense of what the economic imperatives of the day demand. Finally we consider the research agenda.

The search for data

After nearly twenty years we still owe a lot to Heclo and Wildavsky (1981) for their exploitation of the fact that clever Treasury people enjoy explaining how clever they are. The new techniques of the Public

Expenditure Survey system (a coherent annual cycle since 1969) provided a rich source of material and and a research opportunity, for officials could be persuaded to discuss technical generality as a guise for policy investigation. Until it broke down under the pressure of inflation and policy turns, PESC was the Treasury's pride and joy and encouraged them to be systematic in setting out their principles (Goldman 1973). Thain and Wright's recent interview research (1992b) charts the modification of PESC as a 'system' based on the concept of a coherent collective enterprise into a series of 'bilaterals' involving a small group of Treasury officials in continuous dialogue with their opposite numbers in the spending departments, with ad hoc ministerial interventions in the final stages. This process has produced a small, stable policy network with a highly restricted membership which is, as Thain and Wright (1992b) comment, 'neither open nor transparent' (p. 197)

The 'top down' planning system introduced in 1992 with a 'new control total' excluding benefits for the unemployed, and the unified budget to be presented in December from 1993 are of unpredictable impact. But the original system was still going strong in the mid-1970s when an unusually reflective and analytical generation of politicians and officials was in office. Many later produced memoirs and commentaries which may be cross-referenced (Chancellor Denis Healey (1990), his Chief Secretary Joel Barnett (1982), his Second Permanent Secretary in charge of public expenditure Sir Leo Pliatzky (1982), his Permanent Secretary Sir Douglas Wass (1984), and his first political adviser Adrian Ham (1981)). Healey (1990) more than once quotes the old saw that the Treasury knows the price of everything and the value of nothing, but does not give much attention to public expenditure issues at the micro level, emphasising that 'Joel Barnett was so reliable in controlling the details of public expenditure that he took much of that burden from me' (p. 385). As Healey says, the only Labour Chief Secretaries to date (John Diamond from 1964-70, Barnett from 1974-79) were 'Jewish accountant(s) from the North' (ibid., p. 390); presumably the right profile to produce the 'inexhaustible energy and immense good humour' Healey feels the job requires (ibid., p. 390). It is interesting how the post now tends to be held by thrusting young politicians making a name for themselves by assertive relations with spending departments (like David Mellor and Michael Portillo) rather than people who are 'good with figures' (Peter Rees being a Conservative example of this type). One recent Chief Secretary (John Major) has, of course, gone all the way to the top.

Pliatzky (another Mancunian protege of Healey's (1990 p. 79)) achieved a name for himself in the early 1980s as a media pundit; his books are didactic and self-promoting without giving much away (in fact, Pliatzky's career in the Treasury was focussed on the industrial and overseas wings and bypassed social policy until his final post). Wass's Reith Lectures, given shortly after his retirement, are cool and Olympian; on spending issues he says 'the outcome of each battle is determined less by rational argument than by a judgment each party makes of the way the Cabinet would adjudicate in the event of continuing hoistilities between the parties' (1984 p. 14). Ham (described by Healey (1990) as having 'a reciprocated mistrust of all permanent officials' (p. 391)) produced a sharp critique from a hardish left position ('.. two obsessions gripped the senior personnel of the Treasury. One was to 'stop Benn'. The other was to prepare the ground for a tough incomes policy' (Ham 1981 p. 112)).

Barnett's memoirs are the most detailed ministerial account of expenditure-setting. He emphasises the personal, deal-making aspect of the process: the funding of SERPS is settled over a late night drink in the Commons (Barnett, 1982 p. 40), the rate of child benefit during a train journey with Stanley Orme (ibid., p. 53). Inside Cabinet, matters are settled by the accidents of Prime Ministerial favour, or of timing: John Morris gets away with an absurdly low offer on Welsh cuts because it is nearly 1 pm (ibid., p. 103); Albert Booth presents his cases so ineffectually that he tends to win rather than lose sympathy (ibid., p. 130). Barnett's social policy is of an intuitive variety, sometimes seasoned by personal information: 'I felt there was substantial overmanning amongst Health Service ancillary workers' (ibid., p. 60); 'abuse worried me constantly' (ibid., p. 129) (over the Temporary Employment Subsidy, here informed by knowledge of the Lancashire textile industry); 'I felt very strongly that we had done well by the pensioners, while those in work had seen their real income fall' (ibid., p. 131). Technical reform in housing policy is a non-starter because politicians will not bear the transitional costs (ibid., p. 39-40), a point well put by Wass (1984): '.. it has always been difficult to interest ministers in reform because of the slow rate of social pay-off, compared with the short-term political costs of change' (p. 57). Healey (1990) recalls how a joint paper (itself significant) by him and Environment Secretary Shore foundered on such objections from Prime Minister Callaghan (p. 449).

The impression from the insider accounts of the 1970s is of a conceptual structure about social policy being placed in abeyance by the tactical demands of politics. In the 1980s (so far receiving insider discussion from Jock Bruce-Gardyne, Norman Fowler, Nicholas Ridley and Nigel Lawson) there was a much more explicit Treasury philosophy on 'political economy' matters and the Treasury itself was staffed as 'the training college for future Cabinet ministers' (Ridley 1992 p. 162). Most of the Treasury's attention during these years was on macro-economic policy. Public expenditure lost some of its potency as an independent variable, especially in the late 1980s when the buoyancy of tax revenue became the main determinant of the level of public sector borrowing. The Treasury line focussed on efficiency, targeting and incentives. Sometimes this conflicted with Conservative ideology of choice and privatisation, which resulted in the slow pace of rationalising school places and the high take up of fiscal incentives for personal pensions (admitted by Lawson to have been 'quite unnecessarily costly' (Lawson 1992 p. 594)).

Nigel Lawson's memoirs have the bulk and intellectual grip to form an important contribution to the debate. Like Richard Crossman, Lawson has an egotistical swagger which is not necessarily the best way to the truth. What comes through is his defence of the Treasury as the custodian of good sense and clear thinking against complacent, lower calibre spending departments which have usually been captured by interest groups. Coupled with this is a possibility of intervention based on the Chancellor's political weight ('..the Chancellor, if he proceeds with care and caution, can affect the content and not merely the cost of other Ministers' policies and, in a limited number of carefully selected areas, generate the ideas which decisively influence the direction of government policy' (Lawson, 1992 p. 273)). Nor is Lawson immune to Barnett style hunches. He reads Correlli Barnett's *The Audit of War* and launches a Treasury paper on educational reform with 'not a word to DES' (ibid., pp. 607-8); eventually this leads to the Education Reform Act 1988. His election campaigning in 1987 convinces him that the electorate want social security benefits to favour the elderly rather than families (ibid., p. 726), a thought he picked up from Richard Crossman (ibid., p. 595), and he is happy to record the 'long standing ambition of the official Treasury' to freeze child benefit (p. 720). Some of these tales seem, Crossman like, to have improved in the telling: it is instructive to cross check Lawson's account of the bruising conflict with the DHSS over the social security review with that provided by Norman Fowler. But Lawson's confidence in his capacity to reach into policy development in the territory of spending departments was founded on his knowledge that, at least until their final falling out, he enjoyed the direct support of the Prime Minister for Treasury forays across the policy spectrum. 'She considered the Treasury to be her department' (he writes) 'and she ensured that ministerially it was "100% dry"' (ibid., p. 26).

Lawson's use of the term 'official Treasury' to express an institutional view is repeated: 'the ethos of the official Treasury - and for all its qualities, I retain both respect and affection for the Department - is unremittingly austere. They disapprove of tax cuts as much as they dislike increases in expenditure. They cannot imagine what the public have done to deserve tax cuts, which will inevitably be put to frivolous use' (ibid., p. 686). For Lawson, the notion of a Treasury memory and culture amounting to a policy certainly rings true. His friend Jock Bruce-Gardyne (1986) writes in a similar vein; there is the 'philosophical bias of the villagers (civil servants) against the concept of the student loan' (p. 122) and on mortgage relief thresholds 'the treasury was ineradicably opposed. This was an issue on which manadarins and ministers stood shoulder to shoulder' (ibid., p. 200).

'Official' prose

As with the insider accounts, we would expect to find a submerged and politically coded view of the Treasury philosophy in the outputs of the PESC process. Since 1991 these are now published in the form of departmental annual reports, and so have lost some of their Treasury imprimatur; they retain the same careful tone, which may be meaningless or may display the results of a word-for-word fight. The expenditure data themselves are not addressed in this chapter and are quite difficult to analyse because of changes in classification and price base. They may be most significant when there are pre-election reinforcements to expenditure (1986, 1991) or emergency additions to reflect the politically unacceptable optimism of earlier estimates (particularly NHS and (notional) local government spending).

We may classify 'PESC prose' into five kinds:

1.   statements of philosophy (which may be the operational programme objectives of a department, or a careful fudge which cannot be appealed to in policy arguments; in the list of social security priorities, the precise wording has changed almost every year and the caveat 'no particular order of priority' is used some years but not others.);

2.   presentations of changes of policy, where civil service drafting is found at its most bland and pickings are likely to be thin; the Fowler review of SERPS was presented in the terms that the scheme 'will be modified to reduce the emerging costs' (HM Treasury 1987 p.247);

3.   conceptual structures on spending needs (e.g. the estimate of 1 per cent real growth in health spending because of demographic trends was first quoted in HM Treasury 1977 p.80); it echoes Joel Barnett's comment that (in 1976) 'David [Ennals] was technically entitled to some additional expenditure because of demographic changes - the growing number of older patients living longer, and taking up more expenditure, ensured that without an increase there would be an effective cut' (Barnett, 1982 pp. 99-100).

4.   health warnings or 'you won't get away with this next year' (e.g. 'in the difficult economic situation, the Government have only been able to make these improvements (in social security) by strict selection of priorities for the distribution of available funds' (HM Treasury, 1976 p. 103); here we may detect echoes of Whitehall battles;

5.   forecasting errors: 'the demand for education in the coming years is now forecast to grow at a slower rate than was expected 12 months ago' (HM Treasury, 1975 p. 94). This is particularly important over unemployment, where the government refuses to give a forecast but is required to make a working assumption in order to estimate social security and training budgets. It also underlies the dispute between the Treasury and the Department of Employment about the proper response when unemployment falls or rises more steeply than expected.

The most explicit statement of the relationship between economic and social policy under the Conservatives came in the Green Paper *The Next Ten Years* (HM Treasury, 1984). This is perhaps the grimmest statement of the scenario that 'as public spending takes a larger and larger share of GDP, so the public sector steadily encroaches on the rest of the economy' (ibid., p. 20) and 'finance must determine expenditure, not expenditure finance' (ibid., p. 21) (in fact, given the lead times involved this is not quite compatible with the suggestion that the total of public expenditure must be determined first and then adhered to). The paper is deeply pessimistic in tone, asserting the impossibility of securing sustained economic recovery unless the demands for expenditure in social programmes are rigorously restrained. In his memoirs, Chancellor Lawson notes with satisfaction the 'absence of political own goals' (in the form of identification of spending deficiencies) (Lawson, 1992, p. 305). He sees nothing strange in the tone and the lack of hints of the glittering prospects of increased revenue to come, which were to lead only three years later to his reduction of the PSBR to zero and even feverish speculation about paying off the National Debt! In fact, there was a surplus from 1987-88 to 1990-91, but in the first and last years only because of privatisation receipts. Expenditure seemed to pursue a fairly stable trajectory of its own, leaving the overall balance to be determined by the fluctuations of tax receipts (again at largely stable tax rates) according to economic activity. The sharpness of the recession in 1992 led to a plunge into a deficit (£37 bn in 1992-93) of a size unimaginable three years earlier - certainly not imagined by Treasury forecasters.

Treasury organisation and the response of Treasury officials

Most of these themes are reflected in the ways in which the Treasury has chosen to discharge the functions with which it is entrusted. These functions, in conventional analysis, are divided into four: general management of the economy; participation in international economic management; the annual budget-making process; and control of public expenditure. In the former two there is an important and delicate relationship with the Bank of England, one that is prominent in ministerial memoirs but often neglected in studies that focus on the Treasury as the leading player in the Whitehall game.

The areas in which the Treasury's impact on social policy are likely to be at their sharpest and most direct are the third and fourth. Management of the economy is certain to have important consequences for public policies of all kinds; but it is in the specific impact of Treasury interventions on the size and shape of particular departmental programmes that the most immediate influence can be identified. But what outcomes has the exercise of this influence produced and how do they come about? In his eccentric but stimulating polemic, *Social Planning*, Alan Walker (1982) simply asserts: 'The Treasury dominates social planning through the control it exercises on public expenditure' (p. 122). He then goes on, as many have done before and since, to describe the processes by which that control is exercised. But this is not good enough; we need to know not merely how control is exercised (certainly an important subsidiary question) but with what objective, before being able to assess the results.

The classic answer to this is that the Treasury is chiefly interested in public expenditure in aggregate and latterly in total public expenditure as a proportion of GDP (Treasury Bulletin, passim). In this perspective any interest in social policy as such stems simply from the fact that the spending departments with responsibilities in this area take the largest share of expenditure. Similarly, the otherwise rather puzzling form that the Treasury's interest in local government's activities has taken can be explained by the fact that expenditure by local authorities lies (or rather lay) in some measure outside the direct control of the Treasury. It therefore posed a particular problem in management terms (captured by Leo Pliatzky's image of the signal box in which some of the levers aren't connected). Treasury ambivalence about the desirable extent of control is reflected in the exclusion of self-financed local expenditure from the planning total in 1989, but its inclusion in the new control total from 1993.

But an explanation based on the primacy of the 'big picture' won't altogether do. Indeed, some people, at least, within the Treasury are themselves clearly not happy with it. In that fascinating picture of mandarins at play - *But, Chancellor* (Young and Sloman, 1984), the view that Treasury control is merely about reining back the total demands of the big spenders is referred to by one official as 'the usual caricature....it implies that the Treasury is only interested in the totals, and indeed some people believe that that is true. I don't think it is, because we also have a role in trying to achieve value for money, and in encouraging departments to look for that.. . We're interested not only in whether it costs x million pounds, but what that x million pounds is intended to do' (our emphasis) (p. 45). Rather typically, that statement is at once qualified. Another civil servant asserts that there is no such thing as a 'Treasury housing policy', merely 'a housing aspect of a general public expenditure policy' (ibid., p. 44). And the then Second Permanent Secretary in charge of public expenditure, Sir Anthony Rawlinson, pronounces magisterially that Treasury concern is actually 'with the aggregate of the various programmes that make up the whole, and their influence on the economy in the light of the government's general economic strategy' (ibid., p. 44). The Treasury will acknowledge that it intervenes to help departments find the most cost-effective way of achieving government policy objectives, but stops short of avowing a policy of its own.

Clearly, there is some inconsistency here and it is not one that the otherwise generally admirable Treasury openness about the stages and procedures of the public expenditure process, which begins with Heclo and Wildavsky (1981) and has gathered pace over the course of the eighties (cf Likierman (1988), the Treasury's own guide (1986)) has helped to clarify. Some clues can be picked up from other documents. The 1984 Green Paper argued the case for controlling public expenditure on two grounds: first, the 'burden' of taxation and the effects that this has had on enterprise and, second, the tendency of some forms of expenditure to expand continuously under pressure of unsatisfied demands, unless checked. Both of these are orthodox New Right positions; neither is supported by reliable empirical evidence. Nor do they have anything particular to tell us about why control should take any specific form in social policy areas, except to the extent that the much-feared pressure groups are believed through their 'special pleading' (HM Treasury, 1984 p. 20) to exercise a particularly malign influence upon public attitudes towards expenditure in these areas. These arguments are perhaps best viewed as temporary aberrations from the mainstream of customary Treasury arguments, produced by specific political pressures. They belong to the pre-Poll Tax days when Conservative governments could still argue with some degree of consistency against 'throwing money at problems'.

Other explanations therefore need to be sought, and many are available. There is the simple demonology: the Treasury controls social policy expenditure especially harshly because it simply doesn't understand what social expenditure is about. The classic statement here is Aneurin Bevan's in the NHS Tenth Anniversary debate:

> I insist that when the Treasury has decided that it is able to afford certain money for certain purposes it should leave the spending of the money to those who know most about it and about how they can get the most good for the Service. What happens over and over again is that some minor official at the Treasury wipes the dust from his eyes and looks at all these items and sees how he can nibble them away (House of Commons, Hansard, 30 July 1958, vol 592, col 1394).

Such attitudes and such intrusiveness have probably much declined in the PESC era, although undue interference by unduly junior Treasury officials remains a leitmotiv of ministerial memoirs. Then there is the spending department version: the Treasury controls for the sake of controlling, without regard to the consequences of what it is doing, because that is the nature of the beast. However, it is difficult to avoid the impression that this explanation is often much too convenient for the departments themselves. If forced to justify their position to Whitehall colleagues, they can point to the Treasury's intervention as their justification for failure to deliver on their projects. Their benevolent intentions have been thwarted by an all-powerful watchdog with iron teeth: a Treasury which 'never sleeps' (Heseltine, 1987 p. 147). Unfortunately, this alibi is not available, at least for public purposes, to ministers, who have to make the best fist they can of justifying decisions on their spending proposals which may be far removed from their original intentions (cf. Fowler, 1991, ch 11)

But then why should a Treasury watchdog, even one with an insatiable appetite for candle ends, stay awake for some programmes and blink an eye to others? Perhaps it is simply because of a lack of enough time, or people to go around. The Treasury teams shadowing individual spending departments for the purposes of the annual survey are not large (Thain and Wright, 1992a and 1992b). And if it is true that in 1983 there were only ten people in the Treasury dealing with social security (Young and Sloman, 1984, p. 49) that might help to explain why interventions in this highly technical and complex area took the form they did and helped to produce such a lopsided outcome (even in 'pure' public expenditure terms) to the social security review (see below). Perhaps it is because there are other ways of exercising control over the programmes of social policy departments through the greatly enhanced role of the National Audit Office and the sanctions that its reports can impose (publicity when the reports are issued, and public cross-examination in front of the Public Accounts Committee). Or perhaps it is simply because outsiders mistake the nature of the game that is being played. The Treasury are not malicious, or schooled in a set of identical responses, or languidly dilettantish, or too clever for their own good, as critics of various kinds assert (Ham (1981), who see them 'playing out the role which they believe is their prerogative, and which fits in with their culture and perception of the world' (p. ix) and also Thomas Balogh and John Hoskyns). A complex set of moves are being made, involving ministers as well as officials, the full significance of which may be only apparent to insiders. Diana Coyle, herself a former Treasury official, reports an industrialist who has regular dealings with the department as saying: 'They give the impression that they are in a completely different world. You feel that what they say among themselves is not what they say to outsiders' (Coyle, 1992 p. 12).

Territorial and devolved budgeting

Territorial budgeting further explores the Treasury's 'letting go' of expenditure discretion in areas small enough not to affect the aggregate. It was expressed in the 'Barnett formula' of 1978 which tied changes in Scottish and Welsh expenditure to changes in the corresponding English item in effect, the argument was confined to the degree of correspondence. Alongside this, the Secretaries of State could switch expenditure within their 'block' (including health, education and housing spending) without reference to the Treasury. This was intended as the semi-automatic funding mechanism that would allow the block grant system to operate under devolution. The particular circumstances of Northern Ireland have led to particularly high identifiable public expenditure there under separate control mechanisms. In practice, the pressures for United Kingdom policy uniformity and certain specific reservations (e.g. NHS charges) have made this a less fruitful topic for investigation than some might have hoped but it poses interesting questions of how large a programme budget needs to be before the Treasury feels the need to impose full scale bilateral controls.

Continued unease by the Treasury led to the so called 'Portillo formula', announced at the time of the Autumn Statement in November 1992, which adjusts Scotland's formula share to 10.66 per cent, its exact proportion of the population. As before, the formula abates cuts as well as increases and so would work to Scotland's advantage if the trajectory of expenditure is downwards. Scottish Secretary Ian Lang naturally presented this as a victory, a formal acknowledgement by the Treasury that Scotland's needs were higher and could not be expected to converge with England's, but was quoted that 'I think it is important we have a good relationship between the Treasury and ourselves and I was conscious of the fact that the formula was a sticking point in the negotiations' (*The Scotsman* 13 November 1992). The lack of interest in Scottish Office matters in all ministerial memoirs suggests that it sticks some way down the Treasury hierarchy.

Also relevant here are the budgetary frameworks for the new executive agencies, which embody some new freedoms (e.g. the right to use income to finance higher running costs). Nigel Lawson (1992) admits that after the Next Steps report of 1988 'a long battle ensued, resulting in a lengthy written concordat' (p. 392); rather extraordinarily he admits to an oft-surmised hidden agenda, saying that 'the main practical advantage I see is that by creating accounts, boards of directors and saleable assets, future privatisation may prove less difficult' (ibid., p. 393). This is scarcely an accurate characterisation of most of the agencies. The earliest ones (the Vehicle Inspectorate, HMSO) tended to be potentially self financing; the more interesting questions arise when some income is at hand but a degree of permanent Treasury subvention is required. 'Pure' social policy agencies, like the Benefits Agency in DSS, raise different control problems which may only become evident over time should the efficiency objectives of the agency not be realisable within the resources made available to them. Leo Pliatzky (1989), though generally betraying a lack of insider knowledge when he writes of the 1980s, is probably right when he says that 'I doubt whether the Treasury saw this as primarily a matter of Whitehall power politics or whether they had any hostility to the concept of agencies. They would, I think, have been greatly concerned with the problem of reconciling this concept with the Treasury's responsibilities for public service pay and manpower and public expenditure generally' (p. 104).

The long-run themes of Treasury policy

We can summarise our argument by suggesting eight kinds of typical Treasury behaviour it pursues in order to safeguard its own (and in its eyes the public's) interest:

1. preserving its right to intervene when cost implications arise (the turf as well as substance being important); this includes reserving the right to keep coming back at an issue. Norman Fowler (1991) is eloquent on this as he recalls how the Treasury put round a minute trying to reopen the abolition of SERPS two days before the Cabinet was to approve the Green Paper (p. 219) and then (though Fowler is more coy about detail) forced him into 'the worst decision that I had ever to take in government' (ibid., p. 221) when the opposition of the employers and the pensions industry allied itself to the continuing objections of the Treasury to allow SERPS to be preserved after all. This is a particularly interesting case because the Treasury promoted the less ideologically ambitious course of action (in Conservative terms), but for the 'wrong' cost-control reasons. As Nigel Lawson (1992) explains it, the Treasury had no objection to the abolition of SERPS as long as there would not be any compulsory private scheme (p. 591). He (unusually) blames the incompetence of officials for not alerting him until the last minute to the cost implications of Norman Fowler's original proposals (see above).

For the Treasury, this seemed to be a slide-rule issue, and Lawson himself was happy with the freedom not to make provision for old age. The operational principles were a safeguarding of tax revenue and the avoidance of burdens on business, without any sense of a duty to promote social protection across the life-cycle.

2.	reserving its sole proprietorship of 'budget' matters such as tax expenditures and national insurance contributions (a source of frustration to Norman Fowler (1991) during the social security reviews, where he quotes Nigel Lawson as saying 'you have no authority to make proposals on National Insurance' (p. 214), a stance later modified but always available to the Treasury if it wanted to be awkward; as Lawson (1992) puts it, 'holding fast to the hallowed doctrine that taxation is a matter for the Chancellor and must not be put into commission' (p. 596)). The Treasury would also have an interest in trying to ensure that the same policies were not being pursued simultaneously - and hence potentially wastefully - through the tax and benefit systems;

3.	crude economics (work incentives, training, public sector pay) at its worst the Treasury representative sounding off like a pub bore, but a phenomenon known mainly through anecdotes; as Pliatzky (1989) concedes, 'some of those under whom I served or who served under me, although intelligent enough, were ineffectual for one reason or another, unimaginative or indecisive or even neurotic' (p. 163);

4.	crude social philosophy (on matters as diverse as the desirability of female employment, educational opportunities, investment in human capital and the role of private savings), perhaps most characteristically captured at the political level in leaked comments to the Cabinet's Family Policy Group in 1982, such as in Sir Geoffrey Howe and Ferdinand Mount's contribution on the lines of 'teaching children to make better use of their pocket money' (*The Guardian* 17 February 1983), though Nigel Lawson (1992) claims that 'this sounded like a Radical Right manifesto, but its inspiration was mainly Treasury-inspired arithmetic' (p. 303);

5.	selectivity (programmes limited by clientele and time), recently refined into 'targeting' in which the 'deadweight' of universal entitlement is reduced. Concern with effectiveness in reaching target groups and with ensuring that new policies do not create too many losers (or at least not too visibly, as the Poll Tax did) is another recurrent Treasury theme;

6. ongoing bilateral debates with Departments in which small matters get implicated in big (e.g. the DSS under Tony Newton (1989-92) throwing the Treasury scraps in order to keep universal child benefit; and Treasury arguments with the Department of Employment about the merit of different schemes, a process revealed in the leaked letter from Chief Secretary Mellor to Employment Secretary Michael Howard in 1991 (see Unemployment Unit Working Brief November 1991)). The scope here for tactical intrigue to replace policy analysis is evident;

7. using arguments 'on merit' as a high-minded trojan horse to reassert control in areas of particular concern to the Treasury (as in the training instance mentioned above). One particular triumph in this area celebrated by Lawson (1992) is his breaking through the strongly-defended perimeter of the defence budget and securing licence to explore detail on the same basis as for other spending departments (the security services, however, eluded him) (pp. 312-13);

8. finally, dismantling alternative centres of decision making on public finances (especially local authorities) and substituting administratively devolved bodies with no independent sources of public funds. (The collision between the government's general aspiration to devolve responsibility for budgets to local managers wherever possible - increasingly outside traditional departmental structures - and the Treasury's adamantine determination to retain full budgetary control at the centre is likely to be a fertile area for conflict in the near future, as Thain and Wright (1992a and 1992b) point out.

These are ultimately speculative points but they receive enough suggestion from the literature to make it important to research them further in search of empirical backing. In particular, we need to chart changes over time in the relative emphasis the Treasury gives to these various aspects of its purpose.

The research agenda

This chapter has hinted at some of the means through which we might explore Treasury social policy in action, and more will become available. To start with the official record, Cabinet papers from the new era of public expenditure control in the 1960s will soon be accessible to explore the Treasury's motivations as the post Plowden system was being set up, and especially their notions of the controllability of social spending. More recent cases studies are inviting (housing benefit changes in the early 1980s; social security reform in 1985-6; and even the Poll Tax, where Nicholas Ridley's (1991) memoirs suggest that an account of the Treasury's reservations may soon be able to be pieced together (ch 6) and Nigel Lawson (1992) has set out his primarily political objections to the policy (pp. 45-46)). On smaller matters, those which come to the attention of the Public Accounts Committee and require a response from both the Treasury and the spending department are of particular interest. Material assembled by the Treasury Select Committee - including evidence given by Ministers - helps to shed some light on the evolution of the general relationship between the Treasury and spending departments. On the 'fourth term' policy agenda we have the continued development of Next Steps agencies, at the junction of the Treasury's management and financial control functions, as the norm for civil service organisation; and the continued financial uncertainty over Community Care, where the Department of Health's wish for ring fencing of the budget transferred to local authorities from April 1993 ran up against the traditional caution of the Treasury. Developments on the territorial front (local government reorganisation now inevitable, and devolution waiting in the wings) are also good tests of most of our hypotheses.

All researchers into the heart of government have to cope with the problem of how to overcome the lack of truly authoritative recent detail on particular policy issues. This is the area where we find the Treasury at its most sensitive, since they cannot hide behind the fig leaf of explaining technical detail or government policy; the purpose of the research effort is to expose the cracks in the monolith of government. On the other hand, it is now virtually open season on ministerial memoirs about the Thatcher years (especially now that Nigel Lawson has been so free with his records of papers and meetings), and the growing confidence in the respectability of 'contemporary history' by former special advisers and retired Permanent Secretaries is paying dividends. In prospect is a style of social policy research going beyond Treasury bashing to explore the ways that the main economic department grapples with the fact that it cannot control all of social policy but must take a view about the likely social outcomes of its economic objectives.

3 Managing to survive: Dilemmas of changing organisational forms in the public sector

John Clarke and Janet Newman

This chapter is concerned with the place and role of 'management' within the restructuring of the British welfare state. It begins by examining some of the recent arguments about processes of restructuring and connects them to a discussion of the politics of managerialisation. It identifies the claim to the 'right to manage' as a phenomenon associated with a wider programme of restructuring in both Britain and the USA. The final section examines some of the dilemmas which have emerged in the experience of managerialisation within the welfare state.

Restructuring welfare: new state formations

A decade of restructuring of the welfare state has given rise to a growing literature concerned with making sense of the new shapes and structures of state organisation which have emerged. Attention has been directed to different elements of this process of transformation. Some have stressed the subjection of the state to the disciplines of internal and external markets and 'quasi-markets' (e.g. Le Grand, 1990). Some have emphasised the restructuring of public sector labour processes and labour forces (e.g. Pinch, 1989, Cousins, 1990). Others have focussed on shifts in the balance of political forces and relationships around both the central and local state (e.g. Cochrane, 1991). Some have gone so far as to argue that the outlines of a new type of state form can be discerned in the guise of 'post-fordist' or 'post- bureaucratic' modes of organization (e.g. Hoggett, 1991).

The 'discovery' of post-fordism provided a conceptual bridge which linked changes in the organisation of production and distribution of goods and services with an analysis of sub-epochal transformations in the 'regimes of accumulation' of capitalism (see, for example, Piore and Sabel, 1984; and Aglietta, 1979). One central indicator of the shift from fordism to post-fordism has been the move from 'mass' systems to more complexly differentiated systems (in labour processes, in products, in markets, in labour forces). The application of the concept of post-fordism to state restructuring has operated by analogy with this shift from mass to differentiated provision. It suggests that there has been a parallel transition from a bureaucratic, monolithic, producer dominated state providing undifferentiated services to one which is becoming fragmented, flexible, differentiated and 'market driven'. The attraction of this analogy lies in the way it offers a theorised approach to the problems of identifying connections between the phenomena of state restructuring and the processes of wider social and economic transformation of advanced capitalist (or post industrial) societies.

As with the use of the fordism/post-fordism distinction for the analysis of economic restructuring, the attractions of applying it to changes in state forms may be more apparent than real. There is already considerable dispute about its plausibility and accuracy in relation to economic restructuring. Critics have argued that the concept of fordism itself is empirically problematic, suggesting that it over reads the dominance and spread of fordist systems of production and distribution (e.g. Hudson, 1988; Sayer and Walker, 1992). Others have suggested that it is flawed by problems of reductionism and determinism, such that it underestimates the salience of political struggles and strategies (e.g. Rustin, 1989). In particular, this has involved the argument that the focus on post-fordism has distracted attention from the diversity of strategies developed by capital for restructuring in search of profitablity over the last decade which include the revitalisation of both 'fordist' and 'pre-fordist' systems of production and distribution. There are equal difficulties attaching to the argument by analogy to state restructuring. The first is the presumption that the state form developed in post-war advanced capitalist societies can properly be characterised as 'fordist'. In relation to state welfare, for example, such a designation ignores the wealth of difference revealed by comparative analysis in the patterns of welfare provision and organisation in countries which might be thought to be 'fordist' (e.g. Esping-Anderson, 1990). More particularly, the characterisation of the state as 'fordist' runs the risk of misrecognising the specific labour processes of the state, given that, in welfare especially, they have been noticeably labour intensive (rather than mechanised) and have involved complexly discretionary practices of 'people processing' (Gough, 1979; Cochrane, 1989). The application of 'post-fordism' to the analysis of emergent state forms carries the danger of either technological or economic reductionism (depending on which variant of the thesis is taken) and risks underestimating the political struggles involved in attempting to develop and accomplish particular strategies of restructuring.[1] In that context, while admiring the charm of claims like 'one of the few advantages of the term 'post Fordism' is its agnosticism about the future, i.e. it suggests that we're clearer about where we're coming from than where we're going to' (Hoggett, 1991, p. 243), we must beg to differ. Instead we would want to argue that both past and future are more problematic than the binary logic of fordism and post-fordism can allow.[2]

What we want to draw from this rather compressed discussion is the need to be attentive to issues of politics, power and strategies in the analysis of state restructuring. For us, these are the preconditions for focussing on one particular dimension - the impact of managerialism on the welfare state.[3] This is not a claim to have discovered the phenomenon of managerialisation, since it is a theme which is apparent in most of the arguments on restructuring noted earlier, in that management is involved in the coordination of new market relations, new labour processes and forces, new organisational structures and new sets of relationships within and beyond the state. What we do want to argue is that managerialisation is both a central connective thread in the restructuring process and that it is a central component of the political strategy of restructuring.

The politics of managerialisation

To develop this argument it is necessary to return to the focal concerns of the Conservative assault on the welfare state. We would suggest that there have been three central concerns visible since the mid-1970s. The first of these is directed to the economic costs of welfare as imposing an excessive burden on the 'wealth creating' activities of individuals and enterprises. This concern has focussed around public spending and public borrowing and has manifested itself in the stringent fiscal disciplines applied to all aspects of state welfare. The second concerns the social consequences of state welfare: the demoralising, disincentive and dependency producing effects of state provision. This has focussed on the inhibiting results which state provision has had on the freedom, autonomy and responsibility of the individual and has manifested itself both in the efforts to reduce and 'target' benefits and in the encouragement of a more diverse mixed economy of welfare intended to supplant the state's 'monopoly provider' status. The third concern has been rather different. It has focussed on the state itself as the site of power and as a multiplicity of points through which political resistance or opposition might be organised.[4] This has been the core of Conservative attacks on such diverse targets as the 'monopoly provider' role; the power of professional empires; the unresponsiveness of bureaucratic authorities and the activities of 'loony left' (and other) councils. The directions implied by these three concerns do not all point the same way. Reductions in expenditure could, in principle, have been accomplished without 'markets'. So too, more rigourous benefit systems could have been achieved without 'customers'. The economic and social logics of the Conservative attack on welfare have, however, been structured by the political logic of dismantling the welfare state as a site of power. It is this logic which has driven the 'politics of managerialisation'. We must now say a little more about the state and power.

Our starting point is an argument that the development of the welfare state in Britain involved the construction of an internal regime of 'professional bureaucracy' which might be said to embody the Fabian archetype of expertise coupled with the systemic organisation of services through the regulatory principles of administrative categories (see, for example, Clarke, 1943). By 'internal regime' we mean the articulation of modes of power which connect the structures, cultures, relationships and processes of organisational forms in specific configurations. Both bureaucracy and professionalism involve particular modes of power. They lay claim to particular legitimations for the exercise of power (varieties of expertise and neutrality). They exercise particular ways of deploying power (controlling access to resources or establishing normative judgements). They construct relationships of power between themselves and the recipients of their services (as claimants, clients, patients and so on). The welfare state has drawn together these two modes - bureaucracy and professionalism - in combinations as 'bureau-professional regimes'.[5] Such regimes involve different 'balances of power' between the bureaucratic and professional elements in particular settings (compare medicine and social work, for example) but the concept provides a general key to the organisational architecture of the welfare state in Britain. In turn, these bureau-professional regimes were articulated, again in different settings, with organised political power - in central and local governments and in health authorities, for example. Each site also involved the construction of distinctive relationships between the internal regimes of the state, forms of political representation and 'citizens'.

This complex of bureaucratic, professional and political power was identified by the new right in the 1970s as a major stumbling block to a radical reconstruction of the state and its role in British society. It is this which underpins the intensity of the attacks on all three modes of power represented by the welfare state. 'Arrogant' professionals were arraigned alongside 'inflexible' bureaucrats and 'interfering' politicians as preventing efficient, effective and economic public services. But the new right also identified the welfare state as a blockage whose interlocking modes of power might be disentangled and defused by the combination of markets and management - aided by a judicious degree of fiscal strangling through the Treasury or legislative execution where needed (the metropolitan counties and the GLC). Against this background, the restructuring process inaugurated in May 1979 may be viewed as having a number of interlinked objectives: fiscal redistribution by shifting the 'tax burden' and necessitating the reorganisation of welfare; the dislocation of welfare state organisational structures identified as embodying disincentives, dependency and demoralisation (inhibitors to the enterprise culture); and finally the disarticulation of the regimes of organisational and political power identified as the progeny of post war social democracy and as sites of potential political opposition and resistance to the wider programme of reconstruction (Clarke, 1991; Clarke and Langan, 1993).

Managerialisation has proved to be a suitable vehicle for the unlocking of this complex of power in the welfare state. In the process, management has been identified as a transformational force counterposed to each of the old modes of power. By contrast with the professional, the manager is customer focussed and is driven by the search for efficiency rather than abstract 'professional standards'. Compared to the bureaucrat, the manager is flexible and outward looking. Unlike the politician, the manager inhabits the 'real world' of 'good business practices' not the realms of doctrinaire ideology. In the process, it is not surprising that 'better management' has attracted a lot of support and that welfare organisations are becoming thoroughly managerialised, either through importing managers or through the remaking of bureau-professionals into managers (Newman and Clarke, forthcoming). Management, then, is the force elected by the new right to carry through the restructuring of the welfare state. It is the agency which inherits the dismantling of old regimes and provides a new regime (a new mode of power) around which organisations can be structured. The significance of management as a regime lies in the claim that managers 'do the right things'. It is this which underpins management as a mode of power and is associated with an insistent demand that managers must be given the 'freedom' or the 'right to manage'. To grasp the importance of this claim, we must make a small detour via the crisis of U.S. capitalism.

The right to manage: power and prerogative

The managerialisation strategy did not spring fully formed from the hydra head of new right think tanks or the Thatcher cabinet. It draws on a set of analyses and presciptions which were developed about the failings of the American economy in the late 1970s. These were expressed in the domains of 'economics' and 'management' and offered parallel messages that economic decline could be defeated through an onslaught on the individual, corporate and national blockages to enterprise. The economists articulated a vision of the liberated individual (freed from the shackles of the state) at work in the liberated corporation (freed from the shackles of over-regulation and excessive taxation) within the liberated nation (freed from big government) which would guarantee a resurgent America (Moody, 1987 and Clarke, 1991, ch 5). The proponents of the 'new managerialism' articulated a vision of the liberated manager transforming the rule bound, inert and bureaucratically managed corporation into a new and dynamically competitive organism able to deliver 'more from less' (Clarke and Newman, 1993). This also identified a unity of interest between the individual, the corporation and the nation. The enterprising individual would be freed to contribute effectively to the enterprising corporation as part of a free enterprise nation (Rose, 1989, ch. 10).

There are clear rhetorical affinities between these 'liberation' programmes and the new right agenda for social, economic and political reconstruction in Britain and the USA. What is equally important, however, are the strategies deployed on both sides of the Atlantic to clear the ground for the exercise of 'the manager's right to manage'. The 'liberation' of the manager has been more than rhetorical. The late 1970s and 1980s saw sustained attempts to dismantle both extra- and intra-organizational forms of power which blocked the exercise of managerial discretion, ranging from governmental regulation to union organization. A variety of strategies have been used to clear the internal space of the organization for the freer exercise of managerial discretion. Although not wishing to go into detail here, we can note that these include capital mobility, de-unionisation, deregulation, localisation of bargaining, 'sweetheart' deals and 'beauty contests', new labour contracts, new labour forces, changes in industrial relations law and the favourite 'enforcer' of new working practices - large scale unemployment. Such shifts in the balance of power in the workplace by no means commit management to practising the precepts of the 'new managerialism' since there is clearly room for a variety of management styles and tactics to be exercised within the new organisational space created in the name of the managerial prerogative.[6] The core 'flexibility' in these restructuring processes has been the enhanced flexibility (or power) of management (Clarke and Newman, 1993).

The restructuring of the welfare state in Britain has involved a number of methods of dismantling old arrangements: the pressures of fiscal constraint; the imposition of fragmentation through Compulsory Competitive Tendering (CCT); de-monopolisation of service provision either through enforced competition or required 'partnerships'; the introduction of internal trading systems and the combined centralisation and decentralisation of power away from 'intermediate' institutions such as local government. If 'markets' and 'customers' have been the ideological cutting edge of these changes, then 'management' has been the eagerly sought principle of articulation for a new organisational regime for the welfare state. The salience of 'management' for the emergent shape of the welfare state in Britain is located in the way it links the wider context of restructuring to the specific 'problems' identified as requiring change in the organisation of welfare. Management is the necessary corollary of the dismantling of the familiar structures of bureau-professionalism. Managers are those who 'understand' markets; who can extract the untapped potential from the 'human resources'; who are sensitised to the 'needs of the customer'; who can deliver 'results' and who can be relied on to 'do the right thing'. The unlocking of trade union organisation, bureau-professionalism and local political representation requires 'management' to provide an alternative mode of power. At the same time, the process of managerialisation has been able to draw sustenance from the expansion of management education and development, led by the private sector but increasingly applied to those working in the public sector and providing a new vocabulary through which the transformation of the welfare state is increasingly addressed.[7]

It is this context which helps to make sense of managerialisation as a process which is explicitly concerned with organisational power and as a strategy for the recomposition of previous modes of power within and around the welfare state. What is at stake is the diminution of other modes of power in order to establish the conditions for managerial discretion. It is this accomplishment which was proudly announced by the then Secretary of State for Education, Kenneth Clarke, in 1992: 'A measure of the success of our first ten years is that we have restored management to its proper place in our society.' (BBC Radio 4, *Today* programme, 12.3.92.)

Nevertheless, the strategy of managerialisation has not involved the simple displacement of one internal regime by another. The regime of bureau- professionalism has been established deep in the interstices of the welfare state as it has developed in Britain - in its various manifestations it had become the 'taken for granted' way in which public services were organised and provided. It bound together the organisational structures, cultures and routines of welfare with the occupational identities, assumptions and careers of those working within welfare in the post war era. While the various legislative changes of the post-1979 Conservative governments have unlocked many of the structural supports of the old regime, the looked for cultural change in identities, attitudes and practices has been (predictably) harder to accomplish. To some extent, the stubbornness of such dimensions of the old regime explain the sense of constant revolution in the Conservative approach to public welfare as they search for further means of unlocking the past's persistence in the present.

The depth of resistance to change among those in bureau-professional regimes has a number of dimensions, not all of which are encompassed by Conservative explanations about unwillingness to surrender power.[8] One is the profound suspicion about the likely fate of the ethos of 'public service' in the creation of a new mixed economy of welfare with a diminished role for the state. Another is the fear of what happens to both professional and bureaucratic 'standards' in these changes which are viewed as (however inadequately) guaranteeing certain minimum and universal norms of welfare provision. Related to this is a level of scepticism about the rhetoric of markets and management in terms of their ability to 'deliver the goods', even in the absence of fiscal restraint. Defenders of the old regime cast doubt on the transferability of 'good business practice' from the private to public sectors, pointing to differences in conditions, processes and desired outcomes between the two sectors. The specific rhetorical emphasis of the new managerialism (with its stress on missions, visions, corporate enthusiasm and the like) has, if anything, reinforced scepticism, playing into a set of wider cultural categories which distinguish between 'American razzmatazz' and 'British reserve and understatement'.

At stake in these processes are the transformation of bureau-professionals into managed and managers - their subjection to the new discourse of managerialism. Like all discourses the new managerialism aims to construct identities in and through relations of power and practice. In the context of the welfare state, this has involved trying to find the principles which will either subordinate bureau-professional identities to the process of being managed (most visibly in the introduction of 'general management' in the NHS) or will transform bureau-professionals into managers (in local authorities or in locally managed schools, for example). Our focus in the remainder of this chapter is on this latter process - the experience of 'becoming' managers.

Discretion and dilemmas: learning to be managers

Our experience of working with those becoming managers in public sector organisations has highlighted how uncomfortable the process of transformation has proved to to be. There has been no easy transition from old to new 'roles', rather a complex sense of dislocation and uncertainty about the possibilities and prospects of becoming a new manager combined with a sense of confusion and loss about old certainties. It is, we think, necessary to stress the importance of the ways in which the old bureau-professional identities had been 'softened up' and rendered vulnerable by a lengthy period of attacks on the regime of the public sector by the new right dating from the mid-1970s. These ideological assaults combined with other criticisms of the welfare state from diverse political positions (from the left, feminism, anti-racist movements and service user groups) in complicated ways. Together, though, they pointed to structural problems in the old regime and created a degree of uncertainty about the ability of bureau-professionalism to persist as the ordering regime of state welfare. The discovery of managerialism has played into these doubts and uncertainties, being presented as the way of reorganizing which would rescue public welfare from the difficulties it faced.

As a result, any account of the experience of managerialisation must address the 'pull factors' which make the prospect of becoming a manager an attractive one. Despite doubts and scepticism, some find that becoming a manager holds out new possibilities and resolutions to old problems. Probably the strongest of these is the way in which devolved management systems promise solutions to problems of service organisation and delivery in hard pressed public services. For many, devolution has offered the prospect of linking discretion to practice, moving choices closer to the 'front line'. It promises to value 'grounded knowledge' and allow a closer match of resources and action. As such, it addresses the frustrations of those involved in service delivery which are experienced as the combination of resource limits and administrative unresponsiveness at higher levels in the organisation. Such new found 'freedoms' of managerial discretion have proved attractive to those concerned to protect and improve services in a variety of settings. But it is precisely this promise which brings to the surface the first of the dilemmas which we wish to address here - that between managerial and professional identities.

Managerial and professional identities

Professionalism has provided a basis for attempts to defend and improve service standards within the welfare state. Professionals come to 'own' their field of service provision by virtue of training, peer recognition and career development whether in environmental health or teaching. The result is the double edged claim of professionals to know best how to meet needs. While this has been the source of criticism about professional arrogance and paternalism, it has also been a strong institutionalised pressure for the maintenance of 'standards'. Becoming a manager plays on these commitments as strong motivational factors: taking on responsibility gives power in relation to services. At the same time it requires that such commitments be balanced by a recognition of 'organisational realities' (usually budgetary ones) and by taking on board 'corporate' responsibilities. In this way, devolved management has sought to dissolve the characteristic problem of managing professionals (their split loyalties to the organisation and to the profession) not by subjecting them to more management but by turning them into managers. In the process, the tension between organisational and professional commitments become internalised rather than external. Such new managers become the focal point for conflicting identities and loyalties, struggling to reconcile in their identities and practice the previously separated commitments. This process takes place in the context of devolved resources, which carry with them the devolution of resource limits, such that 'hard choices' are pushed down the organisation towards the front line, bringing with them the stress that accompanies trying to balance service commitments and resource limits.[9]

Corporate and local identities

Devolved management systems also contain the seeds of a second dilemma - that of the relationship between centre and periphery or corporate and local interests. The classic bureaucratic structures of state organisations located control in functionally differentiated lines of administration, each represented at the top of the organisational hierarchy by chief officers or their departmental equivalent. As departments have become dissolved, fragmented or decentralised the orthodox linkages of administrative systems no longer represent a stable solution to the problems of coordination. Instead, managers are exhorted to differentiate between the core 'corporate' or 'strategic' functions of the organisation and those other functions which may be effectively delegated, decentralised or contracted out (see, for example, Department of the Environment, 1991). Such solutions carry with them certain problems of implementation.

The first problem is that of identifying what aspects of organisational management can be marked out as matters of corporate or strategic significance. Discussions of this issue often treat it as if the distinction was obvious and natural - suggesting that anybody could tell at a glance if a particular topic was or was not strategic. It is possible that such assumptions betray the general dependence on models drawn from private sector management where, at least nominally, a limited set of strategic objectives can be defined for organisations, relating to profitability, market share, etc. In practice, of course, life can be more complicated than this even in the private sector, but public sector organisations may even have trouble deciding 'what business we're in', always supposing that they wish to identify themselves as being 'in business'. The result is that defining the domain of the 'strategic' is complex, resulting in the uneasy and uncertain production of strategic plans, visions and mission statements which attempt, often for the first time, to articulate a purpose and direction for the organisation or sub-unit. One result of producing such statements is that they create the occasion for dissent (or at least scepticism) and the articulation of conflicting definitions of purpose, direction and interest.

A further difficulty is defining how both to separate the centre from the periphery and still retain forms of integration which avoid the dangers of excessive autonomy for sub-units. Both aspects of this problem are the subject of organisational 'micro-politics' relating to the degree of discretion to be enjoyed by sub-units. Despite the discourse of 'letting go' in the new managerialism, the surrender of control by the organisational centre does not come easily. Both the powers which the centre retains and the forms of control or monitoring which they choose to exercise over the periphery can become the sites of tension. Managers of sub-units often find the promised autonomy accompanying devolution to be excessively hedged around with limits and qualifications and may find their activities become the subject of enhanced, rather than reduced, monitoring and scrutiny.[10] Such reluctance to set the periphery free on the part of the corporate centre is, of course, understandable. Local autonomy can produce unintended consequences where the cumulative effect of local decisions can pull sub-units away from corporately desired directions. The concern of the corporate centre is to promote integration among increasingly disintegrated sections of the organisation leading to a search for 'effective' means of managing unity. These range from the promotion of a 'corporate culture', through performance management systems, to internal contracting, although each carries certain problems as a prospective solution to centre-periphery relations.

The development of corporate cultures through 'symbolic management' has seemed an increasingly attractive option to both private and public sector organisations. Managers are advised that, by careful attention to the symbolic environment, it is possible to promote an integrative culture producing attachment and motivation among staff. As in the earlier discussion of mission statements and related initiative, symbolic management runs the risk of making explicit previously concealed differences of interest and value. Performance measurement is likewise vulnerable to the potential for disputes over what are appropriate objectives and measures, with the possibility of tensions between corporate and local definitions of desired outcomes (to say nothing of the potential difference of user perspectives).[11] Finally, given the increasing salience of 'internal markets' in the public sector, it is not surprising that 'contracting' has been looked to as a potential mode of organisational coordination, establishing a complex of internal customer-supplier relations. This, too, is not a straightforward solution, since the specification of services required raises difficulties. The process may also lead 'customer' departments to question their being limited to internal suppliers (some managers take the language of the market place seriously) and thus add to the centripetal forces at work within the organisation. In particular, service units may resent being 'recharged' for services supplied from and identified with the corporate centre (finance, personnel, etc.). In different ways, these would be integrative devices provide terrains on which the emergent tension between centre and periphery can be played out in new ways rather than resolving them. That is likely to be so, given that the centripetal tendencies are structural features of the changing organisational structures and the managerial regimes being established in them. In broad terms, then, we would suggest that the corporate centre will be engaged in a continual organisational struggle to discipline the potential for greater fragmentation and autonomy for the periphery.

Efficiency and equity

The third dilemma with which we are concerned plays across centre-periphery relations in complex ways. Most of the organisational changes and the promotion of managerialism as a regime have been legitimated through constant reference to the need to improve the 'efficiency' of public sector organisations in order to deliver 'value for money'. The climate of cost consciousness and competitiveness created by the changes sits uncomfortably with other strongly held values developed within the old bureau-professional regime, particularly those concerned with 'equity' of service provision. This is especially visible in considerations of whether the greater flexibility and discretion of service managers can extend to creating different service standards for different customers, notably those able to pay for enhanced standards. We have encountered a recurrent metaphor for this issue in relation to arguments about the quality of service provided. Proponents of differential standards refer to the 'Rolls Royce' and 'Mini' levels of service provision. They argue that both the Rolls and the Mini provide appropriate quality at different price levels and that customers willing to pay for the Rolls Royce level should not be disbarred from obtaining it. The other reference point is that differential service levels should not be prevented by the principle of 'equality of misery'. Such arguments cause considerable discomfort for the defenders of equality of provision who increasingly find themselves trapped by the discourse of 'customer centredness' with its implication that customers' wants are paramount. One further twist to these problems is created by the fact that 'differential' services are not merely the result of customer/market logic but also follow from critiques of the androcentric and ethnocentric assumptions which have underpinned the 'universalism' of much British welfare provision (Williams, 1992).

At this point, efficiency creates a further set of tensions in relation to an expanded sense of equity in terms of equal opportunity agendas for both employment policy and service provision. The demand to do things 'differently' - to change the old ways in response to Equal Opportunities (E.O.) pressures - is easily represented as a costly 'luxury' which can be foregone in the 'hard times' of limited budgets. Different approaches to, for example, staff recruitment and development or the supply of information to service users incur costs of time and other resources in pursuit of objectives which are unlikely to command organisation wide support (Cockburn, 1991). When this is overlaid on greater centre-periphery differentiation, there are particular problems surounding the maintenance of equality initiatives. Given that they have generally been developed and formulated at a corporate level, the implementation and enforcement of E.O. policies becomes more problematic with devolved or decentralised structures. Units and sub units may allow them to fall away, viewing them as 'costs' imposed by the centre or as objectives and practices which are 'not relevant' to the particular concerns of the unit. In part, this disengagement is facilitated by the way in which E.O. policies have often been formulated as general principles. As a result they may provide little purchase on the particular practices and principles of specific service areas. As decentralised and devolved organisational structures take on greater significance, so too does the possibility of such disengagement from corporate commitments.

Competition and cooperation

The final dilemma to which we want to draw attention concerns the relationships between competition and cooperation as approaches to managing in the new public sector. The dominant frame of reference for managers has clearly been that of competition - established in the principles of CCT and the logics assumed to be at work in markets (whether real or quasi, internal or external). Such framing of the management task has led to an assiduous search for new competences - how to create business plans, how to do marketing, how to carry out competitive analysis, how to contract and how to tender for contracts. Such logics in the new public sector are reinforced by the lessons apparently to be learnt from managerial regimes 'out there' - either in the form of 'good business practices' or in the form of the discourse of the new managerialism, both of which are structured around equating successful management with competitive success. It is not surprising that, faced with these pressures, some public sector managers have become enthusiastic converts to the pleasures of competition, not unreasonably equating competitive success with a ruthless approach to cost cutting (particularly labour force costs). 'Macho management' (or what Moss Kanter, 1990, calls 'cowboy management') is one adaptation to the new realities of public sector organisation and its emergence provides powerful testimony to the salience of the 'managerial prerogative'.

This desperate search for the 'competitive edge' is exactly what makes others becoming managers uneasy and uncomfortable and plays a significant role in persuading others not to take on managerial roles and identities. For both these groups, there is a more or less articulated sense that such competitive zeal fails to fit with the ethos, values, style of working which distinguished public sector work for them in the first place. This discomfort is often difficult to express, since it is excluded by a framework which polarises the world of the public sector into choices between the old regime and the new realism and few wish to be positioned as defenders of the old regime. But what is clear is that there is a sense of loss of things valued within the old regime which appear to have no place in the new realism - collegiality, service, professionalism, fair dealing, etc. To a limited extent, some of these concerns can be articulated with aspects of the new managerial discourse, given that it is characterised by contradictory messages (Moss Kanter, 1990). The stress on 'honouring the front line', valuing 'people and process' and having a focus on 'quality' offer partial and unstable points of connection for 'old' values in the sense that they provide a vocabulary through which such concerns can be expressed. But precisely because the discourse is contradictory, such reference points are unstable and provoke uneasiness about 'buying into' the whole discourse by trying to appropriate some of its terms.

We might take the growing salience of 'quality' as an example of these confusions. At present, it is difficult to avoid the sense that everyone is committed to quality (indeed, how could they not be?). But the discovery of 'quality' by central government and senior managements provides a point of leverage for those concerned to find ways of rearticulating old values. It offers a basis for a critique of the competitive/cost cutting approach, allowing its users to position themselves as defenders of quality against those who would destroy it in the search for balanced budgets. It offers a space in the new discourse to which 'professional' values about good practice (and best practice) can be connected. Quality, we would argue, creates a particular space within the discourse of the new managerialism in which very different 'visions' of service can be articulated and contested. But there are problems for those who seek to use it to articulate that which they wish to defend, because, at some point, organisations move to trying to define and operationalise 'quality' as an index of corporate performance. This can prove an elusive task in general and in particular tends to be uncomfortable for those (usually defenders) who object precisely on the grounds that quality is not quantifiable but embedded in knowledges, practices and ways of working.

We have so far treated this as if it was a dilemma simply posed between old and new, but it is more complicated than that formulation allows. The contraditions and 'mixed messages' are not only visible in the managerial discourse but are also present in government policy and practice. Although competition has been the dominant frame of reference for the restructuring of the public sector, there is a second and subordinate frame - that of 'partnership'. This is expressed in a variety of ways - for example, in ideas of the 'enabling authority' and in exhortations to better 'multi-agency working' - which recognise that not all public sector relations can be characterised as market or competitive ones. The logic of partnership is collaborative rather than competitive but is undercut by confusions about the intersection of the two logics (e.g. in community care there are potential contradictions between the local authority's role as enabler and purchaser). Nonetheless, ideas of partnership and collaboration do address some experiences of, and aspirations for, public sector practice ranging from collegiality and team working to service ideals (which are seen to transcend 'local' competitive interest). Unfortunately, managerialism is better equipped to induct competitive managers than it is to advise on building good partnerships: one of our courses evoked the suggestion that there should be a 'Relate' equivalent for public sector managers concerned to create stable relationships.

'Becoming bilingual': living in the discourse of management

These dilemmas (and others which we have not explored here) are an integral part of the experience of those who are 'becoming managers' within the restructuring of public welfare. As such, they link questions of individual identity and direction to the broader concerns of individual and collective survival within the new mixed economy of welfare. We do not use the word 'survival' lightly here, for it is clear among those with whom we have worked that those are the stakes: competitive survival; the survival of a 'public service' ethos; and individual survival in terms of continued employment and continued employment in an identity with which one can live. The advent of managerialisation has disrupted the internal regime of the public sector: changing structures, relationships and identities in the process. For those who were 'bureau-professionals' learning to live in the discourse of management has proved to be a confusing and contradictory experience. One final metaphor sums up this experience - the idea of 'becoming bilingual' or 'learning to talk management'. This metaphor expresses how profound the impact of managerialism on the culture of the public sector has been and how foreign it appears to many of those working within it. It also carries a recognition that old discourses and vocabularies are no longer enough or appropriate. Not to be able to speak management leaves one marginal, disenfranchised or rendered speechless - using words which are no longer recognised. The metaphor also sums up our own ambiguities about the process of managerialisation and our role within it. It references the problems of how to translate between old and new languages; how to learn to use the new effectively and how to 'manage' the tension between speaking a discourse and being spoken by it.

* This chapter is part of a larger programme of work about the managerialisation of the public sector. It draws on the experience of doing management development work with a variety of groups working in the public sector as well as on our own experience of that sector. We are grateful to those who have been involved in these programmes for the ways in which they have talked about the transformations they have been undergoing.

Notes

1.   There is also a problem about the implications of treating the state as an undifferentiated entity, when there are at least arguments to be made that different aspects of the state have been subjected to selective and differentiated forms of restructuring. In particular, what used to be referred to the 'juridico-repressive' state apparatuses (legal and military aspects) have tended to be ignored in the discussion of post-fordism.
2.   We are also concerned that the discussion of post-fordism may take the rhetoric of transformation at its face value - stressing flexibility, decentralisation and customer or demand led provision. While these are aspects of the restructuring of the welfare state, they are not exhaustive descriptions - for example, centralisation has been as significant a component of restructuring as decentralisation.
3.   Although being selective in focusing on welfare, we do not think this is the whole of the state. The restructuring of other sectors cannot be read off from this analysis, although the impact of managerialism on the police is worth noting, see McLaughlin,

forthcoming.

4. This was central to what Stuart Hall had called the 'authoritarian-populism' of Thatcherism as a political ideology in the formulation of a populist opposition between the people and the state as an external, intrusive and oppressive force (Hall, 1989).

5. These arguments draw on a variety of approaches to the study of professionalism in routinised settings. See, for example, Mintzberg, (1983) and Johnson, (1972).

6. A recent American management text is devoted to a celebration of the 'leadership style of Attila the Hun'.

7. The language is now replete with budget centres, trading units, competition, contracts, missions, strategic plans, visions, business plans and the like. One significant impact of this discourse of managment is the way it has focused attention on the means rather than ends of welfare provision against which it is difficult to articulate other discourses.

8. The monopolisation of power by either established professions (the BMA) or other bureau-professional occupations (often lumped together as the 'polyocracy') has been a consistent thread of justification for Conservative welfare changes, especially but not exclusively in the NHS. In the US, neo-conservatives and neo-liberals have articulated this in a more extensive attack on the 'new class' composed of state professionals, drawing or critiques of state power in communist regimes, see Clarke, (1991), ch.5 and Ehrenreich, (1987).

9. For a related discussion of the devolution of stress in the introduction of 'flexible working arrangements' in manufacturing, see Dawson and Webb, (1989).

10. Garson, (1988), provides a chastening account of the uses of new technology in the development of enhanced surveillance within organisations.

11. User perspectives have indeed found it very hard to make an impact on objective setting and performance measures, see Pollitt, (1988). Given the budgetary constraints and governmental scrutiny on public organisations, it is not surprising that measurement has tended to focus on basic 'efficiency' measures. On the problems of objective setting and measurement in 'not for profit' organisations, see Moss Kanter and Summers, (1987).

4 Next steps: Restructuring the Department of Social Security

John Ditch

Introduction

The Department of Social Security is the second largest government department in Whitehall (after Defence) and has a total expenditure of over £70 billions; it employs over 70,000 people; it collects contributions from over 29 million people; it delivers benefits to over 20 million people and makes over one thousand million payments a year. It is government on a big scale, and yet, at the same time, it relates to people in a most direct and personal way. With notable exceptions, it has not been fashionable in research or academic circles to write about the organisation and delivery of benefits in the UK: issues to do with management and administration have been regarded, for better or worse, as being of secondary importance to the exploration of the principles of distribution which underpin the benefits system and the analysis of their distributional consequences. This is surprising, because the DSS is the government department with which most people have most contact. Relatively few people will have regular contact with the Foreign Office, the Ministry of Defence or even the Departments of the Environment or Education & Science (their responsibilities being mediated via local authorities) but most will have contact with the DSS - either as contributors or claimants, and now as customers.

The purpose of this chapter is to review the changes which have occurred in the organisation and delivery of social security benefits over the past decade during which time the DSS split away from the Department of Health; an Operational Strategy to develop and use new technology in aid of benefits administration has been implemented

(Adler & Williams (eds.), 1991); and six new agencies have been established or are at the final stage of planning in Great Britain and there are two related agencies in Northern Ireland. Such changes both reflect and incorporate important ideas about the management of public services, their accountability and the quest for both efficiency and effectiveness. However, at the core of the DSS's activities is a relationship with the public, frequently disadvantaged and vulnerable, who are reliant upon a large and complex public organisation for the provision of financial assistance. For these reasons it is important to examine the relationship between the changes noted above and the principle of equity or fairness.

Social security operations are mostly the direct responsibility of the DSS itself. However the Employment Services Agency (an Executive Agency of the Dept of Employment) acts as an agent in paying benefit to unemployed people and the Social Security Agency (NI) acts as an agent in processing benefits related work which is 'outposted' from some of the London offices. Most national insurance contributions are collected by the Inland Revenue and Housing Benefit together with Community Charge/Council Tax Benefit are administered by local authorities. Within the DSS itself most tasks are now undertaken by Executive Agencies who employ over 97 per cent of DSS staff. It is with the background to, establishment and implications of these agencies that this chapter is mostly concerned; most of the discussion relates to the Benefits Agency. The chapter begins with an overview of DSS operations in terms of its finances, staffing and caseload. There is then a review of the problems faced by the DHSS/DSS during the 1980s and the pressures for reform that were thereby generated followed by a critique of the Departmental response in the form of the Operational Strategy, the 1988 social security reforms and the Next Steps initiative. The chapter concludes with an assessment of the administrative changes and their implications for the conduct and accountability of public policy.

The public finance of social security

Social security is now the largest element of public expenditure, amounting to £65 billion, and accounting for over 31 per cent of the total in 1991 - 1992 (Cm 1914, 1992).

Of this grand total £61.9 billions is spent on benefits and the remainder of £3.2bn (4.9 per cent) is consumed by administration. This figure represents expenditure by both the DSS centrally and local authority expenditure on housing and community charge benefit which amounts to over £5 billion in the year 1990 - 1991. It is important to note, however, that this figure **excludes** £2bn expended in Northern Ireland which is separately accounted for as part of the Northern Ireland block.

Social security expenditure can be broken down into four distinct elements: contributory benefits which account for 55 per cent of the total; non contributory benefits (unrelated to income, such as Attendance Allowance or Child Benefit), 16 per cent; income related benefits, such as Income Support and Housing and Community Charge benefits, 24 per cent; and administration, 5 per cent.

Table 5.1
Estimated average in receipt of selected benefits, 1991-1992

	Millions
Retirement pension	9,930
Invalidity benefit	1,350
Attendance allowance	975
Income support	4,240
Child benefit (children)	12,315
(families)	6,810
Housing benefit	
rent rebate	3,050
rent allowance	1,000
Community charge rebates/benefits	7,845

Source: Cm 1514, (1991) p.14

Expenditure on social security is expected to grow, in real terms, over the next four years at the rate of about 4 per cent per year. This growth is related to an increase in the number of retired people, and a greater number living in residential care and nursing homes; an increase in the number of single parent families and disabled claimants and the prospects for continuing high levels of unemployment (see Kiernan and Wicks, 1990).

The Department has a commitment to reduce the numbers employed to manage and administer the social security system and over the past five years there has been a decline of 4 per cent in the numbers of staff employed. In April 1990 the numbers and deployment of staff was as follows:

Table 5.2
Staff administering the social security programme

Headquarters	4,408
North Fylde Central Office	3,887
Newcastle Central Office	6,336
Regional Organisation:	
a) Local Offices	51,665
b) Regional Offices & other units	4,942
Computer Centres; Information Technology Services Agency	2,937
Resettlement Agency	528
Contributions Unit	6,209
Total	**80,912**

Source: Cm 1514, (1991), p. 42

[Footnote: Staff in the North Fylde Directorate deal mostly with long term disability benefits, war pensions and family credit. At the Newcastle upon Tyne Directorate staff are mainly concerned with contributions, retirement and widow's pension and child benefit.]

Administrative costs average 5.7 per cent of total benefits expenditure, but this masks a range from 1.6 per cent of expenditure on retirement pensions, to 15.2 per cent on Income Support, 20.9 per cent on Unemployment Benefit and 47.1 per cent on the Social Fund. (It should be acknowledged that although these figures are taken from the same table they are subject to qualification: see Cm 1914, (1991) para 112-114).

The Department is generally and as a matter of both principle and practice committed to improving efficiency and achieving economy in the administration of its services. In the financial year 1990-1991 efficiency savings of £92m (equivalent to 4.5 per cent of running costs in that year) were achieved and these are planned to increase to £430m (13.1 per cent of running costs) by 1994-1995. Mostly these savings are to be achieved by the further extension of the Operational Strategy but other contributory factors include: improved 'productivity', especially in the area of fraud investigation and the Social Fund; the amalgamation of local offices into 159 districts with consequent coordination of management services and savings in management posts; the relocation of work to the three out centres (Belfast, Wigan and Glasgow); more competitive procurement policies and market testing (*Competing for Quality*, 1991); the implementation of changes following internal review of services and procedures - see, for example, the scrutinies of debt and fraud (it is planned, for example, that anti fraud measures will achieve savings of at least £382m in 1991-1992); the implementation of energy efficiency programmes.

Problems and pressure points

Over the course of the 1980s the DHSS was subject to a variety of pressures and difficulties. The principal categories were as follows:

Low staff morale;
Poor service to claimants;
Need for better information;
The need for quicker processing of claims;
Poor accommodation/offices;
Evidence of claimant dissatisfaction;
Growing complexity of the social security system, notwithstanding the reforms of the mid 1980s;
The increased cost of administration.

Specific aspects of the administration of social security have been subject to detailed scrutiny by the National Audit Office, Public Accounts Committee, the House of Commons Select Committee and by internal review (Moodie et al, 1988). Although the Social Security Advisory Committee has no formal responsibility for the administration of benefit it has also made detailed comments on these matters.

However, for most benefit recipients there are few, if any, problems. Child Benefit and retirement pensions, proportionate to their total number, generate little difficulty. By way of contrast, Income Support (previously Supplementary Benefit) and Housing Benefit claimants are more likely to have problems and grievances (Russell and Whitworth, 1992). In part this is because these means tested benefits are intended to reflect individual/family circumstances and as these change, so in turn, does the level of benefit. In 1989-90 there were in excess of over 10.2 million such changes compared with 4.18 million new claims for income support. (Cm 1514, 1991 p.45) It is this process of assessment and review which caused so many problems.

For example, in some parts of the country (especially London and other urban centres) there were unacceptable delays in the processing of claims. In 1987 it took an average 6 days to deal with a claim for Supplementary Benefit, but this masked a range of 3 to 17 days. The National Association of Citizens Advice Bureaux, in conjunction with other voluntary organisations and advice agencies, sought a judicial review against the DHSS on the grounds that claims were not being adjudicated within the statutorily allowable 14 days. The appeal was dismissed (see Law Report, 1988).

The Social Security Advisory Committee commented on this issue in their Annual Report for 1988 and noted that a combination of overwork, understaffing and inadequate training were to blame. These were not, however, difficulties solely attributable to the DHSS: many employers in specific parts of the country had difficulty in recruiting and retaining able staff whose skills were being competitively sought by many employers such as banks and insurance companies.

Another problem frequently referred to during the 1980s was the number of inaccurate payments. DHSS figures for 1986/87 indicate a national Supplementary Benefit error rate of 10.4 per cent on a 2 per cent sample. Coupled with claimant concern at the length of time individuals were having to wait before being seen, there was a lack of confidence in the administration of benefits among certain sections of the public (especially, the unemployed, single parents and ethnic minorities). There was an average waiting time of 15 minutes in local offices but in some locations it was necessary to wait for in excess of one hour. Accommodation, for both staff and claimants, was sometimes uncomfortable and lacking privacy. There tended to be a concentration of problems of this kind in inner city offices where it is not unknown for frustration to spill over into violence.

Not all enquiries to a local office were, or are handled on a face to face basis; increasingly the telephone is used to expedite matters and is the preferred mode of approach for many claimants. However this can also be a source of difficulty and frustration: many claimants have to use public telephones; some offices restrict the hours during which they will receive and act upon telephone calls; in many cases the line appears to be constantly engaged. Furthermore, it is sometimes necessary to call more than one office to have a matter dealt with; when the right person in the correct office is found, the relevant case papers may not be readily available.

The inability of many claimants to speak and write in English remains a particular problem. Advice literature has tended to be complicated and ethnic minorities have encountered special difficulties in processing claims for benefit (see NACAB, 1991a). The 1991-1992 publicity and advertising budget for the DSS is £22m (up from £12m in 1990-1991).

£6m will be spent in connection with the new disability working allowance and disability living allowance, the Benefits Enquiry Line and producing information in braille and on audio cassette. Expenditure on the promotion of family credit will remain high at £3.5m and £5m will be spent on general literature and information leaflets.

It would be wrong to give the impression that these problems were typical of all social security offices: the scale of the operation is such that only a small proportion of claimants experienced difficulty. Nevertheless, many claimants did experience problems and although a majority of claimants were content with the service provided this could not, and is not, an excuse for complacency.

The context and response

'The Business of Service' reported on the organisation and location of social security work in Great Britain and recommended redeployment of certain functions and staff. The review team observed some of the best and many of the worst practices in local offices: both are fully reported in what is a remarkably candid review:

> ...some offices pride themselves on virtually a same day service on supplementary benefit claims. Others take 25 working days;

> ...waiting times in offices vary from 10 minutes to 90. Waits of three or four hours are being recorded. The actual interview takes, on average, only about 5 minutes;

> ...accuracy in making payments is declining overall. The declared error rate ranges from the exemplary, 5%, to the awful, 40%;

> ...Freefone is a super initiative which has proved a great success but some groups of customers are still largely unaware of its existence. (Moodie et al, 1988, p.5)

The report also noted that the 'whole person concept', a construct which promised a coherent and integrated approach to meeting the social security needs of claimants, had made little real progress despite having been a departmental objective since 1980. Social security continued to be organised on the basis of benefits rather than around the circumstances of claimants. For example, Income Support remains separately administered from contributory benefits irrespective of the circumstances of claimants. In addition, there is less of a personal basis to the relationship between staff and claimant than previously: there has been a reduction in the number of visits; staff spend less time with individual claimants than previously; staff, even when friendly and well intentioned, are not always very knowledgeable. The report continued:

> The image of social security is poor.. staff think their reputation and credibility on the street are awful. They attribute its awfulness to the inefficient service we provide and to the media stories, with no counter balancing account of any good news (Moodie et al 1988 pp.10-11).

This open and revealing account of the inadequacy and shortcomings is fully acknowledged in the Benefits Agency's first Business Plan.

For many commentators the social security reforms of the mid 1980s have, to a considerable extent, been reduced to budgetary constraint, the introduction of the social fund and the renaming of benefits: but this is an incomplete picture which minimizes an underlying commitment to the simplification of benefits in the interests of both staff and claimants. At a general level these reforms had three objectives: to achieve economies and improve efficiency in the administration of benefit; to relieve staff of routine and monotonous work; to improve the quality of service to the public.

The DSS Agencies: scope, role and practice

The civil service has always been concerned with its capacity to function efficiently but the most recent developments stem from the Fulton Report (1968) and the Heath Government reforms of 1970 - 1974 (the establishment of the Central Policy Review Staff and the introduction of Programme Analysis Review). The Thatcher Government sought, in principle if not in practice, to restrict the scope and scale of government: introducing private sector assumptions (about value for money) and private sector practices (tendering) into the heart of Whitehall. These were stimulated by the series of so called Rayner Reviews conducted by Sir Derek (later Lord) Rayner (of Marks and Spencers) and which worked to three objectives: to promote better value for money in government; to remove obstacles to good management; to encourage quick and effective implementation of feasible changes. These specific reviews are to be seen in the context of broader initiatives such as the introduction of new and comprehensive management and budgeting systems such as The Management Information System for Ministers (MINIS) introduced by Michael Heseltine when at the Dept of the Environment and its more pervasive successor, the Financial Management Initiative (FIN) - see Carter et al 1992, Hennessy, P. 1989). The FMI symbolised the culture of Whitehall in the 1980s with its emphasis on the importance of clarity in the setting of objectives and the need for transparency in the measurement of their attainment. In principle the FMI sought to ensure that all managers, at all levels, should have a clear set of objectives and the means to attain them; that all managers should have clearly defined responsibility for using resources effectively and that they should have the capacity to scrutinize output and value for money; finally, that managers should have access to information, training and the expert advice necessary to function effectively. But although senior management within the DHSS appeared to embrace the ethos of FMI, the Public Accounts Committee found that 'scepticism and mistrust of FMI seems to be widespread among middle and lower management grades' (quoted in Carter et al 1992, p.23).

Arguably the next stage in this programme of bureaucratic management, the Next Steps initiative, has been more concerned with the **refinement** of the policy making process than with its **impact**. But either way the changes which have been implemented amount to some of the most significant ever in the organisation of central government (Efficiency Unit 1988, Efficiency Unit 1991). Consistent with existing practices to promote efficiency and the improvement of management in government the Next Steps report recommended the establishment of semi autonomous agencies to carry out executive functions within a policy and resources framework. The recommendations of the Ibbs Report on Next Steps were accepted by the Prime Minister in February 1988. The programme was implemented almost immediately.

A central or head quarters capability, numbering about 1,200 officials in the case of the DSS, are to be retained at the centre to support Ministers in the management of the social security policy programme; to secure and allocate resources through the annual Public Expenditure Survey and to provide other specialist services across the Department. DSSHQ is organised into three Groups (each headed by a Deputy Secretary): a social security policy group; a resource management and planning group and a solicitors group.

Within the space of three years over 50 agencies have been established, employing almost 300,000 civil servants. The following have been established in the area of social security:

Table 5.3
Social security agencies: staff numbers and establishment date

	Manpower	Date
Resettlement Agency	530	May 1989
Information Technology Services	3,350	April 1990
Social Security Benefits Agency	68,000	April 1991
Social Security Contributions Agency	6,600	April 1991
Social Security Agency (N Ireland)	5,000	July 1991
Child Support Agency	6,000	April 1993
Child Support Agency (N Ireland)	700	April 1993
War Pensions Agency (to be approved)	1,000	April 1994

The Benefits Agency

Not only is the Benefits Agency the largest in terms of manpower and financial turnover but it also consumes about 57 per cent of total DSS administration costs. For reasons of both efficiency and economy large sections of the DSS have been relocated from London, principally to Leeds where the headquarters of the new Benefits Agency is located in premises shared with the Department of Health. The former seven social security regions have been replaced by three 'territories' and these, in turn, are divided into 159 districts. Each district office supports a number of branch or caller offices, is the liaison point for local agencies and frequently undertakes specialist functions (such as Social Fund or fraud work) at a local level.

The Benefits Agency (1991) has assumed responsibility for a substantial proportion of the DSS's operations, and in particular '.. assessing claims for, receiving entitlements to and arranging payments of social security benefits.' (p. 4) Like all other agencies it operates within a 'framework' set down by the Secretary of State on behalf of government which prescribes the policy and resources context. The key elements of the framework are to 'promote the economic, efficient and coherent administration of social security services.' (ibid., p. 4) To achieve this aim a number of specific objectives have been set down:

1. the development of 'an efficient customer oriented benefit delivery service, which is accessible, accurate, prompt, helpful and cost effective and which does not discriminate on the grounds of race, sex, religion or disability.' (ibid., p. 4)

2.   the provision of 'comprehensive information to the public on social security benefits including explanations about how benefits are calculated and indicating rights and procedures of appeal and review.' (ibid., p. 4)

3.   an obligation to contribute to the Department's policy development and evaluation activities; to provide information on the operational implications of current and alternative programme characteristics.

In addition to the Agency's objectives there are a series of management objectives which are more specific and against which performance related pay for the senior executives is determined. These include the need to meet the targets and performance standards as set out in the Business Plan and accepted by the Secretary of State. For example, there are to be cost efficiency savings in the first year of operation of £188.3m; a customer satisfaction level of 85% and specified milestones in the Operational Strategy.

Contributions Agency

The Contributions Agency was established in April 1991. It administers the national insurance scheme and has an annual budget of £122m. Specifically the Agency has responsibility for the maintenance of individuals' records and provides a service to other DSS agencies, other government departments, employers and individual contributors. A particular challenge has been to increase the yield of contributions income, especially from employers and self employed people. The Agency operates the *Social Security Advice Line for Employers* and during 1990-1991 dealt with 132,000 enquiries and held over 200 seminars. As part of the Citizens' Charter initiative the Agency has published the Contributors' and Employers' Charters. Efficiency savings (£4.9m in 1991-1992, £2.6 in 1992-1993) are mostly to be achieved by contracting much of the Agency's (non face to face) work to Newcastle.

Information Technology Services Agency

Established in April 1990 ITSA is responsible for the development and maintenance of all information and communications systems in the DSS.
The key component of its programme is the Operational Strategy the three core elements of which were fully implemented in July 1991. Its annual budget for 1991-92 was £413m and between 1982 and March

1990 total estimated expenditure on the Operational Strategy was £570m and estimated total investment (both development and implementation costs) up to March 1999, will be about £1,800m (House of Commons 1991c, p. 6). The DSS has estimated that annual operational savings by 1995 will be in the order of £150m. The Operational Strategy itself consists of a number of 'live systems' at the heart of which is the Departmental Central Index which holds personal data (name, address and date of birth) for every person allocated a National Insurance Number. It is automatically up dated via any of the satellite systems and these include the Family Credit system, the Local Office project which registers, maintains and pays claims to income support and a parallel system for the Social Fund; the pensions strategy computer system; the Disability Working Allowance and Disability Living Allowance system (which is very similar to the Family Credit system); the National Unemployment Benefit system and an Overseas Branch project which deals with awards of retirement pensions for persons living overseas or who have contributions paid under foreign legislation.

By October 1991 over 5m people had received benefit via the Income Support computer system; the pension computer system has over 10m accounts and produces over 700,000 payments per week; the DSS central index has over 60m records and over 200,000 transactions are conducted every day.

The aims of the Operational Strategy are to improve service to the public through a faster turnaround of claims; a faster response to enquiries and minimising the risk of payment errors; to reduce overheads costs by reducing the numbers of staff required to administer the social security system; by providing more interesting jobs for its staff by eliminating the most routine and boring tasks.

However these objectives have been subject to criticism and there are misgivings about the risks to civil liberties and the ability of the system to cope with exceptional cases which challenge or contradict the expectations of computer programmes (NACAB, 1991b).

The Resettlement Agency

This is the oldest DSS agency and was established in May 1989. It has twin principal aims: to operate hostels for single homeless people with an unsettled way of life and secondly, to replace these hostels by more suitable accommodation, run by local authorities and voluntary organisations. It is a descendant of the Poor Law casual wards for wandering tramps and is the only direct care service provided by the

DSS. Much of the Department's accommodation is of poor quality and is being replaced. For example, the Brighton resettlement unit was closed in March 1991 and was replaced by a wider spread of provision along the south coast. The Resettlement Agency's annual budget is over £20m per year.

Child Support Agency

This was formally launched in April 1993 when it took over and extended the functions and responsibilities of the Child Support Unit, currently located within the DSS. A separate Child Support Agency (with parallel functions and responsibilities) will be established in Northern Ireland. However the Northern Ireland Agency will also provide a service to customers in Great Britain. Indeed from an establishment of 700, over 500 staff will be working on GB cases. In accordance with the provisions of the Child Support Act (1991) the primary task of both agencies will be to make accurate assessments of maintenance on behalf of children and ensure that payment is received regularly. By 1996 it is planned that virtually all divorce cases involving child maintenance will be handled by the Agency. Although the location of the Agency's headquarters has not been decided upon, it is planned that there should be 6 regional centres to deal with the assessment and collection of maintenance payments.

Social Security Agency (Northern Ireland)

Social security legislation in Northern Ireland is legally separate from the Great Britain legislation but it seeks to meet the same policy objectives. The DHSS(NI) acts as an agent for both the DSS and the Department of Health and the Northern Ireland Civil Service has been engaged in a parallel Next Steps programme. The Northern Ireland Social Security Agency came into operation in July 1991 and is responsible for the administration of all social security benefits and the collection of national insurance contributions (other than those collected via PAYE). The Agency employs about 5,000 staff, has an administration budget of £100m and 35 local offices throughout the province. An 'internal market' relationship operates whereby the Northern Ireland Agency provides services on behalf of the Benefits and Contributions Agencies.

Roles and responsibilities

The respective roles and responsibilities of the Secretary of State, Permanent Secretary and Chief Executive are described in the Framework documentation and are crucially important in the development of policy and practice.

The Secretary of State for Social Security retains formal and final responsibility for DSSHQ and all the agencies. However, he delegates responsibility for functioning and performance to an Agency Chief Executive. The Permanent Secretary is, of course, principal advisor to the Secretary of State on all matters relating to policy and finance. In particular, the Permanent Secretary advises the Secretary of State about resource allocation, objectives and targets for the Agency and also monitors the performance of the Chief Executive on his behalf.

The Framework Document prescribes a role for the Chief Executive in relation to both policy development and the operational implications of current and prospective commitments. Far from being a passive or reactive responsibility, the Chief Executive is empowered to make 'proposals to the Secretary of State for changes in the policies and programmes operated by the Agency which are designed to improve the effectiveness with which the Agency meets its overall objectives.' Although there is a proviso that the Chief Executive should consult with the Permanent Secretary there is some ambiguity about what this implies.

It is already clear that the agencies (and their senior staff) are running up against the controlling and centralising tendencies inherent in British Government; the Treasury and parent departments are unwilling to let go of their offspring. As Anne Davies and John Willman (1991) have written:

> The fundamental paradox of Next Steps is that it seeks to develop an enterprise culture in the public services and to focus on outputs and the delivery of services within the input dominated, cash limited, public expenditure system (p. 43).

Their solution is to provide Parliament with greater authority to scrutinize the activities of agencies; to provide freedom of information and revise traditional notions of ministerial responsibility.

Roles and responsibility for policy advice are being blurred and the potential exists for competing channels of information and policy recommendation. The Government's own review of progress of the

77

Next Steps strategy drew attention to the significance of this fracture line. In particular it states that:

> The exclusion of any area from the chief executive's authority should be positively justified (Efficiency Unit, 1991, p. 5).

One interpretation is that this amounts to an invitation for chief executives to exercise their power and influence to the full. Explicitly the Agency provides both operational advice and information; it also keeps in touch with EC developments, including participation in the DSS EC Awareness Group, with a view to learning from the experience of other countries.

Ministers are held accountable to Parliament for all their responsibilities, but Members of Parliament and members of the public are encouraged to write direct to the Agency Chief Executive. Parliamentary questions about Agency operations, routed via the Minister, are passed to the Chief Executive or other member of the Senior Management Team for reply.

In the Benefit Agency's first year it responded to over 250 parliamentary questions, over 2900 letters from MPs and about 90 new complaints investigated by the Parliamentary Commissioner for Administration: new performance targets have been set for this area.

There is an important issue of parliamentary accountability at stake. Whereas ministers are answerable to Parliament for the actions and policies of Departments they are refusing to answer questions about the functions of agencies: these are passed to agency chief executives. The chief executive's reply is not published in Hansard and for a while was only available in the House of Commons library where, in theory at least, it could be seen by other MPs. However the library maintained the file reference to the MP's name rather than date or subject with the result that it was almost impossible to identify topics and questions. The public display of redress of grievances was being made opaque. However, Paul Flynn MP, with the assistance of Tony Lynes, started a slim periodical *Open Lines* which collected all replies and published them privately. This contributed to growing pressure on government to undertake the task on an official basis. The Government recommended to the House of Commons authorities that this should happen and replies are now available through formal channels.

There has been some speculation in the media about the role of the BA in the Government's decision, in September 1991, to amend the rules (Regulation 72) on claiming social security arrears in cases of official error. It was alleged that the prospect of 35,000 claims organised by Strathclyde social work department would have deluged the Agency. It is alleged (*The Guardian* 5/9/91) that the Agency pressed for a rule change to limit claims to those in which there was prima facie evidence that entitlement had been ignored or where a DSS official had 'overlooked or misconstrued' a provision in law.

Citizens' Charter and customer service

The specification of performance targets at all levels within each agency takes forward the development and use of performance indicators. Historically the DSS has been to the forefront of government departments in the use of performance measures. Stimulated by the Fulton Report (1968) the DHSS embraced the Management by Objectives initiative in the early 1970s and established a range of performance indicators, target setting and annual performance review. But the experience was not an unqualified success: the trade unions were highly critical of performance measurement, responsibility for the collection and collation of data was frequently delegated to the most junior staff and the hierarchical aggregation of data tended to mask significant local variations. Most importantly this dalliance with performance indicators encouraged complacency and thereby did little to improve performance. Until the mid 1980s and the introduction of the Quality Assessment Package (QAP) there was little understanding of the need for indicators to measure the quality of service. The QAP, based on surveys of DSS claimants, underlined the importance of three performance indicators as quality measures: caller waiting times; the quality of correspondence and the quality of interviews (see Elam, 1991).

The multiplication of performance indicators has been facilitated by the extensive use of information technology as developed within the framework of the Operational Strategy. But many problems, typical of the public services in general, remain unresolved. For example, the growing concern that the **how** of service delivery detracts from the substantive assessment of **what** is being delivered. The performance of the benefits system can only be fully appreciated when both the delivery mechanisms and the adequacy of benefit are subject to scrutiny and measurement. To focus on inputs, throughput, outputs without regard to outcomes or impacts is as short sighted as it is methodologically deficient. Of central importance is the adequacy of benefits but this is a subject which receives little or no attention within government; despite much prompting from the research community this critically important subject remains at the bottom of the government's policy and research agenda.

The Benefits Agency has committed itself to improved customer service and the creation of better working environments for staff. After criticism of the DSS's treatment of ethnic minorities (NACAB, 1991a) the Benefits Agency has responded with a programme of initiatives including the employment of more interpreters, the establishment of a telephone translation service and improved staff training. There early indications that these developments are appreciated (SSAC, Eighth Report, 1992).

In addition the BA has further developed 'fast stream' reception points at a number of its offices as a means of reducing waiting time; reception areas are being refurbished and in some cases re-designed; greater efforts are being made to improve access to both information and offices for disabled people by, for example, the development of dedicated help lines.

In the first year of its operation the BA did, however, confront difficulties in the processing of claims in some offices. This was a result of (unanticipated) rising levels of unemployment coinciding with declining staff levels as a result of the Operational Strategy. Staff shortage was a particular problem in the South East of England.

The BA Customer Charter declares a commitment to a quality and professional service which promises to be courteous, fair, confidential, private and accessible. The importance of listening and respect are identified, as are obligations imposed by anti discrimination legislation and the Data Protection Act. DSS customers are offered the opportunity to have private interviews to discuss their circumstances. The Charter acknowledges claimant aspirations for a single point of contact with the Agency/Department rather than several different offices and addresses; greater flexibility in opening hours to meet the needs of local communities and a considerable improvement in the quality of accommodation and facilities in local offices. However these are not promised in all locations.

At an operational level the Charter promises prompt and accurate benefit payment specifying the clearance time for claims: Income Support within one week, Family Credit and Child Benefit in three weeks. It is promised that there will be more openness: annual reports (at national and district) levels are to be published along with local information packs which will specify the local standards of performance. By the end of June 1992 all staff having contact with the public are to wear name badges and give their names, on both the telephone and in correspondence. By March 1993 staff in over 100 district offices will be wearing a uniform. One of the more commented upon changes has been to expunge the word 'claimant' from the Benefits Agency vocabulary, and to replace it with 'customer'. While this change in nomenclature is indicative of a new respect for benefit recipients it does exaggerate their capacity to 'exit' if the service does not meet their expectations (Hirschman, 1970).

Senior executives are aware that they will be unable to deliver their plans without the active support of staff at junior and middle management levels. The current risk is that senior staff within each agency may be moving too fast for their own organisation to keep pace. Traditional values and old practices are difficult to displace let alone replace. Moreover the capacity of traditional bureaucratic practices to resist and then incorporate the imposition of new values and procedures has been demonstrated elsewhere (Smith 1960). For that reason there is a considerable investment in the significance of the Benefits Agency Staff Charter (January 1992) and through which there is a commitment to better standards of employment to be achieved through greater flexibility and enhanced motivation. Staff are encouraged to contribute to the planning process through the use of 'suggestions schemes' and there is a commitment to equal opportunities programmes (race, gender and disability). There are to be more childcare facilities for staff and the possibility of new work patterns (including home working and telecommuting) are being examined. The need to change attitudes and reskill staff is reflected in the restructuring of the training division and the creation of new training opportunities including the development of an innovatory MA in Social Security Management at York University. Finally, the Agency recognises the risks associated with stress and seeks to minimize its impact.

Once again, the rhetoric of change is clearly in place and the commitment of senior management to the 'mission' of the agencies is not to be doubted. But motivation, enhanced flexibility and operational discretion are the weasel words of contemporary management speak. To seek change is not to achieve change: the real challenge is to develop a strategy and a capacity which will enable the whole organisation (and its customers) to move forward, at a common pace, from one mode of operation to another.

Conclusion

The restructuring which is occurring within the DSS is profound and it would be short sighted to reduce it to a simple change of clothes and vocabulary. There is both a sense of 'mission' and commitment at the most senior levels within (certainly) the Benefits Agency. The deficiencies and inadequacies to be found in many local offices are recognised, together with the constraints imposed by past practice and policy. There is a will to change and the policy of transparency whereby objectives are made public (at both national and district levels) provide criteria against which performance can be measured. An application of the principle of 'subsidiarity' whereby responsibility for decision making is devolved to the lowest most effective level may enhance motivation and make the system more responsive to local interests. But in advance of evidence coming available it is necessary that power and not just the tough choices and the associated stress is devolved downwards. It is also important that the concomitant risk of variability in service standards is also recognised and guarded against by the prescription and maintenance of basic standards (see NACAB 1991b).

However, even the best laid plans are subject to the realities of the real world and the activities of the Benefits Agency are no different. The absence of an objective which would have committed the Benefits Agency to increase the take up of benefits is a notable omission and has done much to undermine its credibility among claimant and advice groups. Moreover, the broader strategy is informed by a pervasive concern with value for money and the need to achieve savings: this acts to inhibit the capacity of the Agency to refurbish offices, improve information systems and adequately remunerate staff. The requirement that efficiency savings from within the Agencies are returned to the Treasury rather than ploughed back has also drawn unfavourable comment (Benefits Agency 1992). Second, the division of labour between policy and administration is imprecise and the DSSHQ will struggle hard to retain a firm grip of the policy agenda. So long as the Agencies are responsible for the administration of policy (and not its making) then they will have difficulty in convincing customers and staff that they are really in a position to effect real change in the quality and overall adequacy of benefits. This in turn relates to a fundamental difficulty: if a quality service is to live up to prescribed standards there is a major problem in the way. There is an unsatisfactory and entirely artificial division between the means and ends of social security policy. The development of performance measures with respect to the delivery of benefits are to be applauded but they cannot be regarded as measures of the quality of the benefits system per se: such measures must have regard to adequacy and opportunity, issues which at present are deemed to be beyond the scope of the Agencies.

On the other hand, the Agencies are actively pursuing a strategy which will simplify the operation of the benefits system and this must impact, sooner or later, on policy. The problems inherent in operating the Social Fund and policies with respect to 16 and 17 year old people, for example, are inevitably relayed back to the Department and must contribute to a climate of change. But care must be taken that the pursuit of the management of change does not become a goal in its own right: there is sometimes a failure at the highest levels of management to recognise that if a thing is not broken it does not need to be mended. At the same time the difficulties faced by claimants as consequence of living on meagre benefits should become a high priority for policy attention.

This chapter was first presented as a paper at the 26th Annual Conference of the Social Policy Association, Nottingham University, 1992. The author is grateful to those who participated in the subsequent discussion and to Margaret Moodie and Roy Sainsbury for their comments. The author remains responsible for the contents.

Section Two
THE ALLOCATION OF RESOURCES

5   Paying for or providing welfare?

Julian Le Grand

Introduction[1]

The welfare state in Britain, as in most other countries, is actually two welfare states. There is the state that finances or pays for welfare, both through cash payments to individuals and families via the social security system and through the subsidy of welfare services, such as education, health care, housing and social care. And there is the state that provides welfare, through ownership and operation of its own provider units with their own employees and capital assets.[2]

Both forms of welfare state have historically been represented in each area of welfare. Thus in education, the state owns, operates and finances most educational institutions, from nursery schools through to universities. Under the National Health Service (NHS), health care is provided free at the point of use by state owned institutions or by state employed practitioners. Housing is subsidised via Housing Benefit and via the various tax reliefs associated with owner occupation; it is also provided by local governments. Personal social services, field, domiciliary and residential, are provided and subsidised by the state. Social insurance and income support are provided by the state, and subsidised from tax revenues.

However, the balance of these two forms of welfare state is shifting. More specifically, instead of the state both paying for and providing welfare services, its role is becoming increasingly one of paying for services that are provided by independent or semi independent providers operating in internal or 'quasi' markets. This shift is arguably the most important change in the British welfare state for over forty years; and, as such, it is one that has to be high on the research agenda for analysts of social policy.

Since most of the relevant changes have only just been introduced or are in the process of being implemented, it is too early to provide any systematic empirical assessment of their likely effects. However, it is possible to specify the conditions for success (or for the avoidance of failure): conditions that theory suggests will have to be met if they are to have some of the benefits claimed by their advocates, while at the same time avoiding some of the costs claimed by their critics. Further, it is also possible to examine the process of implementation to see whether these conditions are in place - or at least show signs of being put into place.

These will be the tasks of this chapter. It begins with a brief account of the growth of quasi markets in welfare and the consequent reduction in the role of the state as provider. The second section outlines some of the more significant conditions whose fulfilment would appear to be necessary if quasi markets in welfare are to succeed. The third section briefly summarises some of the available evidence on the process of implementation to see what signs there are of the conditions being met. There is a brief conclusion.

The growth of quasi markets

A striking feature of the welfare state during the first two Thatcher administrations from 1979 to 1987 was its preservation. This was confirmed in a recent publication by the London School of Economics Welfare State Programme (Hills, ed. 1990). This found that, contrary to popular perception, indicators of welfare inputs, outputs and outcomes in key areas such as education, health care and community care had either remained constant or had actually risen over the period, even when changes in needs were taken into account. There were significant exceptions, notably in housing and in some areas of social security, but the overall picture was one of a possibly surprising degree of resilience.

More importantly from the point of view of this chapter, the basic form of the welfare state remained intact. Again there were exceptions. By far the most significant was the sale of council houses (Hills and Mullings, 1990; Forrest and Murie, 1991). There was also some contracting out of ancillary services in the NHS; the development of the Assisted Places Scheme for school education (a form of education voucher); and a significant growth in the private finance and provision of some areas of welfare, notably pensions, health care, primary and secondary education and residential care (Le Grand, Winter and Woolley, 1990; Glennerster and Low, 1990a; Evandrou, Falkingham and Glennerster, 1990). Apart from these, however, the basic structure of welfare provision and finance was overall much the same in 1987 as it had been in 1948. The NHS, the personal social services, social security benefits, most education and the (sizeable) remaining council house stock were all still largely both paid for and provided by the state at either central or local level.

But this was to change dramatically in 1988 and 1989 (Le Grand, 1991b). In those years, the Government introduced a series of major changes in key areas of welfare, all with a fundamental similarity. In each case, state finance of the service concerned was to be retained, but the system of service provision was to change, often radically. All involved a decentralisation of decision making; most also involved the introduction of competition in provision. In these cases, the state was to become primarily a purchaser, with state provision being systematically replaced by a system of independent providers competing with one another in internal or quasi markets. The method of finance was also to change. In some cases a centralised state agency would continue to act as the principal purchaser; in others an earmarked budget or voucher would be given directly to potential users, or, more commonly, to agents acting on their behalf who would then allocate the budget as they chose between competing providers.

The first of these changes was the set of reforms to primary and secondary school education introduced as part of the Education Reform Act of 1988 (summarised and discussed in Glennerster, 1991). These included provisions for opting out, open enrolment, formula funding, and the local management of schools (LMS). Under the opting out provisions, schools could choose whether to be funded by their local education authority or by the central government. Under open enrolment, parents could choose the school to which they could send their child within certain limits. Under formula funding, the amount of resources that a school (opted out or not) received depended in large part on the number of pupils it could attract. Both opted out and LMS schools were given control over the internal allocation of their resources, becoming in effect semi independent providers. Together, these reforms amounted to a form of education voucher, with resources being no longer primarily allocated to schools by bureaucratic decision, but by the choices of parents.

The next major quasi market developments were the NHS reforms detailed in the White Paper *Working for patients* (1989a) and implemented in the National Health Service and Community Care Act of 1990 (discussed by, among others, Barr, Glennerster and Le Grand, 1989; Culyer, Maynard and Posnett (eds.), 1990; Klein and Day, 1991; and Maynard, 1991). These involved the splitting of health authorities into purchaser and provider units and the introduction of general practitioner (GP) fund holders, who also acted as purchasers. The provider units were of two kinds: trusts that were essentially independent, and directly managed units that nominally at least were still to be managed by the health authority. The GP fund holding scheme was again a form of voucher, whereby GPs with practices over a certain size held budgets to be spent on a range of secondary care services for each of their patients that they could allocate on behalf of those patients. Although not a voucher scheme in the same sense, the purchasing health authorities and provider units were also intended to operate in a quasi-market environment, with the provider units competing for contracts from the purchasing authorities (and from GP fund holders). By April 1992, the purchaser/provider split was almost complete in all health authorities, and around 160 trusts and 600 GP fund holding practices had been established.

Another set of quasi market proposals appeared in the same Act concerned with community care (Audit Commission, 1992). These were based on the Griffiths report (1988), and the subsequent White Paper *Working for Patients* (1989a). Generally, as in the case of health care, local social service departments were supposed to become primarily purchasing or enabling authorities, buying community care services from independent provider units. And, in another parallel with health, this time to the GP fund holder, it was envisaged that a care manager would be appointed for each client to construct a package of care for the client concerned, based on a pre determined budget. In making up the package of care, the care manager would consider bids from competing organisations, including public, voluntary and private sector agencies. Again, the system can be viewed as essentially a voucher scheme, with care managers allocating budgets on behalf of clients between competing institutions and with the allocation of resources being determined by client choice (as delegated to care managers) instead of by bureaucratic decision.[3] The reforms were phased in from April 1st 1991.

Although I shall be concentrating in this chapter on these changes in school education, health care and community care, it should be noted that similar changes have occurred in other areas of welfare, including housing and social security. Under the 1988 Housing Act, the state continued to subsidise local authority tenants (primarily through Housing Benefit), but tenants were now able to choose their landlords from between competing suppliers. However, transfers of this kind have not been significant in practice, with perhaps the main role of the legislation being to spur local authorities into a more consumer responsive style. Instead, there has been a wave of interest among local authorities in voluntarily divesting themselves of their housing stock, generally to a specially created housing association akin to a management buyout of a monopoly supplier. Even more significant from the quasi markets perspective is the gradual but accelerating phenomenon of the expansion of the housing association movement to supplant local authorities as the main new providers of social housing, while the role of the state as a funder is shifting from general 'bricks and mortar' subsidies to individual means tested subsidy in the form of Housing Benefit. Again, this can be likened to a voucher; indeed its portability extends into the private rented sector.

An executive agency has been set up for social security benefits, with the intention of separating service delivery from policy formulation: essentially a split between purchaser and provider. There were also changes on a more micro-level in social security: the Independent Living Fund, for example, was set up in 1988 to provide cash payments to severely disabled people to enable them to assemble their own package of care (Kestenbaum, 1990; Craig, 1992b).

Given their radical nature, it is not surprising that many of these measures have been highly controversial with equally passionate critics and proponents. Their impact will take several years to be felt; but it is clear that if they continue to be implemented in their present form, the provision of welfare in the 1990s will be very different from that of the previous forty years. Under the 'old' system of welfare local governments owned, managed and directly financed nursery, primary and secondary schools; they owned and managed large stocks of public housing, letting them out to tenants at subsidised rents; they owned and operated residential homes and provided other facilities for the care of children, elderly people and people with physical or mental handicaps. Similarly, the central government owned and managed hospitals and other medical facilities; it funded and provided a GP service.

In the 1990s central government and/or local authorities will still be paying for these activities. But they will no longer be providing the services concerned (or, if they do, their role will be increasingly that of a residual provider). Instead, welfare services will be supplied primarily by a variety of semi independent agencies. Schools will be competing for state financed pupils; independent hospitals of various kinds will be competing with each other for patients; private and voluntary homes will be catering for the clients of local authority social services; housing associations, or even private landlords, will be managing erstwhile council estates.

In passing, it is worth noting that these kinds of welfare changes are by no means unique to a particular government, to a particular system of welfare or even to a particular country. Parallel developments are taking place, or have already done so, in other countries. In much of the rest of Europe, social housing is provided by the equivalent of housing associations. A study of recent reforms in health care in seven European countries concluded that there are 'signs of convergence on the public contract model and increased reliance on market and quasi market relationships that permit governments to regulate at arm's length' (Hurst, 1991, p. 19; see also Van de Ven, 1991). In the United States contracting out has long been a prominent feature of hospital and community services (Propper, 1992).

Indeed, as Hoggett (1990) has pointed out, changes of this kind are not even confined to the public sector. So called 'post-fordist' changes of a similar type are occurring in the private sector, with companies that were previously vertically integrated and tightly controlled from the centre now increasingly contracting out their operations and engaging in other forms of decentralisation. More widely, there is a world wide disenchantment with the perceived inefficiency and unresponsiveness of large scale, centrally planned organisations and a greater reliance on decentralisation and markets, quasi or otherwise; beliefs that have their most obvious expression in Eastern Europe, but are pervasive throughout the West as well.

The fact that these quasi market changes appear to be part of a much bigger social phenomenon make it certain that they are going to be a prominent feature of the British welfare state in the 1990s. It is therefore important that they be examined in an impartial, dispassionate fashion to see whether they yield the benefits their proponents hope, or whether they impose the costs their critics fear. Will they reduce the costs of welfare provision and thereby bring about greater efficiency and resource savings? Or will they prevent sensible planning and thereby create other sources of resource waste? Will they make welfare providers more responsive to the needs and wants of their clients, or replace a relationship of trust by one of exploitation? Will they serve the poor and/or those really in need, or will they simply create two-tier services that discriminate against the needy? It is to these kinds of questions that I now turn.

Conditions for success

As noted in the introduction, the majority of the quasi-market changes are only just being put into place, and it will not be feasible to assess their empirical consequences for several years. However, it is possible to undertake a theoretical exercise specifying the conditions that they will have to meet if they are to succeed, and that is the aim of this section. However, first it is necessary to specify what might be meant in this context by 'success' - or, more generally, what are the appropriate criteria for evaluation.

Criteria for evaluation

It is easy to spend a great deal of time discussing possible criteria for policy evaluation. There are issues concerning their scope (what should be included?), their definition (how should they be specified?) and their ownership (whose criteria: policy-makers, users, researchers?). The proper treatment of any of these could take a chapter on its own. Here I propose to duck all these issues by suggesting, almost without argument, a number of criteria against which the reforms may be judged. They concern efficiency, responsiveness, choice and equity.

I say 'almost' without argument, because I shall make a few comments on these before moving on to apply them. First, **efficiency**. Efficiency considerations have a bad name in some social policy circles, usually because they are identified with proposals for crude cost-cutting regardless of the effects on the quality and quantity of the service concerned. The definition I shall be using is one that economists call X-efficiency and does not make this mistake. Under this definition, a fully efficient service is one where it is impossible to reduce the costs of the service without reducing either the quantity or the quality of the service. It is thus not a euphemism for the emasculation of services.

Second, **responsiveness and choice**. The ability of a service to respond to the needs and wants of its users and the extent to which those users have choices could be viewed as part of the quality of the service and hence merged with the definition of efficiency to produce an omnibus criterion.[4] However, these considerations appear so prominently in many of the policy documents concerning the reforms that it seems important to keep them separate.[5]

Third, **equity**. It seems consistent with most of the policy discussion and hence relatively uncontroversial to define equity in relation to need. More specifically, I shall define an equitable service as one where use is determined primarily by need and not by income, socio economic status, gender, race and so forth.[6]

Now it is possible to specify four conditions that need to be satisfied if these reforms are to achieve the ends of increased efficiency, responsiveness and choice without adverse consequences in terms of increased inequity. They concern market structure, information, motivation and 'cream-skimming'. I look at each in turn.

Market structure

For the market allocation of a service to be efficient, responsive and to offer genuine choice, the market concerned has to be competitive. That is, there should be many providers, each unable to influence the market price by changing their output, and many purchasers, each unable to influence price by changing their purchases. If there are not enough actual providers, and hence not enough competition on the supply side, there should be the potential for competition: that is, there should be an opportunity for new providers to enter the market relatively costlessly. There should also be the possibility of exit from the market: that is, providers should face the risk of bankruptcy, or, more generally, that if they consistently make losses they will cease to be a provider.[7]

The problems that a lack of actual or potential competition among providers can create for markets are obvious. A single dominant provider can use its monopoly power to raise prices and to lower the quantity and the quality of the services they provide. Without the threat of competition it can afford to be unresponsive to the needs and wants of its consumers. And a monopoly by definition offers no choice.

However, it might be thought that a lack of competition among purchasers would present fewer problems, at least from a user perspective. In the case of health care, for example, the district health authorities should operate on behalf of NHS users (both actual and potential) and therefore should exercise any monopoly power that they have in a way that benefits users. Similarly social service departments acting as the principal purchasers of community care should operate on behalf of users.

Also, in several welfare areas, there are dominant providers, who if not actual monopolies are close to being so; again health care provides obvious examples, such as large general hospitals in small cities and towns. In such cases, it could be argued that the presence of these dominant providers makes large purchasers essential; for only then can they exercise a sufficient degree of countervailing power so as to offset the power of the providers.

Unfortunately things are not that simple. Even if those running large purchasing authorities are primarily driven by a concern for user interests, it is far from clear how they will know what those interests are. The problem increases with the size of the authority; the bigger it is, the more difficult it will find the task of keeping in touch with the individuals and groups with whose interests it is supposed to be concerned. Moreover, even if a dominant purchaser does know what the public interest is, it may not always exercise its power so as best to serve that interest in the long term. A purchaser that exploits its monopoly power to drive a hard bargain may sour relationships with providers, lower their morale and motivation, and perhaps eventually drive them out of the business. People who feel inadequately rewarded do not perform well in the short term, and in the long term, they find something else to do.

There is more to the argument that monopoly providers need monopoly purchasers to offset their power. But there is a danger here too that the relationship between the two sides will be too intimate. There will be a relatively small number of people dealing with each other, a large proportion of whom may well have been erstwhile colleagues under the old system. In the circumstances it will be difficult to construct or maintain the distance that a market or bargaining process requires. Instead, the system could become one simply of decentralised budgets, with a management contract between purchaser and provider, but with no real competition on either side.[8]

However, there is one area where it may be important to preserve monopoly purchasing power. This concerns the purchase of labour. Staff in many areas of welfare provision are organised in trade unions or in powerful professional associations which in key respects operate like trade unions. Now the power of a labour supply monopoly can be offset by a monopoly purchaser of labour. However, if there is competition for labour, then the competitors, bidding against one another, will drive up wages. This in turn will put considerable pressure on budgets, leading either to strong political representations for an increase in the budget limit or to reduction in service quality or output - which can then be used as ammunition for a further attempt to raise the budget.

The NHS reforms can be used to illustrate the point (Mayston, 1990; Le Grand, 1991b). The NHS is virtually a monopoly employer and is therefore able to bargain more effectively with the relevant professional associations and trade unions. However, under the quasi-market proposals, the NHS as a monopoly employer is to be broken up. Independent trusts are being set up, which are able to determine pay and conditions for staff. If enough trusts are created, the consequence will be to convert the NHS from a (virtual) monopoly purchaser of labour to a (virtual) monopoly purchaser of services. It will now buy services from competitive hospitals, themselves competing for doctors, nurses and ancillary staff. Economic theory would predict that this change will bring about a widening in the dispersion of wages and salaries and probably a rise in their mean levels as well. This prediction has been borne out in the United States, where hospital wage rates have been found to be higher in competitive than in concentrated labour markets.

This is not to imply that if the salaries or wages of people working in welfare provider units do rise it is automatically undesirable. Monopolies of any kind can be exploitative. Wage rises may have a positive impact on morale and productivity. Also there are differences between the relevant labour markets in Britain and the US that suggest a need for caution in making comparisons (for example, in health care, consultants in Britain can already make large sums from private practice). However, overall, it is fair to say that a real danger for the quasi market developments is that one of the major virtues of a monopolistic public sector - its ability to control the power of the professions and hence an important part of its overall labour costs - will be lost.

Information

An important condition for markets to operate efficiently (in the sense defined above) is that both sides of the market concerned have access to cheap and accurate information, particularly concerning the costs and the quality of the service concerned. Providers must be able to cost their activities so as to be able to price them appropriately. Purchasers must be able to monitor the quality of the service they are purchasing, so as to limit the opportunity for providers to reduce costs by lowering quality.

Costing of activities that have never been properly costed before can itself be a costly activity, as almost anyone working on this problem in the public sector can testify. However, it would not be appropriate to lay all such costs at the door of the quasi market reforms, since in many welfare areas the process of improving costing procedures was already under way (under the Resource Management Initiative in the NHS, for example). This illustrates the fact that, even in a planned system, costing procedures can be an important management tool.

However, there are aspects of the use of costing procedures that are specific to quasi markets. One example is the process of billing. Billing operations, particularly if they involve debt collection, can be expensive, and, together with the expense of the costing and pricing procedures that necessarily accompany them, may be an offsetting factor to any cost reducing tendency of quasi markets.

The monitoring of quality also has to be an essential part of any quasi market system. Otherwise providers may engage in what Williamson (1975; 1985) calls opportunistic behaviour: exploiting their informational advantage to reduce their own costs and hence increase financial surplus at the expense of quality. There are two kinds of opportunistic behaviour to which the theoretical literature draws attention: moral hazard and adverse selection. Moral hazard occurs where providers put fewer resources into the provision of the service than is consistent with the terms of their contract; an example would be where a hospital skimps on its accident and emergency service that it provides under a block contract. Adverse selection occurs where providers possess certain characteristics that may adversely affect the provision of the service and that are known to them but they do not reveal to the purchaser; for instance, a private residential home may try to conceal the dubious financial status of its proprietor from the social services department with which it contracts. In either case there would be a reduction in one or more dimensions of quality. The reduction could be prevented if there were continuous monitoring by the purchaser (of, for instance, the accident and emergency service provided by the hospital, or the financial state of the residential home). But monitoring consumes resources, the cost of which has to be taken into account in any overall assessment of a quasi market's contribution to efficiency.

In theory, opportunistic behaviour should be controlled through the contracting process and its associated enforcement procedures. But there are considerable difficulties involved in practice, as illustrated by Bartlett (1991) with respect to the NHS reforms. NHS contracts can be of three types: block contracts, cost per case contracts, and cost and volume contracts. Under the block contract, the purchaser pays the provider an annual fee in return for access to a defined range of services. Under the cost per case contract, each case has a price set under the contract either on an average cost basis, or where there is unplanned excess capacity, on a marginal cost basis. The cost and volume contracts are essentially a mixture of the other two types of contract. They fund a base-line level of activity to be undertaken by the provider, beyond which all funding is on a cost per case basis.

The cost per case contract is close to a complete contingent claims contract. As such it is obviously subject to the principal difficulty with such contracts: the costs of getting the information necessary to write and to administer them. Block contracts, on the other hand, are incomplete and hence subject to the possibility that opportunistic strategies will be pursued by the provider units, resulting in a reduction in the quality of service provision in some areas, and in others in an over emphasis on prestige treatments and to an increase in the absorption of the 'organisational surplus' in the form of increased perks and side payments to staff. In addition, block contracts involve a shifting of risks on to providers; to protect themselves, providers will try to negotiate fees with a risk premium incorporated within and thereby inflate contract prices. Both of these factors will tend to increase the overall costs of service provision.

Overall, this analysis suggests that any improvement in efficiency due to the introduction of quasi markets may be wholly or partly offset by a number of factors. These include the likelihood that providers will adopt opportunistic strategies in the face of incomplete block contracts; the increased risk premia required by the risk averse providers of services; and the increased administrative costs of fully specified cost per case contracts.

Motivation

The third condition concerns the motivation of both purchasers and providers. Providers must be motivated at least in part by financial considerations. If they are not, they will not respond appropriately to market signals. It makes little sense introducing a market to create profitable opportunities, if the participants in the market are not interested in making profits.

In practice this condition might be difficult to fulfil, particularly during the transition stage from bureaucratic systems to quasi markets. Many people working in welfare services are not commercially or financially motivated, and find it difficult to make the shift from considering, say, the welfare of their users to the financial state of their provider unit.[9]

Issues concerning motivation arise on the purchaser side as well. Purchasers must be motivated to maximise the welfare of users. Now if the purchaser were the user, then, barring outright irrationality, there would be little difficulty in this respect, since a user/purchaser could generally be relied upon to be motivated by concern for his or her own welfare. However, in most of the reforms with which we are concerned, users are not entrusted with the purchasing decision for a variety of reasons. Parents take schooling decisions on behalf of children; GP fund holders take hospitalisation decisions on behalf of their patients; care managers take care decisions on behalf of social service clients. In some cases, such as district health authorities or social service departments, the purchaser is quite remote from the user. In all these situations, where an agent is acting as a purchaser on behalf of users, there clearly is a problem in ensuring that purchasers will act in the interests of users and not pursue their own agendas: a problem that increases the further the distance between purchaser and user.

Cream skimming

Finally, if inequity is to be avoided, there must be restricted opportunities for what is termed cream skimming. Cream skimming is discrimination by purchasers or providers against the expensive or the troublesome user: the chronically ill patient, the incontinent, confused elderly person, the disruptive child from a deprived background. If purchasers or providers can discriminate in favour of the relatively healthy, the competent and the easily educable, that is, if they can skim off the cream, then welfare services will not reach those who need them most.

Cream skimming is often termed adverse selection (see for example Glennerster, 1991) and indeed has much in common with that concept.[10] Both involve selection, and in both cases the consequences are adverse, at least for some groups of users. Also, both arise from an inability of producers to price discriminate. In both cases, if providers could charge the potentially more expensive user a price that was in line with the costs concerned, then there would be no disincentive to provide them with the service that they need.

However, if cream skimming is a form of adverse selection then it is worth noting that it is not quite the same as the adverse selection that was described above under the information heading. Here the problem does not appear to be the result of an imbalance of information, but one of the pricing formula by which providers are funded. For example, if schools received larger weights for potentially expensive children through formula funding, or if fund holding GPs were financed by a formula that included a special weighting for potentially expensive patients,[11] they would have no incentive to cream skim; indeed, if the weighting were large enough, the incentive might be reversed.[12]

Such are some of the conditions that the quasi market structures should meet if they are to achieve success according to the criteria of efficiency, responsiveness, choice and equity. One final point should be noted concerning them. If it is impossible to meet one of the conditions, this does not necessarily imply that the 'second best' position is for the other three to be met. It may be that it is better that another condition be violated so as to 'compensate' for the failure to meet the first condition. For instance, if a particular quasi market is not competitive for structural reasons, it may be preferable to have providers that are not motivated by financial considerations, so that they will be less tempted to exploit their monopoly power. This is a point to which I return in the next section.

The process of implementation

It is too early as yet to say definitively whether these conditions are being fulfilled in practice. However, some studies of which I am aware provide both encouraging and disturbing signs. I do not have the space to describe these studies in detail here; but it may be of interest to relate some of the preliminary results to the theoretical issues discussed above, albeit necessarily rather briefly.

In health care there have been studies relevant to the market structure and information conditions. In a SAUS case study of a health authority (Harrison, L. 1991), the market structure, so far from being competitive, was closer to a bilateral monopoly, with a single purchaser and at best a few providers. However, a King's Fund NAHAT study of the extent of potential competition among hospital providers in the West Midlands suggested that only one quarter of them operated in areas where there was a significant degree of monopoly or oligopoly power (as measured by the Hirschman Herfindahl Index), although these hospitals accounted for 38% of patient episodes (Appleby et al, 1991a; Robinson, 1991a).

The extent of potential competition will depend in part on the willingness of patients to use alternative and perhaps more distant providers. A King's Fund Sheffield project is exploring the views of a sample of patients with respect to choice of hospital for referrals (Mahon, Whitehouse and Wilkin, 1992b). The results suggest that there may be some reluctance on the part of patients to travel, with 38% of the sample not prepared to travel at all, and 36% prepared to travel no further than ten miles.

Moreover, a SAUS review of US experience of hospital quasi markets suggests that as these markets develop over time competition may be of limited effect (Propper, 1992). The long term evolution of a competitive environment appears to lead to a limiting of competition for contracts, a lengthening of contractual relationships and domination by the incumbent of the provider side of the market.

In the SAUS case study (Harrison, L. 1991), the purchaser seemed to be heavily dependent on the providers for information; in particular, it had no independent mechanisms for monitoring quality. Although this has not been investigated systematically, this situation does not seem unrepresentative of the UK as a whole. Moreover information problems do not seem to be confined to health authorities; the Sheffield study mentioned above has also been exploring the views of GPs on patient referrals and found a surprising lack of information on such basics as waiting times for different providers (Mahon, Whitehouse and Wilkin, 1992a).

Also in health, even if efficiency improvements are eventually found to exist, care should be taken before these are attributed to the reforms. Preliminary work on a SAUS King's Fund study (Bartlett and Le Grand, 1992) suggests that the hospitals that were to become opted out trusts were already more efficient than their directly managed counterparts, even before the reform process started.

More generally, there may be a Hawthorn effect from the reforms, with any improvement in efficiency resulting from the process of change itself rather than the specific form the changes have taken. With respect to this it is worth noting that, although the hostility of medical practitioners to the reforms has been widely noted, there has often been a positive attitude among NHS managers towards them. For instance, a King's Fund NAHAT survey of Unit General Managers (Appleby et al, 1991b) found that 84% approved of the changes, with 13% having no reservations at all about their implications.

There have been a number of case studies of community care undertaken at SAUS (Hoyes and Means, 1991; Hoyes, Means and Le Grand, 1992; Means, 1992). Again these illustrate the situation in the relevant quasi markets with respect to competition and information. They found the market structure to be in general more competitive on the provider side than in health, with a combination of profit, non profit and public providers, particularly for residential care. However, there was as yet little competition on the purchaser side, with purchasing being concentrated at the level of the department and with few authorities even considering devolving purchasing to competing care managers.

Even more seriously, there were substantial information gaps. In particular, social service departments had little information concerning costs and even less on outcomes; they also lacked the necessary technology to process information and had little by way of resources to improve that technology (Means and Hoyes, 1992).

Partly in response to these deficiencies, purchasers often preferred to contract with voluntary organisations, whose non profit motivation makes them less likely to exploit their informational advantage and to engage in cream-skimming.[13] This relates to the point made earlier that the consequences of not meeting one condition for success (in this case, information) could be offset by moving away from another condition (in this case, motivation). However, it should also be noted that precisely because voluntary organisations are not profit maximisers, they lack the incentive to be cost minimisers. Hence any gains due to their reluctance to exploit their monopolistic position may be offset by a reduction in efficiency due to the absence of incentives for cost minimisation.

Finally with respect to community care, even if they wished to do so, it does not seem likely that social service departments would have the resources to encourage the growth of new providers, or, more generally, to stimulate the market in a more competitive direction (Hoyes and Means, 1991, p. 30). Again this conforms to US experience in contracting in human services (Propper, 1992).

Hence for health (at least with the district health authority as purchaser) and for community care there seem to be problems meeting some of the conditions for quasi market success, particularly those relating to market structure and information. The situations with respect to GP fund holding and education appear to be rather different. A SAUS case study (Bartlett, 1992) found that, in the case of education, the market structure does seem to be broadly competitive on both sides (although entry and exit on the provider side is limited). Also, the information gap is less than in other areas (although it still exists). Moreover, there do appear to be signs of some surprisingly rapid changes in behaviour in the direction that theory would predict, with parents exercising their opportunities for choice and of schools being motivated to make financial surpluses. However, there also appear to be preliminary signs of cream-skimming, with schools setting up formal or, more commonly, informal means of selection.

This is consistent with Scottish experience, where parents have had stronger rights to choose schools than their English counterparts for several years. A study of admissions into Edinburgh and Dundee secondary schools (Adler and Raab, 1988) found that parents appeared to be choosing more effective schools, but also that there was a growth in inequalities among secondary schools of formerly equal status.

GP fund holding also appears to have considerable potential for improving efficiency and for improving responsiveness to users, as shown by a King's Fund STICERD study (Glennerster, Owens and Matsaganis, 1992). The quasi-market is competitive on both sides. GPs are close to users (or at least much closer than hospital consultants or managers). Even more importantly, GPs have access to the best possible information concerning the quality of care: they can assess a patient's health before he or she goes into hospital and they can assess it when he or she comes out. On the negative side, the costs to providers of negotiating with large numbers of fund holders appears to be high. Also, there is an obvious danger of cream skimming by fund holders in their selection of patients for their lists; a fear to some extent supported by US experience of health maintenance organisations which have a number of similarities to fund holders (Weiner with Ferris 1990) - although as yet there appears to be little sign of this actually happening in the UK (Glennerster, Owens and Matsaganis, 1992, p. 33).

In so far as it is possible to make an assessment at this stage, therefore, education and GP fund holding seem to be closer to meeting the market structure and information conditions for quasi market success than community care and health authority purchasing. However, there is room for concern in both education and fund holding with respect to the other conditions, particularly that of cream skimming.

Conclusion

The quasi market reforms are in their infancy and it is too early to predict their long term consequences. However, we have seen that it is possible to combine theoretical considerations with some of the evidence that is now beginning to emerge on the process of implementation to make some preliminary assessments - or at least to point to areas where there might be possible sources of concern. It is perhaps over simplistic, but we could summarize the argument so far as saying the district health authority and social services reforms do not seem to hold out much prospect of efficiency gains, but may not have much adverse impact on equity either; whereas the education and GP fund holding reforms seem to hold out the prospects of real improvements in efficiency, responsiveness and choice, but may have a detrimental effect on equity.

None of the above discussion is intended to suggest that any of these quasi market changes have failed. They certainly have the potential for creating inefficiency and inequity, but the systems they are intended to replace also had their inefficiencies and inequities. As is always the case in the analysis of social policy, the task of evaluation is finding the 'least worst' system: to compare not perfect systems but imperfect ones.

The 1992 election result means that the reforms will be given time to work their way through. We will then be able to assess them properly - and perhaps thereby to discover whether it is better for the state simply to pay for welfare or to pay for and provide it.

Notes

1. I am grateful to colleagues in the SAUS quasi-market programme for comments on earlier versions of this material. Many of the arguments in this chapter can be found in more developed forms in Le Grand and Bartlett (eds.) (1993)
2. There is also a third form of welfare state: the state that monitors or regulates welfare provision. Important as this role is, it will not be a principal focus of this chapter. Discussion of this taxonomy of the different forms of welfare state, together with a theoretical assessment of the different forms, can be found in Le Grand (1991c) and Le Grand, Propper and Robinson (1992), ch. 10.
3. Ironically there is one aspect of these changes that is moving away from a market system of resource allocation. The budgets that care managers will have, or should have, will be partly financed by eliminating the residential care allowance element in social security. This was in one respect closer to being a genuine voucher than the new system, since the budget allocation was under the control of clients themselves and not, as it now is, under the control of an agent acting on the client's behalf. However, under the new system, the budget will be available to spend on care other than residential care, so in that respect at least it is more market-like than the old system.
4. For example, an efficient service could be defined as one which maximised the difference between the benefits and costs of a service. This would incorporate X-efficiency, in that a service which was X-inefficient would also be inefficient in this sense; but it would explicitly consider the needs and wants of users and the extent to which the responsiveness and choices open to users met those needs and wants. This kind of definition is discussed further in Hoyes, Means and Le Grand (1992).
5. For example, *Working for Patients* (1989a) gives as the two objectives of the reform programme presented: 'to give patients ... better health care and greater choice of the services available' and to provide 'greater ... rewards for those working in the NHS

who successfully respond to local needs and preferences' (pp. 3-4). And *Caring for People* (1989) includes as two of its four 'key components' of community care that services should 'respond flexibly and sensitively to the needs of individuals and their carers' and 'allow a range of options for consumers' (p. 5).

6. Again this seems consistent with the chief policy documents concerned. *Working for Patients* (1989a) has several references to the paramountcy of need and openness to all regardless of income (see, for example, the Prime Minister's foreword); and *Caring for People* (1989) includes as a third key component that services should 'concentrate on those with greatest needs' (p. 5). For a broader discussion as to the meaning of equity in public policy contexts, see Le Grand (1991a).

7. There are market structures other than purely competitive ones that can be efficient: for instance, a monopoly provider with the ability 'perfectly' to price discriminate between its purchasers. However, the conditions necessary for such structures to exist are sufficiently unlikely as to make them little more than curiosa.

8. The dangers involved are illustrated by some of the experience with the Next Steps agencies, where some of the classic examples of bilateral monopolies can be found. Many of these are still locked into departmental organisation. The Benefits Agency states in the introduction to its Framework Document that 'the Agency works within the DSS as a whole'. The most significant risks of this incorporation are duplication and confusion about real responsibilities or 'ownership' of the Agency's activities, which may have a direct bearing on the quality of the service the Agency provides (Davies and Willman, 1991, pp. 29-30). That these dangers are real was confirmed in a Price Waterhouse survey of Next Steps agencies in practice (Price Waterhouse, 1991).

9. Indeed, this is not only difficult for people working in welfare, but probably also for many of those who are studying the quasi market reforms and who might otherwise be sympathetic to them.

10. My treatment of this point has benefited from discussions with my colleague Gervas Huxley.

11. Currently the size of a GP fund holder's budget is determined by past referral patterns; however, it is envisaged that this will be eventually replaced by a formula based on weighted capitation.

12. This is the idea behind the positively discriminating voucher discussed in Le Grand (1989).

13.   Interestingly, this conforms with recent theoretical developments concerning the role of voluntary organisations (see Hansmann, 1987).

6 User empowerment and buying community care: Reflections on the emerging debate about charging policies

Rachel Lart and Robin Means

Introduction

The issue of charging for services like home care, day care, meals on wheels and aids and adaptations is emerging as a crucial one for local authorities in planning and implementing community care. Local authorities can, and do, charge for any or all of these services, but the basis on which such charges are made, how much, for what and from which users, varies between authorities and has more to do with history, elected members' sensitivities and pragmatism than any clearly thought out and rational approach. This results in inequities, not only between authorities which might be expected if local autonomy is to mean anything, but also within authorities, between people receiving different services, or packages of services. In contrast, the framework for charging for local authority residential care has historically been a national one.

The focus of our research, and of this chapter, is the impact of the community care reforms *Caring for People*, (1989) on the users of services in terms of the extent to which users have choice in and control over services. We shall begin by outlining the framework for empowerment used by our research. We shall then review, briefly, the arguments for universal, free welfare provision, and, against this, the arguments for selection, targeting and charging for welfare and the way in which debates on charging for social care have been played out since the second world war.

This debate is now reemerging, particularly in terms of the ability of people to 'self provision'; what is appropriate in the world of, on the one hand, widespread home ownership equity and occupational pensions, and on the other, retrenchment of public spending? (Griffiths Report 1988). This debate is predicated on the idea that the resources locked up in equity and occupational pensions are both substantial and accessible. However empirical work has thrown doubt on this assumption (Oldman 1991, Walker, R. 1988, Bosenquet and Propper 1991).

Examples of emerging charging policies will be drawn from our recent fieldwork on the community care implementation strategies of four contrasting local authorities (Hoyes et al, 1993). Finally some of the implications and likely future issues will be discussed. It is too early for empirical observation of the effects of charging; this chapter attempts to develop theoretical and historical frameworks for the analysis of what these are likely to be in terms of user empowerment.

What is empowerment?

Empowerment of users of services is very much 'flavour of the month'. In Government documents, the idea of involving and empowering users has moved from being something of a side issue to a central rationale for the changes in social care (Department of Health/SSI, 1991). The framework within which our analysis is set uses the contrasting ideas of 'exit' and 'voice' as means to empower people, and draws on the work of Hirschman (1970, 1974), and Taylor et al, (1992).

'Exit' is related to choice on point of entry to a service, and the ability to move from one service to another, in the event of dissatisfaction with the initial service. In its purest form, exit is primarily an economic concept which sees the user as a consumer within a market situation. Preconditions for the success of exit as a strategy for user empowerment are those related to the successful operation of the market: most importantly a sufficient number of providers to constitute competitive supply and thus choice, and an informed and knowledgeable consumer, physically and psychologically able to move between services.

'Voice' refers to the ability of users to influence and change services, while remaining within them. It is primarily a political concept, one which sees users, either individually or collectively, as stakeholders in the process of planning and running services. Preconditions for the success of voice as a strategy for empowerment are clear and accessible consultative and participative mechanisms, information and advocacy, and commitment from authorities to the process of involvement (Taylor et al, 1992).

The two are not mutually exclusive; users may prefer to try to exercise voice before exit, and it may be the threat of the power ultimately to exit that makes voice a realistic option. The means to achieving empowerment suggested within government guidance includes both exit and voice strategies. As part of the broad restructuring of the welfare state which Le Grand (Chapter 5) refers to as the introduction of quasi-markets, the community care changes can clearly be seen in terms of exit. Local authorities are being asked to stimulate a mixed economy of social care which will increase choice, and hence opportunity for exit. Equally, the exhortation to local authorities to include groups representative of users and their carers in planning for community care and in setting service specifications and quality standards are voice mechanisms.

Universalism

The theoretical underpinnings of the case for universal, free welfare have always been associated with the need to avoid the negative consequences of selection such as stigma, and to enhance social integration and cohesion. Universality is taken to represent a commitment to the ideas of equal rights and social equality (Abel-Smith and Titmuss (Eds.) 1987, Townsend 1976).

That it is possible to avoid a second rate, stigmatised welfare service is shown by the National Health Service; historically the vast majority of the population have looked to the NHS for all medical needs, and no stigma has been attached to use of this free, public service. Contrast this with the image of local government social services provision; a last resort when one's personal resources, whether financial or psychological and emotional, have been exhausted. Many personal social services are services aimed at poor, unwilling or unpopular groups (Berry 1988).

A major disincentive to the use of welfare, one linked to the idea of stigma, is the means test (Deacon and Bradshaw 1983). This operates most strongly in the realm of cash benefits; Child Benefit, a 'universal benefit' has a far higher take up rate and social acceptability than does the means tested family credit, in spite of government campaigns to change the image of the latter. The other obvious example is Unemployment Benefit, which is seen as socially less stigmatising than Income Support, even when the actual amounts are the same, because it is based on some notion of entitlement derived from a national insurance record.

Some forms of means testing are not regarded as stigmatising; for example the benefit paid in the form of a student grant, dependent on parental means testing. Even families who have willingly paid several hundred or even thousand pounds a year to educate their children privately up to the age of eighteen will claim this benefit. However, in general, the argument for universality rests on the idea that targeting via means testing has negative effects on take up.

The standard case against means testing is put by Townsend (1976) on these grounds; means testing is inefficient in that, because of the deterrent effect, services and benefits do not reach those who need them; it is also impractical , as it cannot take account of complex individual circumstances; and finally it leads to a divided society and is a distraction from the need to challenge those social institutions which create poverty. As Donnison (1982) has argued, a service targeted at poor people, tends to be a poor service.

Targeting and selectivity

The arguments against universalism and for selectivity have several bases. One is the economic one that demand for universal services outstrips the resources available; make something available to everyone with no costs, either pecuniary or non pecuniary, and too many people will want it. This is an argument for selection and targeting of resources on the grounds of efficiency (Friedman and Friedman, 1985; Davies, in association with Reddin 1978; Mishra, 1984).

Linked to this is the public choice argument about the way in which universal services, provided by the state, tend to become bureaucratic monoliths, with professionally defined criteria for access. There is no mechanism for revealing consumer choice, and no incentive for efficiency in providing services (see Hood 1987 for a fuller discussion of public choice theory). This is a critique of bureaucracy from the perspective of economic analysis, and leads to a preference for small scale, competing providers, funded by unit charges to users, rather than allocations from public funds. This has been part of the 'New Right' critique of the welfare state that has dominated the 1980s. As well as the economic arguments, this critique has included the philosophical perspective that universal welfare contributes to the 'dependency culture', and was thus not only 'ineffective and expensive, but damaging' (Jack 1991).

Sharing the critique of large public bureaucracies, but starting from a very different perspective, that of community development, some writers have pointed to the way public services are often experienced as 'insensitive, inefficient, overstandardised and disabling' (McConnell and Taylor 1988). Such disillusion has been a major factor in the move to more decentralised systems of delivery for local authority services (Hoggett and Hambleton (eds.) 1987).

The overall focus of this chapter, however, is upon paying for services and charging for services rather than upon the universality versus selectivity argument. There is a tendency to see charging and paying for services as the inevitable outcome of a selectivist position, and unnecessary from a universalist position. It is 'ultra vires', for example, for GPs to charge for primary health care services such as district nursing. However, it is possible to pursue a strategy of having services such as those provided by dentists or opticians which are universally available, but which will impose some charge upon most people. Equally many selective services are free to those entitled to receive them.

What can be said is that charging for services can be driven by a variety of motives. They can reflect:

1   a desire to generate income;

2   the need to ration;

3   a dimension of empowerment.

These debates will be returned to later in the chapter. First, however, we are going to ground the discussion by taking an historical look at charging for social care services and then go on to look at emerging local authority approaches to implementing the community care reforms with particular reference to their charging strategies.

Charging for social care services: historical perspectives

This section is mainly concerned with the arrangements which emerged in the late 1940s towards charging for social care services. Perhaps the most interesting case concerned residential care under Part III of the National Assistance Act 1948. Here is an example of provision where empowerment was seen to flow from the introduction of a charge, backed up by the principle of universal availability. During the second world war, public assistance institutions were criticised for their harsh treatment of inmates, especially when these were seen as respectable elderly people who had drifted into such provision because of the disruption of war rather than through what had traditionally been seen as a lifetime of fecklessness. The withdrawal of pension rights, clothing and visiting restrictions did not seem appropriate to war victims (Means and Smith, 1985).

After the war, a committee of civil servants was established to complete the break up of the poor law after the initial Beveridge reforms. Residential care for elderly people was one of the issues to be addressed. The subsequent Rucker Report (see Means and Smith, 1985, pp. 136-42) argued that local authorities should retain responsibility for provision, but that this should be through the development of small homely units, especially for elderly people. However, pension rights were no longer to be removed, but rather:

> as a further step towards breaking away from the old association of parish relief and in particular the conception of an institution for 'destitute persons', we think that a resident in a local authority's home should keep charge of whatever income or other resources he (sic) may have and pay the authority for his (sic) accommodation and maintenance (quoted in Means and Smith, 1985, pp. 138-39).

The report referred to this as a non stigmatising hotel relationship and hence a complete break with the poor law. This 'conception of a "hotel" relationship' would work for most pensioners by them paying to the local authority 21 shillings a week from their 26 shillings pension and keeping 5 shillings for pocket money (ibid., p. 139).

These proposals were incorporated into the National Assistance Act 1948 and the hotel theme was enthusiastically emphasised by Nye Bevan (Minister of Health) when introducing the bill to Parliament:

> .. the whole idea is that welfare authorities should provide them and charge an economic rent for them, so that any old persons who wish to go may go there in exactly the same way as many well to do people have been accustomed to go into residential hotels (ibid., p. 150).

It could be argued that this is much more an exit rather than a voice approach to empowerment, and one in which a charge for services was seen as removing rather than imposing stigma.

It is well documented that the great changes desired by the Rucker Report (See Means and Smith, 1985, pp. 136-42) and Bevan did not occur. *The Last Refuge* by Peter Townsend (1964) painted a terribly depressing picture of local authority residential care. Most residents felt oppressed and isolated. But what does this tell us about charging and empowerment?

This is open to dispute. One response is that paying for care does not reduce stigma especially if the buildings remain the same, staff attitudes remain unchanged and if an inappropriate care package is chosen. In other words, charging has a limited ability to empower. But an alternative response is to stress that empowerment failed to emerge because the exit model failed to emerge. Elderly people could not choose to enter residential 'hotels' in the 1950s. Rather, demand for places soon outstripped supply and hence elderly people seeking residential care needed to submit themselves to assessment by professionals.

The picture with regard to domiciliary services is far more muddled. Most policy makers did not believe elderly people and other care groups should be seen as entitled to home care, day care, meals and other services. This was for a number of reasons. There was a desire to protect the welfare role of the then Assistance Board which was responsible for Supplementary Pensions. There was a concern to develop the welfare role of such organisations as the W(R)VS, the Red Cross and the NOPWC (now Age Concern). There was, also, a desire to avoid unnecessary public expenditure and a fear of undermining the willingness of families (i.e. women) to provide unpaid care (see Means and Smith, 1985).

The actual pattern of local authority responsibilities to provide domiciliary services as well as the powers to fund them through other agencies, which emerged in the late 1940s, is highly complex. What is crucial for our purposes is to recognise is that these responsibilities and powers were limited. The home help service was a discretionary duty and not a mandatory one, and this remained the case until April 1971. It was 'ultra vires' for a local authority to directly provide a meals service rather than find another agency to do so until an amendment to the 1948 Act in 1962. There were broad preventive powers for some specific groups with disabilities but no general power to promote the welfare of elderly people.

This muddled mosaic of services generated an equally muddled mosaic of approaches to charging between different services and between different local authorities (Judge and Matthews, 1980; Judge, (ed.) 1980; Glennerster, 1985). However, what is clear is that civil servants and ministers involved in the drafting of the 1940s legislation saw domiciliary services as appropriate to charge for. But the logic for doing this was markedly different to that applied to residential care. For example, the provision of home help services was confirmed as a power of local authorities by the National Health Service Act 1946 rather than the

113

National Assistance Act 1948, but it was never perceived as a health care service which should be universally free. Rather, Bevan argued in the House of Commons that:

> It is a perfectly reasonable proposition that, where domestic help is needed and the persons concerned are able to provide it for themselves, they should do so, and where they are able to make a contribution they should make it.. it seems to me wholly unjustified that we should provide a service of this sort without any payment whatever (quoted in Glennerster, 1985, p. 147).

The interpretation of these comments by Glennerster (1985) was that Bevan took the view:

> .. that many people already provided themselves with an almost identical service out of their own pockets - a 'char lady' or 'domestic help'. A local authority could not simply begin providing a comparable service free without undermining the private service and landing itself with an intolerable demand for the public equivalent (pp. 147-8).

The 1946 Act and subsequent circulars gave local authorities wide discretion over their home care charging strategy. Section 29 of the National Health Service Act stated that:

> a local health authority may, with the approval of the Minister, recover from persons availing themselves of the domestic help so provided such charges (if any) as the authority consider reasonable, having regard to the means of those persons.

The implementing circular gave local authorities considerable discretion by giving them freedom:

> to determine in each individual case whether any, and if so what, charge - within the limits of the standard charge specified in the tariff - would be reasonable, having regard to the means of the person concerned (quoted in Means and Smith, 1985, p. 265).

The proportion of the gross cost of the home help service raised by such costs has never been large, and declined during the 1970s and early 1980s. The reason for this decline was the growth of elderly clients as a proportion of the overall home help caseload. The majority of these elderly clients were on low incomes and many were in receipt of financial help from National Assistance/Supplementary Benefit. This created conflict between the local authority associations and the NAB/Ministry of Social Security since the former felt the latter should make a contribution to the local authority when claimants received a service. However, the Ministry of Health always took the view that such cases should receive a free service and that any attempt to impose minimum charges in such cases would be 'ultra vires'. Circular 25/65 was very critical of local authority pricing policy in general and claimed: 'some of the present arrangements for charges deter people in genuine and even urgent need of the service from taking full advantage of it' (quoted in Means and Smith, 1985, p. 265).

By the mid 1960s, it was also clear that access to home care was not about a willingness to pay for this service, but an ability to prove entitlement. Demand was outstripping supply, and a number of bureaucratic and professional approaches to rationing was adopted (level of need; presence or absence of carers; date of application, etc.), but few authorities seemed to adopt charging policies as central to their rationing strategies.

In 1985, most of the various charging statutes and clauses were brought under a single Act, namely the Health and Social Services and Social Security Adjudication Act 1983. In terms of charges for local authority services, this specified that:

> an authority providing a service to which this section applies may recover such charge (if any) for it as they consider reasonable. (Part VII, para. 17(1)).

There is one main proviso to this wide degree of local authority discretion. If a service user:

> satisfies the authority providing the service that his [sic] means are insufficient for it to be reasonably practical for him [sic] to pay for the service, the amount which he [sic] would otherwise be obliged to pay for it, the authority should not require him [sic] to pay more for it than it appears to them that it is reasonably practicable for him [sic] to pay (Part 7, para. 17(3)).

Of course, users and local authorities may not necessarily be in agreement about what is meant by reasonable. If a user refuses to pay what is considered by the local authority to be a reasonable charge, his or her service cannot be withdrawn, but the local authority can take steps to recover the debt.

Charging remains an area of great local authority discretion with regard to the direct provision of domiciliary services, and the situation would become even more complicated if we attempted to look at the history of charging by voluntary organisations, who provide services with the support of local authority grants or service agreements.

The impact of the community care reforms: four case studies

But what has been the impact of the community care reforms upon charging policies? Section 3.84 of the White Paper on community care, *Caring for People* (1989), addressed charging issues and indicated that the majority of the arrangements would stay the same. The 1983 Act would continue to cover charging for domiciliary services, and stressed that there was no aspiration to extend this to payment for such services as care package assessment, social work support, and occupational therapy. With regard to residential care, the White Paper indicated a continuance of the system by which residents of local authority homes are charged the full economic cost where they can afford to pay and where the method of determining ability to pay is prescribed nationally. The White Paper went on to stress that these arrangements: 'will be applied to meeting the costs in independent residential and nursing homes when local authorities take over' these responsibilities (ibid., p. 29).

However this rather bland statement covered up the lack of clarity about:

1.   how fees would be set;

2.   how much money would be transferred to local authorities from the social security budget, and

3.   what changes might be made to assessing people's ability to pay, and how much discretion would be given to local authorities for tackling this.

The section on charging is at the very end of the chapter on the roles and responsibilities of social services authorities, and only takes up five paragraphs. The only justification for charging which is offered is as follows:

> In practice many consumers of personal social services cannot afford the full cost of the service, and ability to pay does not and should not in any way influence decisions on the services to be provided. This accords with the Government's general policy on charges for local services: those able to meet all or part of the economic cost should be expected to do so. Moreover, effective costing and charging procedures can be valuable in achieving the best use of resources across the range of personal social services and local social services authorities will be expected to develop them (ibid., p. 28).

However, the early White Paper message may have been that it was to be 'business as usual' with regard to charging but this has not stopped a growing debate and interest in charging by social services authorities.

We will now draw upon our present research which is funded by the Joseph Rowntree Foundation and which involves studying the impact of the community care reforms upon users and carers in four contrasting local authorities. Below is a snapshot of how each is developing its charging policies.

Case Study A is a metropolitan authority which has a combined housing and social services department and a population of 187,000. There is a clear Labour majority on the council. Case Study A has always been hostile to charges for domiciliary services, and members are especially proud of their free home care service. Limited charges are made to cover food costs only for the meals on wheels service and day care (85p per day in early 1992). In recent years, the local authority has funded the development of day care for elderly people by the local Age Concern branch, and this charges £1.50 per day for meals. The General Secretary said she was unsure how this exact figure was arrived at but the assumption is that it covers food costs only. The policies of the voluntary sector providers vary, but overall the emphasis is upon low or nil charging. For example, the local Crossroads Care Attendant Scheme is free to carers in a situation where the national office leaves whether to charge as a local branch decision.

Pressure has been mounting upon this authority to introduce charging. Senior managers decided financial pressures made this inevitable and the Director made a proposal to introduce charges to members during 1991-92, but this was rejected by the majority Labour Group. However, in June 1992, this group had to call an emergency meeting because of the worsening financial position of the local authority. All committees were requested to reduce expenditure and/or increase income by sizeable amounts. An accepted proposal from social services has been the need to introduce home care charges for the first time; this will involve drawing upon Attendance Allowance income of clients where available, but there will be a rigid maximum charge system. The chair perceives this development as a reluctant necessity, yet one which is inequitable and illogical. It will not generate vast sums because most people in Case Study A are on low incomes. It may discourage some people from staying in their own homes rather then entering residential care. Above all, home care is a key service which should be supplied on the basis of need and hence free.

Case Study B is a London borough which presently has a Labour majority on the council and where charging debates have followed a similar path to the previous case study. No charges are made for the home care service. A charge of £1 is made to cover the food costs of the meals on wheels service. This charge was pegged at 60p for six years, but then raised immediately to £1 as a result of poll tax pressures. Voluntary organisations in the borough tend to mirror this approach. For example, the local branches of both Age Concern and the Alzheimer's Disease Society charge users small sums for food and transport, but make no charge for the actual services provided such as day care.

As in Case Study A, senior managers have raised the issue of whether charges for services such as home care should be introduced as a means of generating income, but so far this has always been rejected by members. This has been seen as a less attractive option than reducing some local authority services or grants to other agencies, as a strategy for coping with growing financial pressures.

Case Study C is a county council, which has a hung council, and where there is a very fluid debate between professionals and members about what represents the most appropriate charging strategy. Prior to December 1990 there was a flat rate charge for those not receiving income support. In December 1990, a home care matrix was introduced, based on a system of charging bands. Those on Income Support pay no charge at all; for others, charges are at two levels, currently £8.30 or £16.60. The lower level is paid by those receiving Income Support and Attendance Allowance or those receiving no benefits at all. Those who receive Attendance Allowance but who are not on income support pay the higher charge. These charges are per week regardless of the level of service - hence one might receive less than two hours or as many as sixty hours per week for the same charge.

However, most people who receive services are on Income Support or in receipt of Attendance Allowance. Only 16% of service users receive no benefits and 7% receive Attendance Allowance but no Income Support. As a result, only £750,000 was generated in charges in 1991-92 out of a service expenditure of over £7 million.

The policy remains controversial. The disability movement continue to complain about the use of the Attendance Allowance. Some members want either a means test of the ability to pay or a closer link between the charge and the level of the service. Some professionals feel the income generated is outweighed by the cost of collection.

In December 1991, a report was presented to the social services committee which argued for variable charging levels for those receiving higher levels of service. This was sparked by renewed financial pressures on the social services budget, but the proposals were rejected. At the moment, a thorough review is taking place of the county's charging policy towards both domiciliary services and residential services after April 1993. In general, the statutory and voluntary sectors in this county are happier to charge for services such as day care, meals on wheels and home care than those in the previous two case studies, but there is, as yet, little agreement over the best principles to be applied.

Case Study D is a Conservative controlled county council, currently reviewing its charging policy with the intention of making radical change. At present the authority charges for all services (except, of course, social work, occupational therapy and emergency services). For example, everybody pays a minimum of £1.65 per week for home care. There is then an hourly charge of £2.40, up to £12.00, or five hours, a week. Above five hours, no further charge is made. This is seen by officers as neither fair, nor as yielding sufficient income for the department.

The changes proposed would mean a shift from the idea of charges; fixed amounts with no necessary relationship to costs. Instead, true costs have been worked out for services, and a package, once put together for a user, will be costed. The user will then be assessed financially to determine the level of subsidy to which they are entitled. Some people will be entitled to a full subsidy, and so will receive their package free, unlike the present policy. Others will be asked for a major contribution towards costs, much higher than under the current system. In practice, most people will be entitled to some subsidy, especially if they receive high cost services such as day care.

Preparing this strategy involves firstly working out costs for services, which has been done, and secondly agreeing a formula for the financial assessment, which is still in progress. A paper is due to go to the Social Services Committee in September 1992. As in most authorities, the question of charging policies is politically fraught; while officers and the chair of Social Services see the shift in the basis of charging as both inevitable and necessary, there is likely to be considerable resistance on the part of members from all parties.

Why charge?

There are numerous pressures encouraging our four authorities to place a review of charging quite high on their policy agenda. These pressures must be quite severe since in all four charging is a source of tension between members and officers, with officers tending to see the need to introduce, extend or revolutionise charging policies much more readily than members. It would seem that members 'fear' the charging issue, because it generates negative publicity from the local media, and hence it is seen as a threat to councillor security.

So what are these pressures? How do they relate to the motives we identified earlier?

Charging as a source of income

The context of the emerging debate about charging in our four case studies is the general financial pressures upon local authorities. There is both the tension associated with local government finance in general, but also the more specific issue of how the Department of the Environment judges the amount of money which individual local authorities are deemed to need to spend on social services. The formula underpinning the Standing Spending Assessment (SSA) for social services is both complex and controversial (Harding, 1992). Many local authorities find that their expenditure on social services is far in excess of their SSA; this means that social services in such authorities are consuming income from the DOE, which was allocated to fund other services. But there is little consensus on the reasons for this gap. Does it represent underfunding from central government and the vagaries of the SSA? Or does it represent over-spending by the local authority, or a failure to generate income from charges?

The dominant factor in our four case studies seems to be a desire to generate income in a situation where the ability of local authorities to raise income from local taxation is heavily proscribed. Most members in the Metropolitan authority and the London borough believe domiciliary services should be free, but in the first example they have been driven to accept charging as an income generation device. Most managers in these two authorities now feel there is little alternative but to charge for the same reasons. In the two counties, there is less overt hostility to the principle of charging for domiciliary services, but no clear agreement upon the principles upon which such charging should be based. The debate does seem to be driven by issues of income generation in Case Study 'C', but by a more complex agenda in Case Study 'D'.

Charging as a form of rationing

It is clear that charging is a form of income generation for our four case studies, but is it also a form of rationing? In some ways it is the opposite of this, since income generation through charging is seen as a mechanism to ensure the local authority can afford to provide a service for more people, and hence priority criteria for service allocation can be drawn less rigidly.

Nevertheless, all social services authorities have little choice but to continue to develop assessment systems which distinguish those who are a priority for help from those who are not. Some authors argue that a charge is an excellent test of commitment. As outlined in the earlier part of the chapter, this can be presented in both positive and negative terms. It may stop people consuming a service just because it is free rather than because they really want it; or it may deter poor people with real need from seeking help. However, in all four case studies, the central rationing mechanism is the assessment of need by professionals rather than the use of the price mechanism.

However, there is one important exception to this situation. In case study 'D' there is a strong belief that many people are in a position to pay for all their care needs because of their personal resources. Their proposed new system of costing care packages offers everyone an assessment, but only some people a public subsidy. Wealthy people with care needs in that county may see that as a sign that they are expected to 'self provision' and hence to withdraw themselves completely from the LA system; but others may be only too happy to receive a skilled assessment by local authority staff, and then to go on to pay the full price for the proposed care package.

Empowerment

The third possibility is that charging is perceived as having a role in a strategy of empowerment. Returning to our original themes of exit and voice, charging for services can most easily be linked to exit driven strategies of empowerment, as we discussed briefly in our historical account. Such charges may be part of what Parker (1976) refers to as the 'symbolic' use of charges; an indication that a user is 'paying their way' or standing on their own feet.

There is some evidence that paying something towards the cost of services gives people a sense of control that they would not otherwise have. Small scale research using discussion groups, carried out in Islington, suggested that people felt more able to ask for the kinds of help and services they wanted, when they were paying even small amounts (London Borough of Islington, 1991). Many voluntary sector groups interviewed for our research expressed the idea that charges could give this sense of ownership, although they stressed that a balance had to be kept with the need not to exclude people who could not afford to pay even minimal charges. Some got round this by accepting donations, rather than making charges. However, this kind of informal, discretionary charging is not really appropriate in the context of large scale publicly run services.

The economic analysis implicit in the idea of exit is that only by having control of the resources that pay for a service can a user really have the power to choose between services, or exit from one to another, taking the resources with them. However, the organisational changes for local authorities involved in implementing the community care legislation, namely, the shift from providing care to paying for care provided by other agencies (Le Grand, Chapter 5), does not necessarily involve this radical shift of control of resources to the user. It would be perfectly possible for the 'enabling authority' to continue to allocate services, once purchased, by bureaucratic means, with no transfer of power. The authority would have the power to exit from contracts or service agreements, not the user. For exit to be a reality at the individual level, the user has to be the purchaser, and a charge has to be attached to each service.

One means of giving users this control of resources is by the use of vouchers, an idea which has been mooted for some years now in several areas of social policy. In a sense, the subsidy to private residential care via the social security system was a form of voucher, but one which had to be spent on a particular form of care, with the results that we are all familiar with. There may have been choice for users between those providers of residential care who were prepared to accept the voucher (i.e. accept residents dependent on public subsidy), but users could not choose to spend the resources on other forms of care. It is, of course, to alter this perverse incentive towards residential care and control the ensuing expenditure, that the community care changes are being embarked on.

None of the authorities we are researching is considering the idea of a community care voucher. It could be argued that it is difficult to see how it would fit with the idea of needs led assessment; to an extent a voucher system assumes either a uniform level of entitlement, or a fairly simple categorisation system. That is why the idea can theoretically be applied to education; most people are assumed to be entitled to a similar number of years of education. The basis of needs led assessment is that everyone has an individual set of needs which cannot be met by standardised units of service. The subsidy to residential and nursing home care assumed a very simple binary categorisation of need.

Another way of looking at the issues raised by vouchers would be the handing over of a budget, once allocated on a definition of need, to the user. This form of user control has been the basis of the Independent Living Fund and is being tried on a very small scale in case study B. User controlled budgets lose some of the simplicity of vouchers; the process of defining need, and hence the size of the budget, is more complicated, to take account of individual variations. However, given that some such process is likely to be done anyway, to indicate to care managers the budget or level of resources available for an individual user, the process of handing over control of that budget to the user is a fairly simple next step. The experience of the Independent Living Fund has shown that this form of user control is a relevant and important concept not only for the young disabled, but also for older people with many different kinds of disability, including the most severe (Kestenbaum, 1992).

However, at the time of writing, it is ultra vires for local authorities to hand over cash directly to users of services. Where such schemes are being tried out, a third party such as a voluntary sector organisation acts as a kind of 'banker'.

Returning to the actual or proposed charging policies of the four local authorities, how can we assess their likely impact in terms of our central theme of empowerment?

There are two sets of issues; firstly, whether charges should be made or not, and if so, how their level should be arrived at; and secondly the level and nature of the support given to users to meet charges.

If we take the policies of case studies A and B, where no or minimal charges are made, the basic principle is that services which are needed should be supplied on that basis, and not charged for. In the climate of resource constraints local authorities are facing, this principle is being eroded anyway by the piecemeal introduction of charges. It also means that income generation opportunities are lost, and services are being cut and grants to the voluntary sector being refused or reduced. Tighter priorities have to be imposed and services are rationed more strictly. This is hardly the basis for empowering users. Limited services mean that exit, other than out of services altogether, is hardly an option, while the power of voice mechanisms will be reduced where there are no resources either to enable the exercise of voice or to act on what is said.

Of course, the financial circumstances in which local authorities find themselves are not the consequence of whether they raise charges on social services or not. However, case study D perceives charging as a key part of their response to this situation. They have also reviewed the level and nature of the support which should be given to users in purchasing services. Under the proposed comprehensive charging policy of case study D we can assume that users will fall into four categories:

- not assessed for services, no subsidy
- assessed for services, care package put together, no subsidy offered
- assessed for services, care package put together, some subsidy offered
- assessed for services, care package put together, total subsidy offered

At one end is the option that a user purchases services entirely out of their own resources. To a large extent this already happens. From paying for a gardener to perform tasks no longer found possible, through the purchase of private cleaning and home care services, to the purchase of private residential care, people already 'self provision'. The role of the enabling authority vis a vis this group is to ensure that they have information about the availability and quality of services on which to make decisions. They will be able to buy whatever services the authority continues to provide, if that is their choice. Serving this group adequately in terms of information and regulation of quality is a crucial part of the authority's strategy, as is the provision of services, at a charge, where the market is not sufficiently developed to ensure a choice.

However, it is easy to get carried away with such scenarios. The resources of most potential recipients of residential and domiciliary care are far too low to enable complete self provisioning (Oldman 1991, Walker, R. 1988). Occupational pensions continue to lag behind the rest of Europe (Bosenquet and Propper 1991) and there is no simple mechanism for unlocking equity from owner occupied housing, other than to trade down to a smaller property or to move into residential care (Mackintosh, Means and Leather 1990).

At the other end is the option that a user is entirely publicly funded, after being assessed and a costed package put together. A crucial question, arising from the discussion of universality and selectivity above, is that of how to prevent services used by those dependent on public subsidy from being second rate? The theoretical answer is that within the mixed economy of care, those services purchased with public subsidy may be the same services chosen by those with no public subsidy. The question still remains whether the enabling authority can afford to purchase as good a service for those dependent on public subsidy. Again the question of quality control and regulation is crucial here; the public subsidy may not buy the best, but it has to buy a definable quality. The reality of this will depend on the state of the market; where competition exists quality can be insisted on. Our account of the history of residential care indicates what can happen in the absence of adequate supply and strong quality controls.

The extent to which the total subsidy group are empowered will probably depend less on exit strategies than on voice. At the individual level, the nature of the relationship with assessors and care managers will include the degree to which they are listened to and heard. At the collective level, they need strong representation within the structures of planning and standard setting.

Between these two groups are those people deemed to be within a priority category, and therefore assessed for services, and for whom a costed package is put together, but who are not offered a full subsidy, or any subsidy. Given our caveats about the extent to which assumptions about self provisioning can be questioned, these two groups will in fact include the largest number of people.

They have the choice of accepting the package and paying their assessed contribution to the cost, or of going off to purchase services privately, or of having no services. They can also 'top up' the package from their own resources (as can the total subsidy group). They also, in practice, have the option of accepting the package and refusing to pay; the legal position for authorities in this situation has not yet been established. This confusion is about the status of needs led assessments;

do they confer some kind of entitlement to services, regardless of resources, or are they recommendations as to how needs could be met?

How is this group empowered? Again the voice mechanisms of involvement in decisionmaking are important. But they also have the choice, knowing the cost of their care package and the extent of their own contribution, to choose to use their resources elsewhere, in the way that the first group do. Some may do this. Others may deem the professional services of assessment and care management valuable in their own right, and these are not charged for within the package.

Discussion

The relationship of a policy of charging direct to the user and offering means tested subsidies to a strategy to empower people depends on several factors. Firstly the state of the market; how far is choice of provision a reality, and what power does the authority have to impose quality standards on those services included in packages of care? Secondly the formula used to assess the level of subsidy offered. As with any means test, there is a trade off between the complexity required to achieve fairness between people's very different situations, and the need for a simple, understandable and open formula. As well as the complexity of the formula, there is the level of the subsidy offered and how generous this can be. Here local authorities are working without guidance from central government. Unlike the present situation where authorities are required to charge for residential care and a national formula exists for assessing the subsidy, under the new arrangements the decision whether to charge for and how to subsidise packages of care will be a local one.

For those authorities, like our case study B, where a commitment to the services is being maintained, there is the risk that in the context of tight resources, some services may have to be reduced and eligibility criteria drawn more rigidly. This policy ensures that users do not bear responsibility for paying for care, but with the result that services have to be rationed further and a smaller group of people served. Another of the authorities, case study A, tried to maintain this commitment, but has been forced into a position of introducing a wide range of charges for borough services because of the deteriorating financial position of the local authority.

Local authorities are experiencing extreme pressure to charge for services as a means of generating income. The implications of whatever response to this pressure is chosen, whether to resist and risk reducing availability of services, or to charge and thus shift responsibility for paying for care onto users, need to be thought through in terms of the impact on the authority's approach to empowering users.

7 The restructuring of welfare and social services users: What's in it for them?

Monica Dowling

Introduction

This chapter sets thirteen months participant observation of two social work teams and eighteen independent interviews with social service users in the wider context of government policies towards public welfare and those in poverty. It examines how welfare restructuring affects social services departments; social service users; and the interactions between social service users and social workers. The questions addressed are, in what ways has:

1. the restriction of universal benefits in favour of means tested loans and grants; and

2. the subsidising of private mortgages rather than council housing, exacerbated the difficulties faced by poor social service users and social workers.

The research employed an ethnographic methodology to examine the policy outcomes of these forms of welfare restructuring given that the 'meaning' of government policies for the individual cannot be understood just by looking at statistics on welfare spending, changes in income tax for the wealthy, or even the increasing numbers in poverty.

This study was conducted in two areas within different local authorities - 'Carshire' (with the Silverton social work team) and 'City' (with the City social work team). 'Carshire' is a small, rural, former mining area in Yorkshire while 'City' is the nearby large metropolis where most of the population used to work in a single heavy industry. With the loss of this industry, 'City' is attempting to develop its service sector. In both areas there is high unemployment and poverty.

What is the restructuring of welfare?

Government policies which have brought about a restructuring of welfare include: limiting public spending whilst simultaneously encouraging the private sector to respond to the unmet need; increasing the gap between rich and poor by shifting away from progressive taxation; allowing rises in market incomes whilst cutting the value of benefits in real terms; subsidising private pensions and mortgages; and limiting universal benefits in favour of means tested grants and loans. Walker, (1990c) and Shirley, (1990) note that welfare state restructuring has taken place alongside rising need and inflation and has involved:

> The substitution of voluntary and private welfare for public provision; increasing the role of the informal sector in care; ..... and centralisation of resource control coupled with the decentralisation of operational responsibility, thereby neutralizing any potential power of welfare state users to increase the share of public expenditure devoted to them (Walker, 1990c, p. 21 & p. 33).

Regardless of policies pursued prior to 1979, (Mishra, 1984; Alcock, 1990/1991) the Thatcher Government explicitly set out to restructure welfare because it had very clear ideas about the sort of society it wanted to create - one based on enterprise rather than welfare. Successive Conservative governments have assumed that if welfare aims are sacrificed for the goals of economic growth, entrepreneurs' profits will 'trickle down' to benefit the poor. After fourteen years of Conservative policies, much evidence, (Bradshaw and Holmes 1989; Bryson, 1989a, 1989b; Mack and Lansley, 1985; Piachaud, 1987) including this study, indicates that profits have not trickled down to the poor and that the poor are now poorer and the rich richer (Walker and Walker 1987).

Social service users and the restructuring of social security

What has the restructuring of social security since 1979 meant for the majority of social service users - those who are claiming benefits? Social service users may be aware that they do not have enough to live on but are unlikely to realize that they are managing on significantly less than people in a similar situation prior to 1979. For example Supplementary Benefit rates for a couple with two children aged six and eight in 1965 was £75.87p (at July 1990 prices) - 51% of gross weekly earnings of male manual employees whereas in 1990 the Income Support rates for a similar couple was £84.82p only 38.3% of gross weekly earnings of male manual employees (Walker 1990d). Such a calculation ignores the fact that tax and national insurance have taken an increasing share of earnings, so net earnings have not risen as much, but it does not include figures for dual earning families. If their incomes were included, income support levels would have fallen relatively more. The two Social Security Acts passed in 1980 by the incoming Conservative government explicitly severed the link between benefit upratings and wages, thus keeping uprating amounts to a minimum by linking them to the movement in prices. The Conservative government also made it clear that they were happy to see the value of Child Benefit as a universal benefit eroded and between 1987 and 1990 it was frozen at £7.25 a week. The increase of £1 for the first or oldest child in April 1991 still meant a loss in real terms of 15% since 1979 for those children and 26% for all other children (Walker, 1990d).

Furthermore social service users are less likely to benefit from tax cuts and tax reforms (Taylor-Gooby and Papadakis 1985; Pond, 1989) than the wealthier members of the population. Bennett and Oppenheim (1991, p. 7) develop a 'welfare for the rich and welfare for the poor' example, where a married couple with a single earner on £40,000 per year gain £127.45 a week in mortgage and pensions tax relief whereas an unemployed married couple with two children aged four and six are given £128.61 a week in welfare benefits.

Thus the economic situation of most social service users has worsened considerably compared to the rich and compared to those living on benefit prior to 1979 (Walker and Walker, 1987; Townsend, 1991; Bennett and Oppenheim, 1991).

Social service users' increasing financial need, due to government social security policies was either not recognised by social workers because they took it for granted that social service users were poor or users' financial plight was overlooked because social workers felt powerless to help. Both of these points can be illustrated by examining how the social workers in Carshire and City teams dealt with the issue of the Social Fund.

Under the previous Social Security Act (1980) single payments for essential items such as cookers or beds, had been reorganised to limit demand. However single payments continued to increase from one million in 1981/2 to five and a half million in 1985/6. So the Social Fund which was introduced under the 1986 Social security Act and implemented in April 1988, replaced single payments with a loan scheme (70% of Social Fund finance) with a small number of grants (30% of Social Fund finance) for those re-establishing themselves or wanting to stay in the community. The participant observation part of this study commenced in January 1989 and was able to monitor the progress of policies in relation to the Social Fund ten months after its initial implementation.

In the summer of 1988, Vernon (the Silverton teamleader), welfare rights officers and other team leaders decided to pursue a policy of non-cooperation with the DSS regarding community care grants and Social Fund loans. This was a principled stand. It reflected unease, first, about the difficulty social security claimants would have in paying back loans, thereby creating extra financial need which would result in more pressure on social services departments. Secondly, non-cooperation with DSS was an assertion on the part of social workers that they were not part of the income maintenance system. Social work involvement (which could have resulted in social service users gaining priority over the grant claims of non-users) might well have encouraged claimants to use social services as a second benefit agency. However, not all social workers in the participating teams were aware of these issues and it appeared that social service users rather than DSS staff or the government suffered as a result of the non cooperation policy. By February 1989, both Edward Dent (the principal welfare rights officer) and Vernon (the Silverton teamleader) assured me that all Silverton social workers had received a copy of the non-cooperation policy document (although Vernon subsequently admitted that he was unsure whether the copies had been circulated).   However, when I endeavoured to discuss the policy with individual social workers, none remembered reading the document. They were relieved they did not have to take on more work in relation to the DSS, and were grateful that such a decision had been taken for them by the teamleader and had become departmental policy. Copies of the policy report were finally discovered in a filing cabinet by the Divisional Officer. The local DSS office invited Silverton social workers to a meeting in March 1989 to discuss the Social Fund. The teamleader's response to the invitation was, "I'm not interested in the Social Fund at the moment. We have a non- cooperation policy - I don't want anything to do with it". It was agreed that Brian Lunt, the welfare rights officer, his assistant Malcolm and myself would go to the meeting. The meeting also included probation officers, CAB workers and representatives from voluntary agencies for the Silverton area. Up until March 1989 - the first year of the Social Fund's operation - Silverton DSS had only spent 35.2% of their budget for grants compared to 85.43% for loans. The DSS manager hoped that care organisations would encourage individuals to apply for grants by April 1989, so that their budget was not reduced in subsequent years. The manager explained that the shortfall in the allocation of community care grants was due to: a shortage of Social Fund officers - a turnover rate of four out of five officers in the first year; minimal visiting - DSS were less of a "care" agency and that "home helps may see more"; and that they could not get the information from social services when they wanted to provide a grant. He concluded, "like it or not we are stuck with it (the Social Fund) and so we have to make the best of it for the client."

For social workers and home help organisers in the Silverton team (who knew very little about the Social Fund due to the departmental policy of non-cooperation), it proved difficult to discover social service users who were eligible for community care grants within a month. However a meeting was arranged by the deputy teamleader (Karen) after pressure from the welfare rights officer. Older people in the two neighbourhoods observed, were excluded from claiming a community care grant because their savings exceeded £500. Lorna, (a home help organiser from the Silverton team) commented at the meeting, "I can't think of one elderly person who would get the community care grant, a lot of people have savings of over £500 for their funeral, some people have up to a £1000."

The meeting with social workers and home help organisers thus appeared unsuccessful although Brian the welfare rights officer commented that since the meeting with the local DSS he had had no community care grant applications turned down and had actually secured one award of £500. Social workers in both teams (who were aware of the implications of the Social Security Act) were in the unenviable position of realising that punitive social security policies were affecting the individuals with whom they worked, whilst being unable to do anything about it. The policy of non-cooperation with DSS carried out by the Silverton team had little effect on local or national policy though it had restricted the grants paid out to claimants. A non-cooperation policy did provide some respite for social workers from dealing with users in increasingly desperate financial straits, although City team (who had a policy of determined advocacy regarding the Social Fund) had written to all their users prior to the implementation of the Act stating that they would not be able to receive extra funding from social services, once single payments were withdrawn. On the one hand some social workers (especially in the Silverton team), wished to show their disapproval of the new social security policies which had disadvantaged all claimants and gave social workers unwelcomed power in relation to social security finance and social services users. On the other hand social workers (especially in the City team) were aware that if grant monies available under the Social Fund were not utilized, the government might interpret this outcome as evidence of insuffcient demand.

Mrs Dixon is representative of other social service users interviewed and observed, who have found themselves in increasingly desperate financial straits, which have had an adverse effect on their mental and physical health. Mrs Dixon had experienced financial difficulties since her partner - a miner - had died suddenly on his first week back to work after the miner's strike. She had been disconnected due to an administrative error for non payment of a 72p gas bill. Her budget plan application and normal gas bill had come through a week after she was disconnected. She had been without gas for nine to ten months. The gas reconnection charge was £80 - a figure in excess of the gas charges. Moreover, she had bought a gas cooker because "it was cheaper than electric - I had no gas but a gas cooker. I couldn't feed Mary (her daughter) - she was six years old then."

Although Brian (the welfare rights officer), John (one of the Silverton social workers), the CAB and a solicitor argued on her behalf, the Gas Board refused to reconnect without the charge being paid. These problems coupled with her sudden bereavment, sent Mrs Dixon " over the top". She had a breakdown and was in hospital for three months. While in hospital, her son managed to "blow up" the electric meter - so that when she came out of hospital she was faced with the prospect of using her deceased partner's back pension award to pay for the damaged meter and the reconnection charge. She refused to pay for the gas reconnection.

Mrs Dixon: It's the principle of the thing - I got settled without it. At that time I was fed up with being pushed about. ...the time in hospital hardened me ....Why should I pay the gas board? ...I got an electric cooker and everything, though I hadn't finished paying for the gas cooker.

Mrs Dixon had to take out a Social Fund loan to pay for an electric cooker at £7 a week, (out of a weekly income of £37) but, as a result, had been unable to pay the domestic or the water rates. (Claimants were expected to pay 20% of rates/poll tax after the implementation of the Social Security Act in April, 1988). She had received a letter to say the bailiffs were coming to repossess her furniture, because of non payment of her rates. Although she had appeared lively and cheerful when I had interviewed her three months previously, she now had an expressionless face and voice. "I've spent five to six years of my life facing authorities and getting into trouble - it's not funny you know". John, (her social worker of three years standing) had left, so Tony (who was the duty social worker when she approached social services on this occasion), phoned the rates department who said it was "in the bailiffs hands". Tony phoned the bailiffs who had a pre recorded message on their answer machine. I suggested hiding the furniture with the neighbours, but Mrs Dixon felt this would mean telling the neighbours her troubles which she did not want to do. She eventually decided she would have to sell her furniture to her children because they would give it back to her. Tony suggested firstly that she should ask for the bailiffs' identification; secondly that she should ask them to leave the form (suggesting that she pay £20 a week to clear the debt, an amount she could not afford), which she would then take to her solicitor's. Finally Tony advised her not to sign anything if she could not afford the repayments.

He said to me afterwards that "there was nothing we could do" and that this was "another one for Beverley" - the new social worker. Mrs Dixon had been referred to three different social workers over a number of years. If she was dealing with an urgent financial crisis she would come to see the Duty social worker. Users such as Mrs Dixon were seen as having intractable financial problems and few of the social workers wanted to take them on as an ongoing 'case'.

As a single parent, Mrs Dixon is likely to have lost £2.52 a week with the change from the 1987/88 Supplementary Benefit rates to 1988/89 Income Support rates. The House of Commons Social Security Committee included in these calculations an element for inflation and the extra Income Support allowances which were intended to cover the general rate and water rate contributions which claimants had to make prior to the poll tax. In terms of a market approach to welfare, users coming to social services with financial problems are not the type of 'customer' that could be easily contracted out to the private or voluntary sector - certainly not for profit.

Social service users and the restructuring of the housing market

We have become a nation of homeowners, gaining our 'benefits' from the fiscal system of tax relief, rather than through council housing, where individuals are allocated housing on the basis of need.

The value of mortgage interest tax relief had risen to £4,500 million by 1986/7, more than twice its real level of eight years before, despite the cut in the basic rate of tax. The increase in the real cost of mortgage interest tax relief over the period - £2.4 billion at 1986/7 prices - was the same size as the real fall in net public capital spending on housing (Hills, 1987, ch. 10).

The transfer of housing subsidies from the public sector has resulted in increasing homelessness for those who cannot afford the market price for housing and who thus have years to wait on the council housing list before they would be offered accommodation. It has also meant that council housing like social services, has acquired the stigmatised status of being available only for the poor. Public housing has thus become an unattainable as well as low status housing option for most working class people. Consequently many people who cannot really afford to buy their own property, are being seduced by building societies, banks and the media into taking out mortgages for which they cannot meet payments.

Some commentators stress the easy availability of credit, coupled with aggressive advertising, 'creates a demand, and encourages people to take on commitments to a greater extent than they might if left to their own devices' (Ford, 1991, p. 20).

Until recently mortgages have largely been a middle class preserve. Institutions who lend money do not provide education on how the system works, nor do they have the time or the skills to explain to the predominantly working class people in the areas where the fieldwork was conducted, how and in what ways the market system differs from the public housing system. Brian, the welfare rights officer for the area, commented that some building societies were particularly punitive with customers who could not afford their mortgage repayments during the 1986 miners' strike. It was assumed they would not be able to clear their debts and their houses were therefore repossessed.

Brian: ...they couldn't clear them.. the type of property that was repossessed were the little terraced ones where they had nothing to sell to get into a smaller property.. individual (building society) managers have their quotas.. the ends justifies the means.

One family interviewed could not keep up the mortgage payments during the miners' strike and eventually posted the keys to the house through the letterbox of the building society. They and their six children are now living in a two bedroomed housing association house. Mr Hallam gave the impression that he had not discussed his decision with personnel at the building society, he just became fed up with the worry of not being able to make the repayments. When he found out that a small house near to where he had grown up was empty and available from a housing association, he and his family moved. The living conditions in this house (in which they were interviewed) were extremely cramped, especially for the younger children. During the interview, one of the toddlers became entangled in the kettle flex, whilst another ran out of the back door into the road when Mr and Mrs Hallam were saying goodbye to me at the front. Fortunately the car approaching the toddler was able to stop. Linda, the social worker who visited them was keen for them to move. Mr Hallam was working again, but seemed unwilling to repeat his previous experience of buying a house, even though the housing association had offered to let him buy the house in which he and his family were living. Mrs Hallam, according to Linda was not so keen to stay where they were, but expressed no opposition to Mr Hallam during the interview. They both talked about extending their living accommodation by converting the empty almost derelict shop next door. However Mrs Hallam had apparently said privately to Linda, "Where would I go with six kids?"

It seems that the Thatcher government's housing and economic policies have increased individual wealth (Stark, 1986) at the expense of: local authorities; those who cannot afford to buy their council house and therefore have to put up with deteriorating standards as resources for public housing dwindle; those who are forced out of the housing market into privately rented and housing association accommodation, bed and breakfast or hostels and those who have nowhere to live at all.

Furthermore eighty per cent of outstanding credit is associated with borrowing for housing, and with credit hand in hand goes debt, and in some cases repossession, particularly for low income mortgagees. Janet Ford, (1991, p. 32) describes this process:

> Until the late 1970's home ownership was largely the preserve of the secure professional white collar employee, and skilled craftsworker. In 1979 there were approximately 6 million mortgage loans held. In 1990 there were 9.3 million mortgage loans in force (House of Commons, Hansard, 1990). This expansion is the outcome of several factors, including the increase in the number of households (particularly single person

households); the impact of the right to buy legislation (with discounted prices and supportive financial arrangements); the decline in the quality and quantity of local authority rental property (with associated lengthening waiting lists); the move towards market rents; the deregulation of financial processes and increasingly competitive markets; and the clear desire of many people to own a property.

In the 1980's, the number of home owners grew as mortgage institutions increased their 'down market' lending to compensate for their problems in lending to the third world and domestic industries. Between 1982 and 1986, amongst all households headed by a manual worker, the percentage with mortgages grew from 42.9% to 52.6% (thus exceeding the growth among non manual households). Most were in employment when they entered the tenure (Office of Fair Trading, 1989). In this study too, social workers and users are now tackling problems (although in comparatively small numbers), of low income, debt, and building societies, rather than difficulties with council housing departments. As private institutions are concerned with value for money for their shareholders, they are not necessarily as understanding as a housing department might be if people on low wages or in unstable jobs have a problem meeting their repayments. Public money is effectively being spent on social workers to solve privatised financial problems. In a contracting out culture, perhaps social services departments should bill these private institutions for the cost of sorting out these problems?

On the first day of the fieldwork at Silverton, I listened to a telephone request from Mrs Bagthorpe, a social service user who was in tears and asking for social work help because the Abbey National building society was threatening to evict her and her family (a working husband and four children) over debts of £121.85. As a postgraduate student, presumably regarded as middle class with good earning potential, I had been allowed to continue with my mortgage debt of over £900 for eighteen months without any threat of eviction from the Woolwich building society. Mrs Bagthorpe had already paid £400 off her arrears and could afford £20 that day. However the building society said if the outstanding amount was not paid within forty eight hours the family would be evicted.

Karen, the social worker who had responded to the telephone call from Mrs Bagthorpe said "I would have to go to charities... to use Section 1 money , you would have to go to committee to get that sort of money". She was not able to convince the building society manager that Mrs Bagthorpe would be able to pay the debt off by the following Monday from her child allowance and disability allowance (one of her children was handicapped). The building society manager said, "This has happened a number of times in the last few years" - referring to Mrs Bagthorpe getting behind with her payments. Karen then rang the Homeless Families Officer who "twisted the arm" of the building society and arranged with them that the money "would be paid one way or another" by the following Monday. He commented to Karen that Mrs Bagthorpe had "got up someone's nose". Karen then rang Mrs Bagthorpe back and said, "You must pay the money by the following Monday otherwise it destroys social services' credibility". Mrs Bagthorpe told Karen that she had learned her lesson. Mrs Bagthorpe's request for help had come on the same day that her handicapped daughter Marilyn (whose life expectancy was unlikely to exceed a further five years) had had two fits at school.

I interviewed Mrs Bagthorpe later on in the fieldwork and she maintained that she had had no trouble with the mortgage repayments since, that she had "learned her lesson" and that "it wouldn't happen again".

Interviewer: If you ever did get in the same situation again, would you go back to social services?

Mrs Bagthorpe: I don't know, I don't think it would work this time with the building society. If they tried that approach again from [with] the building society, I think they'd say "Oh no you did it before and she didn't keep her side of the bargain". They wouldn't be able to persuade the building society again I don't think."

Interviewer: So it wouldn't be worth you going back to social services?

Mrs Bagthorpe: No it'd have to be a moneylender I suppose which would probably make it worse all round wouldn't it - because its silly borrowing money to pay off arrears isn't it?

Interviewer: I wouldn't be as definite as that about not going back to social services, because you've got your three children. (Marilyn, her handicapped daughter had died since the original crisis). It's up to you but I wouldn't be too definite about it.

Mrs Bagthorpe: Alright flower, I won't get in that situation again [laughs].

Mrs Bagthorpe had no idea of the differing policies that were pursued as far as repayments of mortgage debts were concerned with people of different backgrounds, living in different parts of the country and being of the wrong sex or race. Although Mrs Bagthorpe was at home with her children, she seemed to be responsible for the mortgage repayments. She complained that although her husband was good company when he was in, he was out a lot and did not help with the children. Her use of the word "I" throughout the interview when talking about the mortgage and her plan to use money she had access to - Child Benefit and Disability Allowance - implied that she held herself responsible for the debt. This was her second mortgage (she had been responsible for the mortgage and two other children in a previous marriage). She had none of her own kin family living locally to help her financially or in other ways.

Parker (1987) has argued that the roots of debt may lie in the pattern of financial allocation adopted, and the inadequate allocation to women for day to day budgeting may push them to miss payments due. A number of studies have indicated that the internal allocation of resources is informed by a cultural acceptance by both men and women that a portion of the household's money is 'protected' as 'the man's money' (Morris, 1984). Parker has shown how even when debts are incurred the 'man's money' remains protected. Ford's (1990) study of owner occupiers in default reported that the majority of households effected some reorganisation and reallocation of finances when the mortgage crisis became sufficiently serious. The reallocations were not equitable but the inequalities were reduced.

> Even where commitments have been the man's responsibility, women may manage them when they become debts because of their role as day to day financial managers. Here the assumption is that it is they who can re-jig the budgets and make economies, an assumption women often confirm, but only by personally bearing the brunt of any economies.. debt involves negotiating with creditors, visiting their offices, undertaking to make certain payments. Women are also often seen as "free" to undertake this work, either because their own employment is part time, or regarded as less significant than the man's, or because they are "at home" all day involved with tasks that are accorded little priority or prestige (Ford, 1991, p. 81).

Brady's (1987) in depth study of seven families in debt reported that women had a higher incidence of self-assessed mental health problems than men. Stress factors he associated with debt included: the stigma of debt; financial adversity; attempts to cope financially; the guilt and blame associated with failure and the isolation of women. Lone mothers according to the PSI survey of credit and debt, had an 'exceptional' level of risk. 'The combination of low income with family responsibilities makes lone parents the population group at greatest risk of debt, alongside unemployed families with children' (Berthoud and Kempson, 1992 p. 182). These findings were backed up by the fieldwork.

Mrs Crale came to social services as a one parent family with two children dependent on income support whose husband was claiming tax relief for the mortgaged house that his wife and children were living in. He was working in Saudia Arabia and was having an affair with a nurse. This had eventually split up the marriage, and while the husband and his mistress were apparently having expensive holidays, his wife was claiming social security and food vouchers from social services because she did not have enough to live on. Because the couple were not legally separated or divorced - Mrs Crale still seemed to be hoping that he would come back to her - no adequate financial provision had been made for her or the children.

Mrs Crale: I came (to social services) to see if anyone could help me 'cos my house was actually up for sale at the time and I was going to be homeless.. nothing really happened (as a result of the first visit to social services), because my husband decided he was quite happy for the house not to be sold - "it's not fair" he said, "because of the boys".

Interviewer: So what happened the second time you came in?

Mrs Crale: I came down because I had no money for food and owed £26 for the gas bill and I owed £11, two weeks electric that was,.. so it left me with virtually nothing to live on.. . I know I bought ten cigarettes but I have to.. . But I was just really upset because I'd nothing for the children and I can't stand to see kids go hungry.

Mr Crale was not helping with the bills but had agreed to a voluntary payment of £20 per week for the children which was taken off Mrs Crale's income support which went down from £74 a week to £54 a week.

Mrs Crale: It's a lot of money I know (the £80 a month maintenance), but when you've got bills to pay and clothes for the children and when it's school I've got to give them money for dinners and get them tea, and because its the holidays they want to go to the swimming baths and cinema.. it's a hell of a struggle, it's terrible.. I just wish he'd come back.

They had no problems with money when they were married:

Mrs Crale: He was great, he was fabulous, he helped me in every way possible, he's given me a lovely home and we always had food in.. brilliant with the kids.. he's just a womanizer.

Interviewer: You didn't have any problems with housekeeping before he left?

Mrs Crale: No it's only since he left I got myself into a mess with money.. because with his job I was getting £350 a week for a wage. He paid all his wages home into a bank account.. he said to me "that's for the mortgage and everything else".. it was great you can understand it.

Interviewer: So you dropped from £350 a week to £74 a week apart from the mortgage. That's a big drop!

Mrs Crale: It's terrible I've always been used to having that money.

Mrs Crale had received advice from social services regarding council housing and on her second visit a £10 food voucher to feed the children was obtained. Mrs Crale, unlike Mrs Bagthorpe had financial problems because of a sudden drop in income rather than persistent low income. Her house and its furnishings and her clothes, were of a higher standard than most social service users I visited. However she and her sons may have to get used to different accommodation and a lower standard of living.

Sullivan (1986) and Tunnard (1973) indicate that divorced and separated women face considerable housing difficulties. They may initially remain in the matrimonial home, but the costs prove prohibitive and debts result. They may experience 'forced' moves out of single owner occupancy into public renting, sharing or even homelessness. Owner occupation for women on their own with children may figure in the rise in mortgage statistics - from £18,956 million in 1973 to £255,811 million in 1989 (BSA Bulletin and Financial Statistics 1974-1989). However female lone parents inclusion in these statistics may be a temporary phenomenon to be replaced by others in a similar situation. As Ford (1991 p. 60) notes,

> .. where the lone parent who remains in the matrimonial home following the dissolution of a relationship is a woman, the available income is, in many cases, low and there is a high risk of mortgage default.

More lucrative employment opportunities, better childcare facilities, and fairer maintenance and access arrangements could change this scenario in the future. However the restructuring of the housing market has meant that women who cannot afford to maintain a mortgage are marginalised like all the other non owner occupiers, in some cases having to rely on bed and breakfast accommodation.

It was fairly unusual, in the City team, for social services to be asked for help with mortgage problems, in that they were seen as middle class problems, not the problems of the poor. However as Ford (1991, p. 27) comments, ".. in many cases they do have household earnings that are below the low pay threshold as defined by the Low Pay Unit or the Council of Europe." For example, Keith in the City team could get no free legal help for June's mortgage problem, because the Law Centres would not deal with the buying of council houses - "they were against it in principle". June had been discharged from Rampton mental hospital on appeal. She had been there since she was 13 and she was now 22. Loan sharks had told her she could buy her council flat at £5 a week, the total cost being £1000 and the deposit being £25. She would not agree to sign anything until she had talked to Keith. He was taking her to a solicitors for half an hour's legal advice for £5, as she had already paid the deposit. We are all dependent on government organisations, only some of them are labelled welfare organisations (Titmuss, 1958). It is these organisations that the government expects us to secure our independence from. In June's case it seems clear that becoming independent from her social worker, and dependent on a private financial organisation in order to secure her 'emancipation' from institutional care and from council housing would have resulted in exploitation. She would also of course have benefited from tax relief if the arrangement had been genuine. All individuals gain from the state in different ways depending on their income, despite the differing terminologies that are used to describe our indebtedness to the state. Benefits are regarded as an example of government generosity whilst tax relief on mortgages and pensions are seen as relieving the burden of government taxation. As Cook (1989, p. 26) notes:

... recent evidence suggests that the gap between rich and poor has widened since 1979 (Byrne, 1987; CPAG, 1988). Yet the myth of the redistributive 'Robin Hood' state remains ideologically powerful, and buttresses the allied myth of the over-taxed or 'harassed' tax-payer.

Those on benefit are net beneficiaries for the time they are claiming, which may be preceded by years of being net contributors; however they are still seen as 'scroungers'. Those claiming tax relief are seen as net contributors, despite the fact that they may have for example inherited capital, without working to contribute to the tax system. Tax relief on mortgages did not commence in 1979, but as Johnson (1990, p. 156) comments:

> The ideology of the three Thatcher governments is more clearly demonstrated in housing than in any other area of social policy....Between 1978/79 and 1989/90 government expenditure on housing in real terms declined by 79 per cent.

Tax relief to the individual home owner has taken the resources that were previously allocated for the whole community. This individualistic concept of redistribution does not account for those who cannot get onto the first rung of the owner-occupier ladder or who get onto it and then slip off, due to redundancy, low wages, loss of pay or marital breakdown.

Many of the social service users with financial and housing problems were female lone parents with young or school age children. As it is mostly women who take the main caring role when marriages split up, it is they who are most likely to suffer from the effects of social security and housing restructuring. Social services are involved in the privatisation of the housing market because they are dealing with the casualties of it. There has been an increase in money advice centres, but there is a current imbalance between the supply (limited), and the demand (great). Moreover the stability of such centres is extremely fragile given the current squeeze on local authority resources. It has been suggested that creditors have some responsibility to support the casualties of the credit system. Social workers would probably prefer to see the government and/or creditors supporting money advice centres rather than social work departments, thereby reducing the services expected of social workers. They are clearly not just dealing with the casualties of mortgage repossessions, but also the immense shortage of council housing. Social service users with marital and/or poverty problems cannot be rehoused satisfactorily when in need.

> Compulsory mechanisms to fund money advice - for example, a levy on creditors - are discussed from time to time and may yet be necessary ...... The underlying problems that give rise to much of the debt, particularly in low income households, have been influenced and structured not only by the policies of some creditors, but centrally by the economic and welfare policies pursued by successive governments in the 1980's (Ford, 1991, p. 103).

Summary and conclusions

This chapter has demonstrated how the restructuring of the social security system and the housing market has created additional pressures for social service users and social workers. The restructuring of welfare creates more hardship for the poor, and more work for those who deal with them.

One of the fundamental disputes in discussions about the restructuring of welfare is whether the welfare state should provide for all citizens or only the poor. In terms of value for money and cost effectiveness, further research could demonstrate that increasing benefits by say £20 per person per week might prove more economical than current expenditure on professional time in the DSS, welfare rights offices, voluntary agencies and social services departments devoted to sorting out the financial difficulties of claimants and social service users. Although cost effectiveness is a consideration in evaluating the relative merits of means tested and universal benefits, what is important is the political philosophy that lies behind restructuring. Conservatives who believe in a New Right ideology would be unlikely to increase basic income support even if it were less expensive, because of their fear that individuals would become dependant on the state.

Conservative policy makers suggest the welfare state should be a residual service that does not drain the economy whereas theorists on the left such as Titmuss (1974), Cook (1989) and Le Grand (1982) suggest that the middle and upper classes have benefited the most from universal services, as well as their own fiscal 'welfare state'.

The logical outcome of both these sets of ideas is that the poor should be targeted or treated more generously. In this sense perhaps social services should develop as a service for the poor and work at negating the public's attitude of these people as undeserving (*Caring for Quality* Conference, 1990). However other studies (Titmuss 1970; Taylor-Gooby and Papadakis 1985) have shown that services that are developed only for a powerless group of users are marginalised, whereas universalistic forms of welfare are more likely to be retained. Social services departments with few middle class users, lead Conservative policy makers to propose that this part of the welfare state is not necessary. Social services do not represent value for money for those who do not use it. As Chris Patten argues:

> Is it really necessary for some of our big cities to have approaching 10,000 or so social workers and related staff on their pay-rolls? Are such large groups of people appropriate, any more than it is appropriate for one local authority to own vast holdings of council houses and flats....? (The Times, 3.1.91).

Council housing has been successfully restructured, social security less so as yet, while health and education have proved less rewarding to restructure in terms of public opinion, because of the large numbers of middle class people who use these services or who work in them. With the attempts to create a market in health and social services, it is difficult to imagine how those who have suffered as a result of the restructuring of social security and housing will cope. Packages of care which do not involve financial support may not prove very useful. How for example, will the provision of Section 1 money (replaced by Section 18 under the Childrens Act 1989), continue to be part of a social worker's role as a manager of resources? Will social workers be able to 'buy in' welfare rights on a private basis or will all financial work be passed over to social workers as a continuing public service? Will welfare rights as part of a social services department continue to exist? The reason social workers were not willing to cooperate with the Social Fund was partially because they did not want to be closely associated with the social security system. But do they want to be completely divorced from it, so that social service users become increasingly destitute and social workers have no power or funds to support them? For example the Child Support Act (1992) offers little in the way of conciliatory services for parents so that social workers may well have to pick up the emotional as well as financial problems that result. It is likely that lone parents who are already clients of social services will be the 'parent with care' claiming Income Support. If they refuse to name the father of their children because of fears of violence (which are not accepted as 'legitimate'), 20% of their benefit will be stopped - for six months initially. Social workers have few policies or guidelines for dealing with financial problems associated with the restructuring of welfare.

This fieldwork commenced as the restructuring of social security and social welfare began. It seems more research needs to be conducted as social workers become managers of care under the Community Care Act (1990), if we are to understand what effect this may have on social service users. Social workers like health professionals, have had very little training on how to manage both finance and individuals. The two social work teams I observed may find it difficult to manage the sort of community care changes being expected for practical rather than ideological reasons. Resistance to internal markets and privatisation should not be seen as resistance to change. The need to discover better ways of working with social service users is accepted by all those engaged in the caring professions. After all the community social worker was an invention of the progressive 1960's and 1970's and many arguments were put forward then for social workers to work with groups rather than individuals on a casework basis. Research on the restructured caring roles would be one way of identifying mismatches between the public and private sectors, as would a greater dialogue between all professionals in the caring field. Such discussion which could take place through trade unions, professional organisations, and other networks could lead to the development of constructive policy initiatives for the future.

The way forward involves: pointing out how a market ideology cannot practically fit with caring for people; being aware of how the restructuring of social security and housing has reduced the incomes and choices of those coming to social services for help; developing policies in liaison with welfare rights agencies that empower users by giving them what most well off people have - an income with which to choose; and applying other philosophies and social policies that have proved to be successful in other countries (Munday, (ed.) 1989).

Section Three
THE IMPACT OF CHANGE

8 Payment for caring – Mapping a territory

Clare Ungerson

The issue of payment for care is, as I shall argue in this chapter, of increasing interest to the social policy community. It raises traditional questions of equity, quality, professionalization, as well as being a topic that is appropriately addressed by the now well established feminist perspective on social policy. In this chapter I will outline why the topic is growing in importance in Britain, and also point up some of the dilemmas (many of them moral) that arise from considering the issues involved.

Definitions

It is, as I think this chapter will make clear, rather difficult to delineate what constitutes payment for caring. In many ways it is easier and simpler to decide what we are not interested in. I am not interested in the payment, organised within a private market, between individuals, one a care giver and the other the care receiver; in other words, I am not talking about domestic service, privately organised and generally, unless the payments come to the notice of the tax authorities, invisible. What does concern me are the caring relationships involving the receipt of income, from whatever source, on the part of the care giver, and the receipt of care on the part of the person with needs, with some element of public intervention, organisation, subvention. A wide variety of such public interventions may exist: they could include tax allowances for those who receive payment; tax allowances for those who give payment; social security payments for those who give care (but not, I think, social security payments for those who receive care - such as an Attendance Allowance or Disability Premium - unless it is specifically tied to the costs of paying for care as is the case with the British Independent Living Fund); payments, generally nominal and/or called 'expenses', given to volunteers, either directly paid by a voluntary or statutory agency, or paid by the care receiver, but organised and regulated by a voluntary or statutory agency.

It should already be clear that it makes little sense to use the term 'payment' in the singular since there may be such a variety of forms, levels, organisation and origins of payment. Moreover, although there is an element of exchange in these relationships, in the sense that care is given and taken, and at some point the carer's income is raised as the result of that giving of care, these are not ordinary exchange relationships where, in return for services rendered, payment is made. There are some forms of 'payment' which are not explicitly designed to pay for caring services; items like payment for 'out of pocket' expenses, the 'hotel' costs of caring, compensation for not participating in the labour market, may well have originally been intended for some other purpose but have come to be regarded by many care givers as a form of pay.

As if this were not complicated enough, we also need to establish what, in the context of this discussion, is meant by 'care'. Mindful of the claims made by many feminists, for example, that 'care' should be defined by its personal, individualised nature and the dyadic relationship between carer and cared for rather than the way in which it is organised, who delivers it, or the demographic profile of who receives it (Ungerson (1990) and Thomas (forthcoming)), it is arguable that we should include the care of children without special needs when they are cared for by their parent/s. There are, for example, countries where there are very substantial payments by municipalities to mothers who care for their pre school children (Finland for example); and it might well be possible to make an argument that universal child benefits such as exist in Britain constitute, at least partially, a payment for care. Ultimately, largely for expedience and simplicity's sake, I have decided to exclude the care of 'normal' children when they are cared for by their own parent/s. In contrast, because of the nature of the public organisation, intervention and subvention of fostering, I include the care of children when they are cared for by publicly recognised surrogate parents (but not adoptive parents).

Why is the topic important?

In a recent study of payment for caring funded by the Joseph Rowntree Foundation, Diana Leat found an extraordinary mixture of arrangements, rationales for and levels of payments in this country (Leat with Ungerson, 1993). Much of the mixture (a polite word for 'muddle') results from the variety of sources of payment - from social security to local authorities to voluntary organisations; but it also arises out of apparently genuine confusions as to whether such payments are for work, compensation for out of pocket expenses incurred by volunteers, the 'hotel' costs of caring rather than the caring itself, and whether, significantly, they are compensations for not working - but caring. At the core of these difficulties is a central issue about what constitutes 'work' and what constitutes 'care' and whether the two activities are distinguishable.

One might well ask if there is much point in trying to make sense of this muddle. Are we not trying to knit together transactions which, empirically, have nothing in common in terms of objectives, assumptions, beneficiaries, institutional setting, and construe them as a single issue, and then attack them, unfairly, for inconsistency, and contradiction? Of course that is possible. But I want to suggest that there are contextual factors, both practical and conceptual, why they should both be addressed as a single issue, and are of growing importance.

First, there are practical contextual reasons, deriving both from social and economic trends, and from policy trends. In the case of the social and economic trends, it is the way in which these trends threaten the supply of unpaid informal carers which leads to the consideration of payment for care as a way of generating further and possibly different sources of supply. The most important of the social trends is the entry, over the past thirty years, of the vast majority of women of working age into the paid labour market. While much of this paid work is on a part time basis, hence not necessarily preventing women from spending at least some of their time in informal care, this 'economic activity' nevertheless raises the question about the security of future supply of informal carers and the competition between the world of paid work and the world of care for women's time. Moroeover it is possible that for the women themselves, many of whom are employed in the personal services, it raises the question as to why they should be paid for carrying out certain tasks in the public domain but not in the private domain. Secondly, the changes in family formation and biography brought about by the loosening, through divorce and cohabitation, of marriage, raises

151

a question about the future operation of family obligations (Finch, 1989). It seems likely that as families increasingly contain members who are related by the marriage of their parents rather than by blood, there will be concomitant loosening up of kinship and care obligations between step relations. There may have to be some counterweight in the form of monetary remuneration in order to generate the same supply of care, based on traditional kinship obligations, as can currently, with safety and empirical evidence, be assumed to exist (Ungerson, 1987; Qureshi and Walker, 1989).

The policy, as opposed to the social, trends are rather less to do with supply of carers and are due more, as we shall see, to the reorganisation of demand. However, there is one interesting exception to this statement: this is the recent decision, by the British government, to abandon altogether the earnings disregards for old age pensioners. While this decision was taken within a context of a fear of imminent labour shortage in the late eighties, and the perceived need, therefore, to encourage pensioners to remain in the paid labour market, the recession and high unemployment of the early nineties have not led to a reversal of this policy. Indeed, it is extremely unlikely that once an earnings disregard has been dropped, particularly for such a large group of recipients, it can with any political impunity be reimposed. Hence it may be that in future, should the economy recover, the supply of informal carers from active pensioners is also threatened by competition with the paid labour market, and that payment for care, even for those above the 'official' retirement age, will also have to be carefully considered. But rather more important as far as policy trends are concerned are the implications of the National Health Service and Community Care Act, 1990. As far as community care is concerned, there are two main changes: first is the switch from social security funding of private residential care to the local authority funding of domiciliary care; second is the change in role for local authority social service departments from being mainly concerned with provision of services to being mainly concerned with enabling the development of non-statutory providers, and ensuring that those who need services are maximally provided with income (usually from benefits) to purchase and pay for them, and optimally provided with a 'package' of services from statutory, non profit, and for-profit providers. Many local authorities have also introduced purchaser/provider splits within their social service departments and devolved care-purchasing budgets to frontline social workers, now known as 'care managers'.

The effects of these changes in the organisation and financing of social care are yet to work through, especially since the full changes have only just been implemented in April 1993. But one particular aspect is already clear: they are likely to (indeed, they are intended to) commodify the personal social services; and most of these services consist of caring labour. A number of pressures are likely to lead to the recruitment of such labour using a 'quasi kin' model of care, but with a form of payment attached. First, the switch away from the funding of residential care to the funding of domiciliary care means that there will be rapidly increasing numbers of very frail individuals, living in their own homes, and without the insurance of twenty four hour surveillance provided by residential care. Typically the frail are most in need of care at times outside 'normal' working hours - early in the morning, late at night, and at meal times. It is for these reasons that informal care, which is often proffered by co-residents of the person being cared for (Green, 1988), is generally assumed to work best as a substitute for residential care, because care can be provided on a twenty four hour basis and at these crucial moments in a care recipient's day. But if, as a result of the social trends outlined above, the availability of kin-based informal carers is reduced or non-existent then how can reliable and continuous care be assured? One of the obvious ways is to introduce the idea of flexible labour willing to work as the need arises and at unusual times, and contracted to do so. In these circumstances any underlying idea of moral commitment, whether taking the form of generalised altruism or a personalised form of commitment through a weak relationship as neighbour, friend or family, has to be reinforced. The development of the contract to provide caring services, reinforced by the linkage of nominal pay, in combination with labour (usually women's) that is prepared to be especially flexible, is a growing feature of British social care thinking, if not yet a widespread feature of practice (Qureshi, Challis and Davies, 1989). While at the moment generally restricted to the recruitment and maintenance of caring strangers, there is no conceptual or practical reason why the idea of the contract linked with payment should not be used to pay 'informal' carers, where the originating informality of the relationship appears to need more formal and regularised reinforcement.

A second pressure to pay for care arises out of the idea that payment can at least introduce an element of control. As residential care declines, or remains static relative to the expected growth in domiciliary care, care workers will increasingly work on their own and will be able to act independently, invisibly (except to the person they are caring for), and hence, potentially - unaccountably. Payment can be used to enforce reliability, introduces the power to hire and to fire, to formulate job descriptions, and to establish occupational hierarchy and structure.

How well payment does in practice introduce control over quality of service delivery depends on many factors, not least the way in which the payment is organised and who is responsible for monitoring and evaluation : the client, the agency or the social service department (for a discussion see Leat and Gay, 1987). Nevertheless, the introduction of payment into caring relationship does, at least in theory, offer a sanction - the withdrawal of payment and the ending of a contract - should the care prove to be inadequate and/or unreliable.

A third pressure for payment is that, as a result of the new financial regimes being introduced in social service departments, social workers will, through devolved budgets and purchaser/provider splits, increasingly have the means as well as the responsibility to purchase care from whatever source they can find. Payment for care will almost inevitably ensue, whether it be directly to the care provider, or to an agency such as a voluntary organisation. If the payment is made in the first instance to a contracted voluntary organisation or private for profit agency, than they in turn, in order to maintain control and reliability, will tend to have to pay the care providers even if, in the case of voluntary organisations, they call these care workers 'volunteers'. Moreover, in a severely cash limited situation, rather than pay the full cost of care provided by personnel employed by the local authority, voluntary organisations or for profit private agencies, there will be considerable pressure to find care which can be provided at less than full cost and for nominal payments - hence, the presentation of such care as 'quasi kin' and 'quasi voluntary', and the potential search for carers claiming benefits, such as income support, or even Invalid Care Allowance, for which small 'top-up' payments are all that is needed, or, indeed, desired by the care-giver.

Thus there are strong, possibly irresistible, pressures both as a result of the perceived shortages of unpaid informal carers, and as a result of the reorganisation of the financing of demand, that are likely to lead to payment for care. For that reason alone, if we are interested in how payment for welfare will look in the early twenty first century, the subject is worthy of treating as a single topic - even though the justification for such payments, their level and their institutional context may vary considerably. The signs that such a trend is already in place are everywhere: payment for care schemes are becoming more and more widespread (see for example, Leat and Gay, 1987; Horton and Berthoud, 1990; Qureshi, Challis and Davies, 1989; Thornton, 1989) and apply to a wide variety of caring relationships, from foster care for children and elderly people, to payment for carers to live in the homes of people with special needs arising out of age and/or disability.

Similarly there are signs that informal carers in receipt of Invalid Care Allowance are increasingly treating ICA as a form of payment (and a very inadequate one at that); in a recent study of ICA by McLaughlin, 'most carers and ex-carers ... perceived ICA to be 'payment' for caring' (McLaughlin, 1991, p. 48).

But quite apart from the way in which social and policy trends are encouraging payment/s for care and are likely to continue to do so, there are also conceptual contextual factors which mean that the issue should be treated as a single one, and it is to these issues that we now turn.

Contexts and concepts: two traditions

The feminist perspective: The first conceptual reason is to do with twentieth century feminism. The distinction between the 'public' domain and the 'private' domain, which has run like a deep fissure through European and North American thought and social practice since the industrial revolution, has been for almost as long a period, subject to the fierce and critical scrutiny of feminist writers - ranging from the so-called 'material feminists' of the turn of the century in north America (Hayden, 1981) to the socialist feminists of the 1970's and the 1980's. For all these feminists there was a central understanding: what took place in the home was a) a social construct and not a natural event and b) was similar to and, some would argue, the same as the paid work which took place in the public domain. Hence the efforts of the material feminists to design housing and urban settlements that collectivised housework, and the efforts of later socialist feminists to analyse domestic labour as productive labour in the marxist sense. Some feminists of the second wave went beyond marxism and developed a campaign for 'wages for housework'. The history of the practical impact of the north American material feminists, whose ideas were actually translated into concrete, most notably in Britain in the quadrangle Ebenezer Howard and his wife lived in in Letchworth Garden City, is a sorry one (kitchens have long since been installed in all the experiments in kitchenless housing) (Pearson, 1988). But the idea of the social construction of domestic labour has a more lasting quality, and within social policy has been translated into mainstream (I earnestly hope) thinking by, for example, the classically and resonantly titled collection *A Labour of Love: women, work and caring* (Finch and Groves (ed.) 1983). Debates about the relationship between care and work have continued since then (see for example, Ungerson, 1990;

Graham, 1991; Thomas, forthcoming) although it is noticeable that this debate tends to take place in sociology journals rather than those of social policy, reflecting perhaps the founding paper of the sociologist Margaret Stacey (Stacey, 1981). Thus an interest in payment for care derives directly from this tradition of breaking down the conceptual boundary between public and private in both feminist sociology and social policy thinking. It has to be said, though, that the emphasis in this tradition, when it comes to look at caring, is on what is normally known as 'informal' care, carried out by kin, in their own homes or in the home of the relative for whom they are caring. So far, little of feminist thinking has addressed the question of care given by strangers which is also traditionally unpaid but is increasingly paid - namely that of volunteers (for an account of paid volunteering, analysed from a feminist standpoint, see Baldock and Ungerson, 1991). Yet there are interesting developments of payment for such volunteers, many of whom work with one needy person in their own home. These volunteers are often treated in the literature and in practice as quasi kin. Challis and Davies note with approval the way boundaries can shift between 'formal' and 'informal' care in the context of paid volunteering:

> The social workers saw helpers as having a separate and distinct contribution to make to the care of the elderly. It was not simply care to meet basic instrumental needs of daily living, however important this was, but care with an affective basis which in many respects resembled informal care ... For these people, a relationship had developed with the elderly person whom they helped and the tasks and activities undertaken had broadened out, albeit within the original planned approach. (Challis and Davies, 1986a, p. 142)

and Tinker quotes one such scheme's job description for volunteers paid

£10 a week as:

> to give help to one elderly person (usually a close neighbour) on a flexible basis, i.e. as and when needed in conjunction with statutory help e.g. home help if needed (Tinker, 1984, Table 4.1).

Thus the difficulty of establishing a conceptual boundary between public and private, care and work, is as applicable to voluntary caring as it is to kin-based care.

The social administration perspective

The second conceptual context derives from the way in which the topic raises questions traditional to mainstream social administration. A fundamental question is whether cash relationships are incompatible with care relationships, an argument that has roots back to the work of Octavia Hill and other nineteenth century female philanthropists, and, more recently, Titmuss (1970). But if one assumes such payments, then, secondly, there are questions as to whether their basis should be general, universal and citizenship based, or particular, selective and conditional. Moreover, arising out of the wide variety of routes to and organisation of payment/s for care, there are questions about fairness and equity between different kinds of care workers, and different kinds of caring relationship and dependency. Finally, the development of such payments raises the question both of the working conditions of those who deliver welfare, and of whether and how an occupational structure should be developed for those engaged in this caring work.

The feminist and traditional issues: laying out the territory

Using feminism for making judgements

The feminist issue concerning the relationship between the public and private domains, and the allied attempt to break down the division between public and private worlds both conceptually and empirically, raises the question about 'wages for housework' which has dogged and divided feminism throughout the century (Malos, (ed.) 1980). The arguments for and against translating the conditions of the public world of work into the private world of the home are now so sewn into the fabric of feminism that it is verging on the banal to repeat them: against are the arguments that payments for housework would trap housewives and carers in the home; that the payment of one person to service the household would ensure that demeaning and isolating tasks are never shared; that women ought to find financial autonomy through the labour market rather than perpetuate their dependency on either male partners or the state. In favour of such payments are the arguments that they recognise the unpaid work currently undertaken in the home; that they provide carers, particularly women, with their own reliable source of income; that they compensate for not undertaking paid work in the conventional labour market.

In my view the longevity of this debate, with its heady mixture of value judgement combined with few empirically testable questions, indicates that it is a fruitless exercise to attempt to decide, in general, whether or not 'wages for housework' (or payment for some subset of caring relationships within the home) is, in general, in women's interests or against them. The most one can do is attempt to agree on a general set of criteria for judging whether or not a particular scheme of payment (be it a social security payment or from a social service agency) is in the interests of all those involved in the caring relationship; and, if one uses a specifically feminist analysis, whether a particular scheme is in the interests of women carers. If one accepts this point, then I tentatively suggest below some, at least, of the criteria we must be concerned with:

1. Does the scheme specifically seek out carers on the grounds that they are likely to be available and willing to undertake care for less than full pay because they have an income from another source - their male partner, benefits from the state with low earnings disregards, part-time paid work which does not reach tax and national insurance thresholds?

2. Does the scheme specifically exclude women - or particular subsets such as married women - on the grounds that they are likely to provide unpaid care anyway?

3. Is the level of payments to carers, whether they are informally caring for kin, friends or neighbours, or recruited as caring strangers, simply a reflection of the minimum pay thought necessary to ensure the supply of and control of carers, where caring is presented as something different from work?

4. Or is it a reflection of prevailing wage-rates for similar fully paid work; does it reflect the amount of time spent caring and the 'unsocial' hours involved; does it reflect the complexity and difficulty of the tasks involved?

This is by no means a complete list of possible criteria for which much more thought and space is needed; it does not for example include any criteria for judging the scheme as far as the care recipient is concerned. However, I do suggest that if one is trying to judge a scheme and its related payments as far as carers are concerned, and within a feminist framework, then, if the answers to any one of questions 1-3 are in the affirmative, then the scheme is not in the interests of carers in general and women carers in particular. Indeed, such a scheme would be positively bad, particularly for women carers, since if any of these three criteria are fulfilled then women are likely to be further embedded into a way of life - and a life course - so graphically described by Laura Balbo as 'piecing and patching' (Balbo, 1987). Answers in the affirmative to question 4 indicate a scheme which is arguably positively in the interests of all carers since a level of payment is indicated that reflects both the social and economic value of such work. Such payments may of course raise other problems, not least of the professionalization of care, some of which we refer to below.

Using social administration to delineate issues

Altruism and quality: As far as the traditional social administration issues are concerned, I am going to be just as - if not more - preliminary in my remarks. The question of there being an inherent contradiction between love and care on the one hand, and payment on the other, is an extremely complicated one and a hypothesis that is difficult to test. Much of the discussion about the effects of payment are about whether or not it is likely to generate lower quality care than when love is the sole motivator to care. These issues are closely and carefully considered in Diana Leat's work (Leat and Gay, 1987; Leat, 1990). But such discussion tends to assume that love and its more general counterpart, altruism, are the only alternatives to payment, and that it is love that payment in some sense corrupts. In my own work, looking at the care of elderly people, I came to the conclusion that love may initiate a caring relationship, but that, for a mixture of reasons, love becomes decreasingly important in the commitment to long-term informal care and that, for women particularly, feelings of affection are replaced strongly by the need to maintain an emotional distance and by a sense of duty arising out of kinship (Ungerson, 1987). If that is the case, then payment is clearly quite compatible both with an attempt at emotional distancing, and with a sense of duty. Moreover, what is empirically established beyond a doubt is that high quality care, both formal and informal, takes place with or without payment, and, in exactly the same way, low quality care, both formal and informal, occurs with or without payment. In other words, when it comes to the quality of the caring relationship, and the quality of care that is delivered within it, there are a great many determinants involved, of which payment is almost certainly not one. However, in contradiction to the argument that payment corrupts love and therefore quality, it is probable (and is certainly assumed to be the case in a number of community care innovations) that payment linked to a contract does, at the very minimum, guarantee reliability of care.

University and selectivity: general and particular: But this brings me to the second 'traditional' social administration concern I have identified - namely, the question as to whether these payments should be based on some general criteria of what constitutes a carer, or be based on more particular criteria that specify the tasks that a carer must fulfill before he or she becomes eligible for payment. (This categorisation of the basis for payments is extremely simplistic, and needs a great deal more consideration and categories.) There clearly are payments which fall into the general, rather than the particularistic, category.   The paradigmatic example of such general payment is the British Invalid Care Allowance (ICA) which assumes that the existence of a relationship between two people (but not necessarily a kin relationship) in combination with a need, as demonstrated by receipt of Attendance Allowance, generates care. This underlying assumption is demonstrated by the fact that although ICA is surrounded by all kinds of eligibility tests related to earnings and benefits received by both the ICA recipient and the person in need (McLaughlin, 1991), the payment is not conditional on care actually being carried out. Nobody in receipt of Invalid Care Allowance is inspected to see that they do in fact provide a minimum of 35 hours a week of care, and the nature of what constitutes 'care' is left entirely unspecified. This is what I mean by a payment that is founded on a 'general, universal and citizenship' basis (p. 141). It is based, just like Child Benefit, on an assumption that a relationship, in this particular case quite loosely defined, generates a right to a universal benefit. (Similar payments, based on similar principles, can be made through the tax system.) In contrast, there are payments which are made contingent upon actual acts of 'care' taking place. Such systems of payment usually find some way of enforcing that contingency through, for example, the use of contracts or the use of some kind of inspectorate.   In Britain the prime example is the recruitment, payment and contracting of 'paid volunteers', 'good neighbours', 'community care helpers', who are normally paid on condition that certain tasks of care are undertaken. Some kind of 'quality control' through monitoring by the organising agency may also be involved. This is what I mean by payments that are 'particular, selective and conditional' (p. 141).

Neither model, as they are evolving in Britain at the moment, actually generates much in the way of 'pay': ICA is currently (1992) £31-25p a week; similarly earnings from paid volunteering can be minute and bear just as little relation as ICA does to what is actually earned by those in the 'caring professions' (a point I return to in more detail below). If we look at the level of ICA, it is not surprising that, given political and financial restraints, and that the payments are provided on a general basis, that the payment is so low. But there is an added paradox about ICA. It is noticeable that this benefit, although intended to constitute compensation for lost earnings, is actually set at 60% of the level of long-term national insurance benefits; this means that it is absurdly low in relation both to possible earnings and to needs (McLaughlin, 1991, p. 5). But the reason for such a low level is in order to ensure that the contributory principle, which is the foundation of almost all other non means tested benefits, is maintained. Hence there are two kinds of universal benefit: the one based on rights generated by contributions allied to an assumption of need, the other based on rights generated by a relationship and assumptions about work undertaken within that relationship -which in turn is assumed to carry with it opportunity costs. The trouble is that an insurance system that pools risks only works if it is assumed that that what is covered are involuntary risks. Despite the fact that there are aspects to caring that are essentially involuntary (carers frequently report, for example, that they feel compelled to care), it is also the case that there are voluntary elements to it, in the sense that even within a kin network and a system of gendered obligation, it is sometimes something of a mystery as to why particular individuals emerge as carers (Ungerson, 1987). Hence it would be difficult for caring to be construed as an insurable risk (although it is not impossible to do so). It is, paradoxically, precisely the element 'work' 'voluntarily' undertaken and of its concomitant, 'pay', which ensures the very low level of ICA.

But as I have already suggested, both the general and the particular model of payment for care share exceptionally low levels of 'pay'. Payment for care schemes typically pay according to some criteria other than those of the market. Pay levels most often relate to some deliberate confusion of 'work' with 'care' so that the payments involved are explicitly said to be nominal and charitable, or to cover standardised expenses and not to pay for the actual tasks of care involved. But it is also striking what variety of levels of pay exist between schemes: in 1981-2 Tinker found visiting wardens paid between £21 and £140 a week, 'neighbourly helps' who look after one person in their district paid up to £10 a week, and emergency telephone information officers earned between £80 and £120 a week (Tinker, 1984).

Equity: This brings me to the third issue I identified as arising out of the social administration tradition - namely, the question of fairness and equity to care workers and between different kinds of care workers. In fact it is something of an exaggeration to claim this issue as part of the social administration tradition: we attend far more to questions of fairness and equity when looking at the benefits and services received by those in need, than when we look at the working conditions of those who service them. Nevertheless, the question of the pay of care-workers has a great many knock-on effects for other social administration concerns - the needs and poverty of low paid workers, the position of pensioners with a chequered occupational history and a history of low pay, the impact of earnings disregards and marginal tax rates on labour market behaviour, the institutionalisation of married women's dependency on their male partners (to name but a few). In many schemes the 'pay' is extraordinarily low, bears absolutely no relation either to the difficulty of the tasks or the hours involved, and despite being rather similar to what many 'fully paid' local authority home helps undertake, bears little or no relation to the levels of pay that they are able to command. John Baldock and I have argued elsewhere that even though 'paid volunteers' on the whole claim high rates of satisfaction with their lot (Qureshi, Challis and Davis, 1989) this hybrid form of occupation, combining paid work with unpaid care, nevertheless constitutes a form of exploitation, particularly of women (Baldock and Ungerson, 1991). Pay, of course, is only one element of 'working conditions'; also included should be the rights of such workers to leave (holiday, sick and compassionate), redundancy payments, occupational injury protection etc, as well as rights to be consulted about the needs and care package of the person/s they are caring for. So far we know relatively little about the kinds of contracts that such care workers sign, and how far the contracts are designed to protect their interests as well as those of the agency organising the scheme and the interests of the person/s they care for. Diana Leat's recent work indicates exceptional muddle and diversity in precisely this area.

Professionalization: The question of contracts brings me to the final traditional social administration concern that I have identified as relevant to the issue of payment for care. This is the whole topic of the professionalization of care work. There are two traditional approaches to this question: the first using a feminist perspective, the second using a social policy perspective. Feminists are traditionally wary of professionalization; it smacks of over specialism and over control, particularly in the context of medical care (Oakley, 1981); the history of professionalization in both social and medical care has been a sorry tale of masculinisation of previously female dominated and controlled occupations (Hearn, 1982). Social policy analysts are not so sure: on the one hand they may be unhappy about the way in which professionals with vested interests determine both the policy formulation process and its implementation; on the other, social policy teachers in particular have played an energetic proactive role in the process of credentialising all aspects of social care in Britain throughout this century.

When it comes to considering the particular case of payment for care, one can see that, once payment is introduced, a hierarchy of workers naturally develops, consisting of budget managers and hirers and firers at the top of the hierarchy, and hands-on workers at the bottom. Eventually many of the paid workers at the bottom will wish to better themselves and move up the structure, while the managers are continuously concerned that, through payment, they are getting both a high quality service, and value for money. Inevitably, pressures for training, with complementary credentials, develop from both the top and the bottom of the hierarchy. Such 'skilling' processes are likely to lead precisely to the divisions of labour and specialisms that feminists have reason to dislike. Moreover, even though the tiny payments to 'volunteers' are intended precisely to avoid over tight divisions of labour by representing the work undertaken as 'what a relative would do' and hence highly general, I would argue that payment for care schemes contain their own inbuilt pressure for tight divisions of labour. This is particularly the case in payment for care schemes like the Kent Community Care scheme, where small aspects of care are shaved off the whole 'package', routinised and made subject to a contract (a typical agreement would involve a contract to get a frail elderly person out of bed everyday, make them their breakfast, and reverse the process late at night.) While the push towards professionalization may not be so obvious here, a division of labour is part of the rationale of the contract. Other forms of 'paid volunteering' particularly those, like the Crossroads Care Attendant Scheme, or the Helping Hand scheme in York, which are designed to provide respite care for generalist informal carers, are more likely to move towards professionalization and credentialism than towards a strict division of labour. But for both kinds of scheme, it is the existence of the payment that initiates an inevitable trend. For feminists there is a hard knot to entangle: if they support payment for care, and 'proper' payment at that, then they have to face the possibility that professionalization and specialism are likely to ensue, with all the problems of power, masculinisation, and the further marginalisation of unpaid domestic labour, that these processes are likely to bring about.

Conclusion

This chapter is intended to be a beginning rather than a conclusion: a marker that there is a territory out there that is slowly acquiring a literature, but needs more detailed consideration and analysis. I have tried to lay out some of the issues involved in this area, but, on the whole, have not reached any particular conclusions about them. It has to be said, however, that my interest in payment for care stems from the initial shock and dismay I felt when I realised what very small amounts of money were being offered by many 'payment for care' schemes (and by the Invalid Care Allowance), and later confusion when I realised, through the work of others, and through meeting, in the course of my daily life, a handful of paid volunteers, that such 'work' and 'pay' is attractive to many (most of them women) who give their services to care, often in very difficult and demanding circumstances. Clearly, confusion between the world of 'work' and that of 'care' has a social and a personal reality that is not unattractive, at least to those initially engaged in it. What I have tried to demonstrate in this chapter is the need to describe that confusing reality as it is, in order, eventually, to reach conclusions as to what it ought to be.

9   Rationing versus choice: Tensions and options. Cash and care for disabled and older people and their carers

Gary Craig and Caroline Glendinning

Introduction

Our aim in this chapter is to examine some of the relationships between the purchase and the provision of help and support to disabled and elderly people. How is such help 'purchased', in the broadest senses? To what extent do the various methods of purchasing and providing help and support in fact reflect devices for rationing resources; and how equitable are these rationing devices? How far are choices maximised, both for disabled and/or elderly people and for informal care givers? What are the implications of the different funding mechanisms for the relationships between those who give and those who receive assistance? These issues are assuming critical importance at a time when all local authorities, facing the community care changes with limited resources, are having to make difficult decisions about prioritising demands on those resources and about who should be required to contribute to the costs of care.

In the UK, social security 'cash' policies for disabled and elderly people and for informal care givers have by and large developed in isolation from welfare ('care') policies concerned with the meeting of social and health care needs. Unusually, the House of Commons Social Services Committee (House of Commons, 1990b) has acknowledged the important link between social security support for disabled and frail elderly people and informal carers and the success of 'community care' policies in general. Otherwise, the issue of how best to provide the financial support necessary for 'community care' at an individual level has generally not been at the centre of policy discussions. Thus the major. developments in 'community care' policies, from the Audit Commission Report of 1986 (Audit Commission, 1986), through the Griffiths report (Griffiths, 1988) to the community care White Paper *Caring for People*, (1989) apparently took place with little reference to the review of social security provision for disabled people (and, to a much lesser extent, informal carers) which was taking place over the same period (DSS, 1990).

The transfer of cash resources from the national social security budget to local authorities effective from April 1993 shifted money from one statutory allocative system to another. At the same time policy statements have repeatedly emphasised the crucial importance of informal 'carers' to the success of the community care initiative as a whole (Parker, 1990; Twigg and Atkin, 1991; Glendinning 1992a, 1992d). Yet there has been relatively little discussion, in official policy debates, of whether, rather than simply transferring resources from one statutory agency to another, resources should also - or instead - be directed from the statutory to the informal sector. Moreover, if this were to take place, to whom might such resources be directed? To disabled and elderly people? To family and informal supporters? Or perhaps to independent brokers and advocates? To what extent would each option represent a fair and equitable device for rationing resources; and to what extent would the choice of those involved (a key indicator of success for the government) be maximised?

We would not wish to imply that none of these issues has been considered at all - indeed, far from it. In fact, each of the three foregoing options has been advocated by often dedicated and committed proponents and, as we will describe, there are organised and articulate lobbies backing each. Instead our aim in this chapter is to try to consider the different options together; to contrast the various arguments for and against; and to evaluate them within a discussion of the two concepts of rationing and choice around which this chapter is structured.

We have highlighted these two particular concepts because they seem to be of crucial importance in current policy debates. Demographic pressures, especially the anticipated increase in the numbers of elderly people (Henwood, 1990a; Walker, 1990b), and associated concerns to constrain the growth in public expenditure on statutory services have encouraged the development of rationing mechanisms in relation to an increasingly wide range of public welfare provision. The growing importance, especially during the 1980s, of means testing as the main strategy for determining access to social security benefits (Lister 1989) is one illustration of this trend. Similarly, it has been argued

(Glendinning, 1991, 1992b) that the 'community care' changes now taking place may represent little more than the introduction of a further mechanism for rationing access to state funds for residential care, which has hitherto been available solely on the basis of financial need and without regard to any 'social' or health care needs. We would argue here that the strategies which are used to ration access to services; the criteria which are employed to make decisions in individual cases; and the mechanisms for challenging rationing strategies at both a macro and an individual level should begin to be opened up for debate, in a similar manner to the increasingly explicit discussions about the bases on which health care resources are rationed (see for example Williams, 1988; Cochrane et al, 1991).

On the other hand, much of the political rhetoric and policy analyses of the past decade have emphasised the enhancement of choice as an important and desirable goal. Both from the perspective of the 'New Right' (Flynn, 1989) and from the standpoint of organisations of service users (Davis, 1986), traditional modes of allocating and delivering statutory services have been criticised as offering little or no choice to users. The exercise of choice of course depends upon a range of options being available from which the 'consumer' can select the most appropriate (and the most affordable) for her/his needs. Thus, enhancing the purchasing power of the health and social care service 'consumer' and thereby stimulating the development of a range of different services within the welfare 'market place', has been the goal of much of the social policy analysis emerging from right wing commentators in recent years (Laing, 1991). The notions of 'choice' and 'rationing' will therefore provide both a structure and some important evaluative criteria for the discussion which follows.

We will, in the following sections of this chapter, first describe briefly the diverse range of funding mechanisms by which help and support to disabled and elderly people living in 'the community' are currently funded. We will then discuss in more detail two contrasting alternative models, each of which has been proposed by a range of commentators. Again, in our attempt to bring together a number of different arguments and perspectives, we will attempt wherever possible to ensure that the discussion which follows is applicable to both younger and older disabled people. Both research and policy discussions have hitherto tended to focus on one or the other. *The Way Ahead* (DSS, 1990) for example, reflects the widespread treatment of disabled people below and above retirement age as two entirely separate groups for policy purposes - a strategy which has been criticised as both divisive and ageist and which has led to the exclusion of many older people from entitlement to disability benefits (Walker, 1990a; Walker and Walker, 1991). We too would argue that the issues to be discussed in this chapter are as relevant to younger disabled people as they are to older people who need physical or social support; how should we go about providing a range of support and assistance to disabled and elderly people in ways which maximise choice and independence - the choice and independence, moreover, of both disabled and elderly people themselves and those family and neighbourhood members who provide them with help and support on a day to day basis?

Recent mechanisms for funding care/assistance

Through the social security system

To disabled people through the Attendance Allowance/ Attendance component of the Disability Living Allowance. The original intention behind the Attendance Allowance was to help meet the general extra costs of disability (attendance needs were the mechanism for 'targeting' the benefit). However it is clear that among many disabled people the allowance is used to meet ordinary everyday living costs (Berthoud and Horton, 1990). However, there is also a growing public assumption that the purpose of the allowance is to pay for attendance and assistance needs. Thus local authorities increasingly (AMA, 1991; George, 1991) require the allowance to be contributed towards the costs of home help/home support services.

(Until April 1993) to disabled people through Income Support allowances for private nursing home/residential care home fees.

(Until 1988) to disabled people through Supplementary Benefit additional requirements for private domestic assistance (up to the costs of a full time living in helper).

To working age carers who have no more than minimal earnings from paid work, through Invalid Care Allowance (ICA).

There is widespread evidence that these payments are too low, both on their own - for disabled people to purchase all the care they need

(Berthoud and Horton, 1990); for the levels of fees which are increasingly charged by private residential care and nursing homes (House of Commons, 1991b); and for informal carers who have no other sources of income to remain out of poverty (Glendinning, 1989, 1992a; McLaughlin, 1991). In this context, notions of choice are not very relevant.

Through the Independent Living Fund

The ILF was established in 1988 to 'cushion' the effects of the large losses experienced by some disabled people in the course of the switch from SB to IS - especially those who were likely to lose high levels of additional requirements for domestic assistance. The ILF allocated relatively large sums of money to pay for both personal and respite assistance for both younger and older (an earlier upper age limit of 75 has now been removed) adult disabled people. In some respects, the ILF exhibits all the worst aspects of the discretionary allocation of money: a detailed social work assessment; eligibility rules which have shifted from year to year depending on the state of the budget; decisions made by an autonomous, independent body with no clear channels of accountability to government or users; and an arbitrary and limited life (with the Fund being terminated in its present form, with new applications ceasing, as from April 1993). However the ILF has also revealed some of the vast reservoir of unmet need for personal assistance and support - demand has continually outstripped budget projections (Craig, 1992a); it has proved popular with disabled people; and it provides some very important lessons about the extent to which giving disabled people the money to purchase their own personal assistance is (and sometimes is not) empowering (Kestenbaum, 1990, 1992).

From the private resources of elderly and disabled people themselves

Increasing numbers of elderly and disabled people are finding that they are making contributions from their own financial resources towards the costs of the assistance and support they need. This is partly because of the growing practice on the part of local authorities to impose charges for home help and other services (Oldman, 1991; George, 1991; McGlone, 1992); partly it is accounted for by the purchase of services from the private market. Parker (1990) estimated that in 1986 around 1 million retired households purchased private domestic help. There are some interesting issues to be explored here about whether, as charging for statutory services increases, choices are made between public and private sources of care (Parker, 1990), although the evidence from one recent study of elderly people (Allen, Hogg and Peace, 1992, ch. 4) suggests that such choices may as yet be relatively uncommon. We also do not know to what extent the charges levied on local authority services might also act as a deterrent to potential users.

Moreover, there is a growing interest in trying to increase the extent to which long term needs for assistance and support, among elderly people in particular, are funded from care users' own resources. Potential sources of funds might include the resources which are tied up in home ownership and long term care insurance schemes (as advocated by Griffiths). In order for this to be a viable policy option, there must be sufficient resources to provide for an adequate basic income **plus** the additional resources needed to purchase care. The evidence suggests that this is generally not the case. First, the OPCS disability surveys (Martin, Meltzer and Elliot, 1988; Martin and White, 1988) showed that disabled people both above and below pension age have lower than average personal and household incomes; and have extra costs, though these were probably seriously underestimated (Thompson, P., Lavery, M. and Curtice, J. 1990; House of Commons, 1990b). Of particular importance are the lower incomes of many disabled older people - and their explicit exclusion from many of the extra costs benefits available to younger disabled people (Walker, 1990a; Walker and Walker, 1991). The OPCS surveys also found that a third of Attendance Allowance recipients were also dependent on Income Support. This must lead us to consider seriously whether the publicly funded 'community care' programmes we are talking about will in fact largely be for those on social assistance benefits.

Secondly, many studies have shown that the majority of disabled people both above and below pension age are less likely to have other private financial resources - savings, investments, occupational welfare benefits etc. - than their non disabled counterparts (Townsend, 1979; Martin and White, 1988; Dalley (Ed.), 1991; Oldman, 1991).

Thirdly, there is evidence that the levels of resources tied up in home ownership, which some commentators have earmarked for the potential purchase of care services, may be exaggerated, at least in the immediate future. The average equity available from home ownership was recently estimated, on the basis of the English Housing Conditions Survey, to be £38,750 (Mackintosh, Means and Leather, 1990). In contrast, Gibbs (1991) estimates that a capital sum of £70,000 would be needed to yield sufficient income to fund a shared room in a residential care home at a cost of £150 a week (very much the bottom end of the market). Even the widened home ownership of the past decade is unlikely to make very much impact on the availability and distribution of resources among older people in the foreseeable future, particularly given recent falls in property values. As Oldman (1991) points out, equity release schemes tend to be available only to those who are already relatively affluent; who live in well maintained homes; and who are already very elderly.

Finally, there is no evidence that commercial insurance companies are manifesting a great deal of enthusiasm for long term care insurance schemes (Henwood, 1990b; Oldman, 1991); other types of commercial equity release schemes may also have very limited potential (Gibbs, 1991).

Hidden subsidies - the resources of other household and family members

Other members of the household and family can also experience the financial consequences of the assistance needed by a disabled or elderly person, both directly through providing that care themselves and indirectly, through paying for someone else to provide it. Studies of the help given on an informal and family basis have shown that carers are likely to have lost or foregone earnings and pensions; that they incur extra spending on items associated with their care giving activities (such as laundry equipment, furniture and household alterations); and that lowered living standards may be experienced by other household and family members because of the costs (both direct and indirect) of providing assistance to the disabled or elderly member (Baldwin, 1985; Glendinning 1989, 1992a; Evandrou, 1990; Caring Costs, 1991; McLaughlin, 1991). It should also be noted that we know relatively little about the financial effects on relatives (including spouses) of having to 'top up' Income Support payments to meet the fees charged by private residential homes. This is likely to have been a major financial pressure for some people in recent years, and will continue to be so following the new arrangements for funding residential care.

From local authorities and health authorities

The range of services, the manner in which they are accessed and the methods by which they are delivered are increasingly under scrutiny, partly because of repeated criticisms by users - both younger and older disabled people (Oliver and Barnes, 1991; Allen, Hogg and Peace, 1992); and partly because of the government's own expressed wish that local authorities should move from a 'service driven' to a 'needs led' approach in developing community care services (see e.g. *Caring for People*, 1989 and subsequent guidance documents e.g. DH, 1990a). Nevertheless, there is considerable evidence that, as yet, the range of comprehensive information necessary for disabled and elderly people to exercise choices between all the various service options is not widely available (Glendinning, 1987; Bynoe, Oliver and Barnes, 1991; Bewley and Glendinning, 1992); and that the 'packages' of care from statutory sources received by very many disabled and elderly people are relatively small, especially when compared with the help provided by informal and family sources (Qureshi and Walker, 1989; Martin, White and Meltzer, 1989). As one recent study of elderly people notes:

> There was little evidence in this research that elderly people were able to act as 'informed consumers' in their use of care services, either in the community or in the residential sector. ..there was a clear unmet need for comprehensive booklets describing the health and social care services available from as many sources as possible, with information on how access to them might be gained by elderly people. (Allen, Hogg and Peace, 1992, pp 297-8).

At present, then, we seem to have the **worst** of all possible worlds. The levels of income available from social security benefits for both disabled and elderly people are low. This and their relative lack of other, private, resources make them very weak 'consumers' (both actual and potential) within a welfare 'market'. Consequently, very many disabled and elderly people are de facto dependent on care provided informally by household and family members - whether they wish it or not - because of their lack of money to purchase alternative services in the private market. Furthermore, the relatives and friends who provide assistance on an informal basis are themselves at risk of impoverishment as a consequence of giving substantial amounts of help. Within the public sector, both information about services and access to them is rationed and controlled by professional gatekeepers and administrative procedures. This is likely to increase still further with the introduction of comprehensive assessment procedures by local authorities in 1993.

In the next two sections of this chapter we examine critically two of the main options for developing policies in this area. Both sets of discussions will draw upon the foregoing critique and both will, again, revolve around the key issues of rationing and choice.

Social security provision for informal carers

Key features

The main intention of current social security provision for informal carers is to replace earnings which have been lost or foregone because of heavy commitments to provide personal help and support. However, because Invalid Care Allowance (ICA), a non contributory benefit, was introduced at a time when there was a desire to maintain a clear 'contributory preference', the level of the benefit has always been very low and is still less than 80 per cent of the single adult Income Support rate. This means that its effectiveness as an income maintenance benefit has always been compromised (McLaughlin, 1991). Furthermore, because ICA is only payable to those who are providing assistance for at least 35 hours a week and who have earnings of no more than £40 a week, it assumes, if not encourages, carers to withdraw from the labour market while providing care (McLaughlin, 1991; Glendinning, 1992a).

There is no social security support at all for carers who are themselves over retirement age and only very limited protection of the future state pension entitlements of those still of working age. Protection of entitlements to other national insurance benefits (especially unemployment benefit after care giving ends) was actually removed in 1988.

The impact on the relationship between the disabled person and the carer

Despite the principle articulated in the 1974 White Paper which first proposed the introduction of ICA (DHSS, 1974), that carers should have an income which renders them financially independent of the person receiving assistance, this goal has not been achieved with the present system of provision.

First, eligibility for the ICA depends upon the disabled person's receipt of the Attendance Allowance or one of the two higher attendance components of the Disability Living Allowance. The failure by a disabled or elderly person to claim or qualify for one of these benefits (for whatever reason - and there have been considerable administrative difficulties since Disabled Living Allowance (DLA) was introduced in 1992) therefore has a direct effect on a carer's benefit entitlement (Glendinning, 1992a). This direct relationship between one person's benefit receipt and another's social security entitlement is

173

unprecedented outside of marriage and marriage type relationships.

Secondly, research has shown that some groups of carers are likely to have lower personal incomes than either those to whom they are giving assistance (Glendinning, 1989, 1992a; McLaughlin, 1991), or than non carers (Evandrou, 1990). This means that when household incomes, patterns of consumption and expenditure are examined, they are likely to reveal a degree of financial dependency by carers on those for whom they are providing assistance. Glendinning's (1989, 1992a) research showed this to be particularly marked among daughters and sons who were not currently married and who had given up paid work to look after an elderly parent.

The value of care giving work

Because ICA is an earnings replacement benefit for people who have either minimal or no contact with the labour market, it embodies an implicit assumption that the work involved in providing upwards of 35 hours a week help and support to a disabled or elderly person is not 'real' work. This in turn reflects assumptions which are deeply embedded within a gendered division of labour, that the types of activities which are carried out, often by women and largely within the private domestic domain of the home and family, are neither regarded as 'work', nor assigned any economic value.

Challenging this assumption is an important step in challenging the much wider sexual division of labour of which it forms part, not only for women care givers but also for the 2.5 million men who consider themselves to be informal carers (Green, 1988). As Land writes:

> Too many women are not free to choose not to care without either damaging those whom they care about or their own self esteem. Worse, those who do, face tasks and experiences little valued, supported or acknowledged in material terms, and their reward is too often poverty which may extend years after the caring has ceased. (Land, 1991, p 18)

Baldock and Ungerson (1991) in the same volume comment:

> ... it is women's subordinated and isolated social position and the economic constraints on their labour market activity and remuneration which leads them into accepting - and gaining considerable satisfaction from - nominal payment for hard caring work. (p 154)

The context in which they are writing is that of 'community care' schemes which 'employ' paid 'volunteers', but exactly the same conclusions could be drawn about informal and family based care giving which is 'paid for' by ICA.

Strategies for change - carers

From the above discussion we might conclude that one necessary strategy for change would be to make some substantial improvements to the current levels and coverage of social security provision for informal and family carers. Within the present structure of social security provision, these improvements could include raising the level of ICA at least to the levels of other long term benefits such as Invalidity Benefit and state retirement pension; improving the protection of carers' entitlements to national insurance benefits; and introducing a new allowance to help meet the extra costs of care giving (this measure would also direct some financial help towards carers who are themselves over pension age). There are strong lobbies behind a strategy such as this. Carers' organisations and some disability organisations have argued strongly for them (Disability Alliance, 1987; Caring Costs, 1991; Disability Manifesto, 1991). They would also need to be accompanied by a range of workplace based initiatives which would help working age carers to remain in the labour market for a long as possible (Glendinning, 1992c).

However, it is difficult to envisage any marked improvement in the levels of social security provision for informal and family carers within the present political and economic climate. Nor, in the longer term, does it seem likely that carers will stand much chance of improving either the financial or the social acknowledgement of their work within the framework of the highly residualised social security system which now exists (Lister, 1989; Deacon, 1990; Craig, 1992c). Moreover, simply improving social security provision within the current framework would do little to challenge the assumption that providing assistance and help, especially on a more or less full time basis, is not really 'work'. This suggests that a more radical approach may be needed, which moves away from the present structure of 'earnings replacement' and 'extra costs' benefits, towards a system which allocates payment in explicit recognition of the work which is done in providing assistance. Here one begins to look at the experiences of paid care givers (Leat and Gay, 1987; Leat, 1990); and also at the experiences of other countries such as Norway and Finland, which allocate home care allowances on this type of basis and which are discussed in Clare Ungerson's chapter in this volume.

However here one also immediately encounters the issue of how far available resources are likely to fall short of the vast amount of assistance which is actually being given (computed recently as being of the order of £25 billion - Family Policy Study Centre, 1989) - both now and in the future. There is a very real dilemma between, on the one hand, recognising the value of care giving work by making payments in explicit recognition of it and, on the other hand, having to ration resources in such a way that care givers are seriously underpaid for the work that they do. This latter scenario is a common source of criticism of the system of Home Care Allowance in Finland, for example (Sipila and Levy, forthcoming), because it runs the risk of actually increasing the institutionalisation of care giving as 'women's work', rather than reducing it.

Purchasing assistance - the argument for direct payments

The critique of 'care' giving

A growing set of arguments have been articulated from within the disability movement which challenge the whole language of 'care', as inappropriate for describing the assistance which disabled people need. It is argued that the terminology both creates and sustains a dependency which is socially constructed:

> We believe that these social barriers are the true cause of disability and that the solution to the independence of disabled people lies in using their direct experience to inform social policy.. (Wood 1991, p. 202; see also Keith, 1992).

Equally important are the challenges to the assumption that care needs should 'normally' be met within the family, and that family based care is 'best'. On the contrary, it is argued that an absence of choice over how and by whom needs for personal care are met is a dependency which is highly oppressive:

> ... where there are no options other than dependence on a relative or partner, then this can be 'the most exploitative of all forms of so called care ... for it exploits both the carer and the person receiving care'... (Brisenden, quoted in Morris 1991, p 164).

176

It is important to note that these views are not just the sole prerogative of the more politically active members of the disability movement. There are strong similarities here with the expressed wishes of older people for 'intimacy at a distance' - for relationships which do not make them feel unduly dependent on and indebted to their relatives (Waerness, 1990, p 118). The older people interviewed by Wilson (1991) in London also 'clearly stated that they did not like to impose on their relatives or burden them' (p 4).

These critiques of 'care' giving - particularly the giving of assistance which assumes a very unequal relationship between giver and receiver - are paralleled by an increasing antagonism towards the ways in which formal service provision is controlled and delivered by professionals (Oliver 1990, p. 90). This control - and the antagonism which accompanies it - is likely to be even more marked since April 1993, when access to residential and other services became more rigorously controlled because of the enhanced functions of 'assessment' within the new 'community care' arrangements.

The campaign for direct payments

The campaign for direct payments is one response to the critique outlined above. The allocation of payments by local authorities directly to disabled people would, it is argued, enable them to purchase (and thereby be in control of) the assistance necessary to meet their personal care needs. Although the campaign has been orchestrated primarily by sections of the Disability Movement, the principles which underlie it have wide ranging support from some unlikely bed fellows. For example, the Wagner Committee on the future of residential care (Wagner, 1988), argued for a system of vouchers or allowances based on an assessment of an elderly person's care needs. Similarly Laing, associated with the IEA:

> ... has put forward arrangement for direct payments to
> elderly care users, stressing that it would meet the
> objectives of choice and control, and stimulate supply side
> innovation in the care market. (Craig, 1992b, p. 48)

The government's response to these arguments has been to reaffirm that direct payments are technically illegal (a position recently restated by the Secretary of State for Health). However in response to a survey by RADAR, 60 per cent of local authorities admitted that they made direct or indirect (i.e. via a third party) payments (Browne, 1990). What are the arguments for and against increasing (and legalising) the

177

use of such payments to pay for personal assistance?

One of the strongest arguments in favour of direct payments is that they enable the person who needs assistance to be in control of the timing and manner in which that assistance is provided. This is in contrast to the **lack** of control which many disabled and elderly people currently experience in relation to domiciliary services they receive from statutory health and social welfare agencies. The interviews carried out with a sample of direct payment recipients, those given help by the Independent Living Fund, provide a stark - and depressing - picture of the lack of continuity, unpredictable timing and restricted tasks which frequently characterise the inputs of home helps and community nursing staff, in comparison to the assistance purchased with ILF payments (Kestenbaum, 1992). Moreover, it is far from clear how the introduction of case management and the development of a 'mixed economy' of community care services will address and remedy these shortcomings.

Secondly, the wider use of direct payments would implicitly challenge the assumption that the provision of personal assistance by a close relative is necessarily 'best'. This seems particularly salient at a time when the development of community care services seem, from our reading of community care plans, to incorporate informal and family carers as providers in a 'package' of services to a greater extent than ever before (Twigg and Atkin, 1991).

From a supply side perspective, as Laing noted, direct payments would help to stimulate innovation in the range of provision within the social care market. They would also enhance the choice, control and independence of service users.

Finally, if a disabled person chose to use a direct payment to pay a member of the family or household to provide the assistance s/he needed, this could have far reaching effects on their interpersonal relationship. It would help to balance a hitherto very unequal relationship, enhancing the power of the disabled person and providing her/him with some means of reciprocating the help which is provided. If the payment to a relative or friend was formalised to some extent, this could also have the effect of enhancing the status of the helper too. No longer would s/he be receiving no payment at all, or only a token social security payment for being 'out of the labour market', but would receive a payment in direct acknowledgement of the personal assistance work s/he performed. However, we need to know much more about the impact which such payments could make on the giving and receiving of personal assistance within families; the willingness of each party to make and accept payment; and the interaction of payments with the more complex expectations and feelings of obligation and duty, which are in any case likely to vary according to factors such as the age, gender and nature of the kinship ties between the people involved (Leat, 1990).

However there are a number of counter arguments which also need to be addressed. Some of these centre around larger scale issues of resource allocation and administrative controls. It is likely that government opposition to the extension of direct payments centres around a mistrust of the ability of local authorities to administer a system of cash payments within overall public expenditure controls. This anxiety has undoubtedly been increased by the rocketing expenditure on the Independent Living Fund since 1988 years (Craig, 1992a). Such reluctance is also to some extent shared by the local authorities themselves, who might be expected to show some reluctance at taking on a greater role in the allocation of financial welfare to individuals, out of a desire to preserve the traditional dichotomy within Great Britain between central and local government and their associated separate systems of fiscal and service welfare (Craig, 1992b, p.48; Craig, 1992d). Local authority dispensation of direct payments might also open the way to even greater territorial inequities than exist at present.

This inevitably raises the question of how direct payments should be awarded: to whom; in respect of which particular service needs; and for how much. Some form of means testing would seem to be inevitable, particularly in view of the means testing associated with the charges levied on local authority services and which have become more widespread as local authorities have taken over responsibility for residential care (Craig, 1992b. pp. 12-15). Similarly, some kind of 'passporting' qualification would seem to be administratively attractive. For example, it has been suggested that receipt of the Attendance or Disability Living Allowance should be a proxy indicator of need for personal assistance and therefore form a basic eligibility requirement for a direct payment *Community Care*, (30 May 1991). However it is important that the lessons learned in the context of social security policy are not overlooked here. Means tested eligibility for a direct payment immediately opens up the danger of a 'poverty/service' trap, whereby an increase in income from earnings (or, possibly, benefits) results in a reduction in the level of payment, so that the disabled or elderly person is no better off if s/he wishes to (or has no choice but to) maintain her/his level of service inputs. Passporting arrangements have also been heavily criticised in the context of the change from the former Supplementary Benefit additional requirements for disability related expenditure to Income Support 'client' group 'premiums', where entitlement is dependent solely upon receipt of one of a small number of other benefits (Disability Alliance, 1987; Andrews and Jacobs, 1990). At its worst, such passporting arrangements would simply amplify and extend into the arena of service provision the problems and inconsistencies which have apparently characterised decision making in relation to disability benefits (Bradshaw and Lawton, 1980; Buckle, 1986; Cooke, Hirst and Bradshaw, 1987; Disability Alliance, 1987).

There are other barriers to be overcome as well. One of these is the power accorded to professional social work judgements in the determination of 'needs' and the appropriate methods of meeting those needs. Thus the British Association of Social Workers, for example, has endorsed the campaign for direct payments but with the qualification that social workers should then advise and arrange services on the disabled person's behalf (cited in Sapey and Hewitt, 1991. p. 49; see also George, 1992).

Finally, at an individual level, the experience of the Independent Living Fund has indicated some of the difficulties which individual disabled and elderly people may experience in making use of direct payments. People who are relatively isolated, either geographically or socially, may have difficulty in accessing local networks in order to find suitable assistants. Such feelings may make others reluctant to use more formal methods of recruitment, such as placing advertisements in local shop windows or local newspapers. Feelings of vulnerability may also characterise early relationships with newly employed assistants, especially if good working relationships are not easily established. A considerable amount of energy may be needed to recruit and manage assistants and helpers, especially if complicated rotas and timetables are involved (Macfarlane, 1990). Time and energy are also required to fulfil employer related obligations, arranging payments, administering PAYE and perhaps drawing up contracts of employment. In these circumstances, some disabled and elderly people have turned to private care agencies, in the expectation that they will be able to manage at least the recruitment, administrative and quality control problems. However there are still relatively few private organisations providing domiciliary care services (compared to those offering residential care), and charges are often high (Kestenbaum, 1990, 1992).

In some areas, organisations of disabled people have recognised these problems and begun to organise training and support programmes for those who want to employ their own personal assistants in this way. Such programmes would need to be much more securely funded and widely available to provide the necessary basis for a substantial expansion of the system of direct payments. It also remains to be seen how far the quality assurance mechanisms which can be built into service contracts, the Regulation and Inspection Units being established by local authority social services departments and their new complaints procedures might together address some of the problems of regulation and quality control which have been experienced by ILF beneficiaries.

Furthermore, while there has been a very substantial body of research on the experiences of those caring 'informally' for a close family member (and, to a lesser extent on those who are employed as paid 'volunteers' - see Qureshi, Challis and Davies, 1989), to date there has been little attention given to the experiences of those who are employed to provide personal assistance, as distinct from being expected to provide it out of love, duty, filial obligation or altruism. In the same way in which research on informal care giving has been (rightly) criticised for ignoring the voice of the person to whom assistance is being given (Morris, 1991; Keith, 1992), it is important that the experiences of paid care workers are also not overlooked, in an emphasis on empowering disabled and elderly people. At the very least, there is a need to explore issues such as minimum working standards and conditions, training and support, especially in view of the relatively isolated situations in which some personal assistants may be working.

Conclusions

The issues discussed in this chapter connect with a number of other important concerns. These include the extent to which policies also explicitly motivate and sustain the supply of informal care giving; with 'supply side' concerns to stimulate the range and choice of services available in the welfare 'market'; with feminist concerns to assign proper recognition and value to the work which women carry out on a largely unpaid basis within the home; with the ascendency of a social rather than a medical model of disability; and with issues of 'empowerment' for service users. They also have implications for intergenerational transfers of inheritance and wealth; and for the relationships and patterns of reciprocity established between family members of different generations which incorporate expectations of future inheritance. This latter concern has caused some commentators to express anxieties about the dangers of intergenerational conflict (although there seems to be little evidence of this so far - see Walker, 1990b). Nevertheless, there are potential implications for taxation and inheritance policies and, perhaps, for the assistance which family members are prepared to give, if future generations feel themselves to have been 'deprived' of an anticipated inheritance because of the need to pay for the current generation's care needs.

Ultimately in this chapter we have raised more questions than we have answered, and this is both deliberate and, to a large degree, inevitable. The issues are complex and they reflect many conflicting points of view, subjective perspectives and vested interests. In raising them we have attempted to address some fundamental questions concerning the roles of the state, the social welfare 'market' and the family (particularly women within the family) in providing personal assistance and support. While we may not have provided any definitive answers, we hope that this chapter has made some contribution to debates which will be revealed as increasingly important, once the dust has settled round the initial impact of the community care reforms. Each of these tangential issues are covered in more detail by other chapters in this volume; separately and together, they provide starting points for discussions about the real meaning of choice and control in the context of those reforms.

Note

The issues discussed in this chapter are addressed at greater length in:

Glendinning, C. (1992), *The Costs of Informal Care: Looking Inside the Household*, SPRU/HMDO.

Craig, G. (1992), *Cash or Care: A Question of Choice? Cash, Community Care and User Participation*, SPRU, University of York.

10 The NHS reforms: Managing the market in health care

Roland Petchey

Introduction

Evaluating the first year of operation of the NHS internal market is no straightforward task. The first, obvious, complication is the scale of the reform, accepted to be the most wide ranging and fundamental revision of the NHS since its inception in 1948. A second complication is the lack of detail concerning the organisational structures that might be required to support the operation of the internal market. By contrast with earlier reforms (1974 or 1982, for instance) which had contained clear prescriptions for organisational change, the focus of the 1991-2 reform was rather less precise. Structures were effectively left to crystallise out of the process of implementing only vaguely specified change. Such was the 'organisational indeterminacy' of the reform and the degree of local variation that it fostered that it was extremely difficult to make coherent sense of the emergent shape of the NHS.

This neglect of organisational detail may be attributed to a number of factors. One is the speed of the Prime Ministerial review which led to the reforms and the complexity (possibly underestimated) of the task that was being tackled. Right up to the eve of publication of the White Paper (*Working for Patients*, 1989a), Department of Health project teams were still attempting to put flesh on to the bones of the policies they were responsible for implementing. The vagueness even of the subsequent Working Papers (*Working for Patients*, 1989b) attests the continuing difficulty they experienced. Another factor is the timetable for the reforms, which had been thrown out by the NHS 'crisis' to which the Review had been an emergency response. Implementation during the run up to the 1992 General Election meant that change needed to be introduced with minimum disturbance of the status quo (a requirement which induced a degree of schizophrenia into Government handling of the reform). A third factor is the thrust of the analysis which informed the reforms. This identified the existing administrative structure of the NHS as a bureaucratic deadweight, suffocating the immediate producers of health care. Little thought seems to have been given to what might replace them. This hostility towards vertical organisation is a feature of the attack on bureau-professionalism elsewhere in the public sector (Clarke and Newman, Chapter 4).

Underlying all of this, however, was a much more fundamental source of ambiguity, unresolved in the Prime Ministerial review and persisting throughout the implementation. I refer to continuing uncertainty over the balance to be struck between market forces and non-market considerations in determining service provision in a 'managed market'. Whether strategic planning will be completely abandoned, whether Ministers will be prepared to grant purchasers and providers a completely free hand seems inherently unlikely given that they (the Ministers, that is) will continue to be accountable to Parliament for NHS spending. At the moment, though, the scope of central planning, the circumstances under which local service decisions might be overruled and the mechanisms by which it might be done remain unclear. There are parallels in this respect with education where there has been similar indecision over the accountability of opted-out schools. There are important differences between education and health, though. For one thing, the fragmentation of health care provision is on a much larger scale. In addition, after the Griffiths management reforms of 1984 and a decade of managerial appointments HAs are regarded as politically dependable in a way that local authorities quite clearly are not. As a result, the NHS reforms confront the government with a number of very real organisational dilemmas.

Structural innovation, 1991-2

Nevertheless, although the reforms were little concerned with structures, this does not mean that they were unaffected. Even during the first year of implementation, a number of structural innovations occurred which may turn out to represent the shape of the NHS to come, even though it was difficult to discern a consistent overall pattern. Some of these innovations arose from local initiatives, others were centrally sponsored. An example of a local initiative was the formation of purchasing consortia out of neighbouring DHAs in an attempt to obtain efficiencies of scale and reduce transaction costs. The most notable of these is SLCA, the South London Commissioning Agency, formed out of Lewisham, N. Southwark, Camberwell and W. Lambeth HAs and responsible for purchasing health care on behalf of 600,000 residents (Ham, 1992). A similar but more formalised arrangement was the planned series of mergers of DHAs in Yorkshire region. These would produce enlarged authorities, responsible for populations of up to three quarters of a million people and coterminous with Family Health Service Authorities (FHSA) and local authorities. Such developments may prove to be a mixed blessing. On the one hand they provide a potential basis for regaining the coordination with community health and social services which was lost with the abolition of AHAs in 1974. They also offer the possibility of tilting the balance of power away from the traditionally dominant providers towards purchasers of health care. On the other hand, their scale raises anxiety about potential remoteness and their sensitivity to local needs among the populations for whom they are purchasing services. An example of a potentially significant central initiative is the series of pilot studies into the feasibility of forming small general practices into fund holding consortia (Beecham, 1991). If successful these would open the way for the extension of the General Practice Fund Holding scheme among practices which are currently ineligible because they do not meet the list size criterion. Originally the limit had been set at 11,000 (double the average practice size), subsequently it was reduced to 9,000 and is scheduled to be relaxed still further to 7,000 in April 1993. Thus, a scheme which was originally envisaged as being limited to larger practices could ultimately come to be extended throughout the general practice sector.

By the end of the year the above changes were either under way or else well advanced in the planning process. Elsewhere, however, the organisational indeterminacy referred to earlier prevailed as the abiding uncertainty over the balance between management and market freedom was intensified by the politics of implementation. Nowhere was this clearer than in the indecision over the future relationship between FHSAs and DHSAs. The anticipated decline of their direct management responsibilities due to the continuing expansion of the Trust hospital and general practice fund holding schemes clearly raised the possibility of their being merged. For a while there were indications that this might be on the agenda. However, subsequently it was rumoured that, at least in London, such mergers might not be acceptable. The Tomlinson enquiry into London health services was reported as having been 'shocked' by the extent to which community budgets had been raided by some large London hospital trusts (Sheldon,

1992a and 1992b). Government cooling towards the idea of merger (which would require primary legislation) was suggested by the failure to include it in the Queen's Speech.

Even greater uncertainty surrounded the future of RHAs. Initially it seemed virtually certain that they too would simply be allowed to wither on the vine as their direct management responsibilities dwindled, but subsequently there were signs that they might be reprieved, albeit possibly in smaller numbers and with significantly reduced functions. This apparent stay of sentence seemed to be a recognition of the problems of direct central monitoring of thousands of independent provider units and hundreds of purchasers. The next (but possibly not the last) twist in what bore all the hallmarks of a long-running affair (of the 'on-off-on' variety) was the suggested abolition of RHAs and the transfer of their remaining functions to the six newly established 'outposts'of the NHS Management Executive. These were set up in April 1991 (amid considerable secrecy) to monitor trust finances and performance and as a response to the failure of the Executive's trusts unit to subject to adequate scrutiny the business plans of many applicants in the first wave of trusts in early 1991 (Butler, 1992a; Ham et al, 1992). The replacement of RHAs by a regional tier of the NHSME would represent the culmination of a process of substituting managerial for political accountability that can be traced back to the Griffith reforms of 1983. It would also represent a further and marked twist in the spiral of centralisation. Whatever its eventual outcome, the saga serves to demonstrate both the earlier lack of attention to the structures that would be necessary to manage the operation of the internal market and the difficulty of the political decisions arising from the attempt to depoliticise the provision of health care by substituting the power of exit (via the market) for the power of voice. As Paton (1992, p. 22) graphically puts it,

> As in other areas of policy, the government has been forced to centralise ruthlessly in order to 'decentralise' - but then has discovered it is astride a tiger from which it cannot dismount.

This is a point to which I will return in my concluding discussion.

Implementation of the internal market

Reference has already been made to the political sensitivity of the reforms, introduced as they were during the run up to a general election in which it was widely (but incorrectly as it turned out) expected that the NHS would be the central issue. Harrison, S. (1991) has distinguished between 'political difficulty' and 'Party politics', where the former refers to the questionable legitimacy of DHAs (as appointed rather than elected bodies) in rationing health care. While his distinction is conceptually valid and possibly significant in the longer term, in practice it was politics in the Party political sense rather than any other which dominated the first year of implementation. Even if DHAs had had the data they needed to make rationing decisions, one must suspect that they would not have been permitted to do so for fear of the Party political consequences of radically restructuring existing patterns of provision. 'Party politics', in other words, ensured that 'political difficulties' were never given a chance of raising their potentially ugly heads at least during the first year of operation of the internal market. The fact that decisions about the health services in London were entrusted to a committee of enquiry rather than being left to market forces is ample evidence of the way that the depoliticisation of the NHS remained sensitive to electoral politics.

Accordingly, word went out from the NHS Management Executive to Regions and Districts that major shifts in service patterns would not be welcome; what was being sought was 'smooth take off'. The success of this heavy 'steer' from the centre was indicated by the NAHAT 1991 Autumn Survey which found that 75 per cent (by value) of contracts had been placed with the local district (i.e. the traditional provider) (NAHAT, 1991). All the evidence, in other words, points to the hardly remarkable conclusion that in its first year the managed market was very intensively managed indeed. These strenuous efforts to avoid hostages to political fortune notwithstanding, the first year of the health care market was not entirely free of incident. It had been widely anticipated that any potential difficulties would be more rapidly realised in Greater London than elsewhere, and so it turned out. This was because London, with its population density, its transport network and its concentration of providers, supplied the ideal conditions for the rapid development of the market. There were other features of health care in London, however, which were always going to pose problems. The first of these was the heavy dependency of inner city hospitals on cross boundary flows of patients from Outer London; research by the King's Fund Institute revealed that of the half million acute in-patient episodes in Inner London almost 20 per cent involved non-residents. The second was the differential cost of hospital care between Inner and Outer London; in Outer London the average cost per inpatient episode was £630, in Inner London it was £790 against a national average of £564

(King's Fund Commission on the Future of London's Acute Health Services, 1992).

The ability of the Inner London hospitals to compete financially was further compromised by the system of capital charges imposed on NHS providers as an incentive to utilise their capital assets efficiently and to place them on a more equal footing with the private sector. Variations in land values meant that inner city hospitals had to face (and pass on in their prices) much higher capital charges than did their suburban competitors. Charing Cross Hospital, for instance, in desirable Fulham was confronted with capital charges that amounted to 35 per cent of its budget (against a national average of 16-17 per cent). In order to protect the Inner London hospitals from too rapid a contraction of their market share, the budgets of London purchasers had been adjusted upwards to take account of the higher costs of their traditional providers. It had been hoped that this device, along with the exhortation to 'smooth take off', would ensure a smooth transition to the market but in practice it failed to do so. Some London health authorities soon realised that their adjusted budgets could purchase an even greater volume of health care if they diverted patients away from their traditional providers in Central London towards cheaper suburban hospitals. By December 1991 Guy's Hospital was reported as attempting to recover £1.6m it was 'owed' (morally, if not contractually) by London HAs who had been funded to purchase services from it but who had spent that money elsewhere. By the end of the financial year Middlesex and University College hospitals had accumulated a £14m deficit. The attempt to place a 'lifebelt' around London health services was continued into 1992-3 with the four Thames regions being given an additional £46m to help deal with the problems faced by London hospitals. Whether this was sufficient was already being questioned only three months into the financial year (Butler, 1992b) and Middlesex/UCH were anticipating a year end £20m deficit as a result of a predicted 10 per cent fall in demand for services as a result of shire purchasers switching to cheaper local providers. A further adverse consequence of changed referral patterns was that, as they lost work to their suburban competitors, Inner London hospitals were forced to pass on their higher unit costs to already hard pressed inner city health authorities (Limb and Sheldon, 1992).

The internal market and NHS efficiency

The question that remains to be asked is: is there any evidence that the reforms have improved NHS efficiency? Discussion of NHS efficiency is universally agreed to be fraught with difficulty at the best of times, given the problems of specifying and measuring outputs and inputs. An election year (1992) in which the NHS was a political football was far from the best of times. Nevertheless, the Government attempted to answer the question. In what was clearly intended as a pre-emptive strike against Labour the NHS Management Executive in January published a review of the first six months of the reforms which claimed,

> Changes in the way the NHS is organised.. are leading to improvements in the quality of care, greater responsiveness to individuals and even better value for money.. (NHS Management Executive, 1992, p. 2)

These claims have been disputed (eg. Clarke and McKee, 1992; Radical Statistics Health Group, 1992; Seng, Lessof and McKee, 1993) but they did appear to be corroborated by the absence of those traditional indicators of inactivity, i.e. hospital beds temporarily closed as a year end cost saving exercise. They were rather more authoritatively confirmed by the publication of the NAHAT financial survey (NAHAT, 1992). This revealed that numbers of inpatients had increased by 3.5 per cent; day cases by 31 per cent; total outpatient attendances by 3.2 per cent and new outpatient attendances by 2.3 per cent.

The NAHAT survey also offered confirmation of the Government's claims on waiting list reductions, although it observed that it was necessary to make allowances for reductions achieved clerically rather than clinically. Even here, though, there were subsequent indications that the momentum that saw the virtual elimination of waits of more than two years might not have been sustained beyond the election, and that the achievement might in any case have been partially offset by a rise in waits of between one and two years (Limb, 1992). Concern that this might be occurring had, in fact, been expressed as early as the Spring of 1991 by the Health Committee in its report on waiting lists (House of Commons 1991a). Further anxiety was voiced that the prioritisation of reducing long waits had been at the expense of clinically more urgent cases that had not been waiting so long (Pope, 1992a:1992b: Radical Statistics Health Group, 1992). On balance, though, there was evidence that the first year of the internal market witnessed record levels of NHS activity.

Before we could concede the causal linkage claimed by the NHSME, however, it would be necessary to eliminate alternative explanations such as increased funding. Analysis of NHS spending and activity between 1979-1992 carried out by the Nuffield Institute in fact points very strongly towards this alternative explanation (Brindle, 1992; Thunhurst, personal communication). Whereas there had been virtually zero real growth in NHS funding during the 1980s, in 1990-1 and 1991-2 NHS expenditure grew in real terms by 2.8 and 4.1 percent respectively. In other words, almost all of the real growth that took place during the decade coincided precisely with the run up to the implementation of the internal market (and the General Election). It must, therefore, be included in any explanation of increased activity. This conclusion is confirmed by NAHAT who observe:

> The underlying causes for the rises cannot.. be isolated with absolute certainty. Clearly, the large rise in financial resources last year enabled more care to be provided.. . The increase in day case work reflects plans started some years ago to build day case units as new medical techniques allowed more patients to receive treatment without overnight stays in hospital.. . The extent to which the reforms.. have contributed to the observed increases in activity (or, conversely have acted to limit the other positive factors) is impossible to judge. (NAHAT, 1992, pp. 26-7)

The claim that waiting list reductions are evidence of the success of the reforms is even more questionable. For one thing, as has already been suggested, waiting lists can be reduced by means other than increased clinical activity. Apart from clerical reductions, alternative strategies for dealing with embarrassing lists include simply abolishing them entirely, as in the case of North East Thames RHA and varicose vein surgery, or delaying outpatient appointments so that patients have to wait before they are admitted on to the official waiting list. In any case, the elimination of two year waits can hardly be attributed to the internal market. Rather, it is the culmination of a centrally coordinated drive (the 'Waiting List Initiative') which began in July 1986 in the course of which a total of £156m was spent, with a further £39m planned for 1992-3. It thus clearly predates the reforms. What it validates is not the market solution but the power of politically determined priorities and additional targeted expenditure. Finally, the Health Committee was extremely doubtful that the initiative had contributed to NHS efficiency:

> We received no evidence that would contradict the view that the £119m already allocated to reduce waiting lists

190

could have been better spent. (House of Commons 1991a, para. 26).

The pattern of trading in the first year of the market was so limited by political and technical constraints that it would be unsafe to generalise from it. Nevertheless I would conclude that there is so far no evidence to compel the conclusion that the reforms have led to any increase in NHS efficiency. I would go beyond this and suggest that there is evidence which points in quite the opposite direction, towards the conclusion, in other words, that far from improving efficiency they have actually reduced it at least in certain respects.

The internal market and NHS inefficiency

There are three areas, I believe, where evidence suggesting reduced efficiency may be found: the General Practice Fund Holding (GPFH) scheme; tax relief on the private health insurance (PHI) premiums of the over 60s; transaction and implementation costs. I will discuss each of these in turn.

General Practice Fundholder (GPFH) scheme

The first area where I believe it is possible to discern evidence implying reduced efficiency is the GPFH scheme. Although it is clearly too early for definitive judgements, there are aspects of the scheme which raise doubts about the consistency of the Government's position on variations in performance. As was widely remarked at the time, *Working for Patients* (1989a) did not offer a detailed analysis of the NHS. This makes it all the more significant that, among the very few statistics it did contain, data on variations in performance between providers should have figured so prominently - variation of 50 per cent in acute hospital treatment costs, for example, or of 100 per cent in GP prescribing costs. In other words, in the absence of any reliable direct measure, variation was taken to be an indicator of the existence of inefficiency. The budget setting process for GPFHs implies a quite different attitude towards variation. Pending development of a capitation funding formula sufficiently sensitive for use with the small populations associated with general practices, it was decided that in the interim GPFHs would be funded on a historical basis, that is, they would be given a budget that would allow them to maintain their existing activity and referral patterns. Setting budgets on this basis revealed massive variations in per capita allocations between practices. Variations of more than 400 per cent in the case of drug budgets, more than 300 per cent for hospital inpatient treatment budgets and 150 per cent overall were found in a study of fifteen practices in London and the Home Counties (Glennerster, Owens and Matsaganis, 1992). This pattern was confirmed nationally by Day and Klein (1991). The scale of variation was such that it seems unlikely that it will prove to be correlated with deprivation or need.

Glennerster, Owens and Matsagnis (1992) comment that fundholding 'has revealed rather than created these variations' (p. 23). I would argue that it did rather more than just reveal them; it reinforced them by building them into practice budgets. Instead of seeking to eliminate these variations (or the inefficiency they represent) the Government was actually rewarding higher spending inefficient practices with higher budget allocations and penalising the more efficient with lower budget allocations. The implication that 'easy money' was available to GPFHs is reinforced by reports that by January 1992 some were anticipating saving six figure sums from their hospital treament budgets by the end of the financial year ('Hart', 1992). By the year end GPFHs in West Midlands RHA had saved a total of £1.7m - an average of £51,000 per practice (Anonymous,1992a). It is hardly surprising that health authorities and hospital managers were reported as calling for the immediate introduction of capitation funding for GPFHs as a means of stemming losses from DHA budgets (Sheldon, 1992a and 1992b). That they should have done so is an indication that the scheme has entailed costs for other actors in the internal market. DHAs were faced with the costs of the uncertainty arising from the unpredictability of GPFH purchasing decisions, or of having to maintain a service on a lower throughput when GPFHs refer elsewhere. Providers had to develop much more detailed service costings than were required by their major customers,the DHAs, who were limited to the less information costly block contracts during the first year of the internal market. The fact that these costs cannot readily be quantified does not make them any less real, nor should they be overlooked because they fell outside the GPFH sector.

Private health insurance (PHI) premium tax relief

The second area where efficiency is almost certain to have been impaired is tax relief on PHI premiums for the over 60s. Here, the evidence is rather more secure because, although part of the reform package, this particular scheme has been in operation for two years, having been introduced in the Budget of 1990. The consequences of this measure had already been analysed by Propper and Maynard (1990) who predicted that the loss of Exchequer revenue would substantially outstrip any gain in terms of total expenditure on health care. It is apparent that this pessimistic prediction has been fulfilled. The revenue cost to the Treasury of tax relief was estimated to be about £60m for the year 1991-2 (Hansard, 1 May 1991, c215w), while the number of people claiming relief was put at 330,000 (Hansard, 6 December 1991, c251). The costs to insurers too were not insignificant. BUPA was reported as having invested £3m in an attempt to tap the anticipated new market, but failed to recover its investment. Western Provident Association spent in excess of £1m only to find that they recruited just 120 new subscribers (Millar, 1991). As Laing (1991b) put it:

> ... tax relief for PHI policies for over 60 year olds ... did little to expand demand in that sector of the market. The main effect appears to have been a switch from nonqualifying to qualifying policies.

The costs of the PHI tax relief scheme do not end with the losses directly incurred by the Treasury or the insurance industry, however. As Propper and Maynard (1990) anticipated, the tax subsidisation of private health will have moved the market away from, rather than towards greater efficiency. By reducing the market price below that which existing subscribers had already shown willing to pay it will have reduced the efficiency of this particular sector of the health care market. At the same time as it has reduced efficiency, it will also have reduced equity. It is known that PHI subscribers are of above average income (OPCS, 1990). Tax relief therefore represents a reduction in vertical equity by redistributing purchasing power from lower to higher income groups. Since the wealthy are also likely to be more healthy, the scheme also reduces equity of access, since the more healthy gain access to health care at the expense of those whose need is greater.

Transaction and implementation costs

Although proponents of markets have been critical of the costs of bureaucratic organisation it has been suggested that they have been less willing to acknowledge the costs of transactions in the market place. Bartlett (1991) has explored this aspect of quasi-markets such as the reformed NHS by means of Williamson's (1975) 'markets and hierarchies' approach. It is argued that, far from being a distortion of the market, bureaucratic 'internal' organisation can in fact be a rational response to market failure. Under certain circumstances it is either extremely costly or else impossible to specify in advance in a written contract every contingency which might affect a market exchange. He gives as an instance, variations in health status between patients for major surgery. An elderly unstable diabetic is clearly going to require a greater volume of hospital treatment than a younger fitter patient. The difficulty of writing such contingencies into it means that the contract will inevitably be an incomplete specification of the rights and obligations of the two parties. This creates scope for opportunistic behaviour. For example, a provider could seek to increase profits by trimming the quality of care, a purchaser to reduce costs by manipulating information or concealing intentions (for instance, about the number of cases it will be referring under a block contract or their health status).

Within the framework of a market two solutions are available to the problem of incomplete contracts. The first is to try to make them more complete specifications by incorporating as many contingencies as possible, but this would require a vastly increased input of information resources. The alternative is increased monitoring of performance in an attempt to ensure contract compliance. In the context of health care neither solution would be straightforward, given the inherent difficulties in specifying and monitoring compliance with care plans that are essentially 'customised' to each individual patient. Either would add significantly to the transaction costs of operating the internal market.

There are other options available but each of these entails a degree of departure (partial in one case, total in the other) from the competitive market. One, neglected by Bartlett (1991) but explored usefully by Hughes and Dingwall (1991), relies on the development of 'private orderings' or gentlemen's agreements between purchasers and providers. Although such informal understandings between trading partners are the norm in the commercial sector it seems unlikely that the Government will regard them as acceptable in the NHS since they would undermine the formal separation of providers and purchasers on which the reforms hinge. The final option is even less likely to be politically acceptable since it runs quite counter to the reforms and would represent a reversion towards the traditionally organised NHS. This is the suspension of the market through the internalisation of trading within vertically integrated organisations. Interestingly, some sort of combination of these last two solutions would seem to have been the outcome of the most recent health market simulation exercise ("Rubber Windmill III") in April 1992:

If in Rubber Windmill I the market crashed, then in Rubber Windmill III the market froze into a pattern of entrenched institutional and clinical interests. ... Collaborative partnership and 'preferred purchaser' arrangements ... virtually neutralised the free workings of a market. ... Under pressure, purchasers protected preferred contracting relationships at the expense of cheaper contracts to non-local trusts. Providers ... seemed suspiciously willing to accept almost any change ... in return for negotiated block contracts which ... removed the dangers of competition (Liddell and Parston, 1992, p. 19).

The health service managers who have been 'gaming' the internal market since 1990 thus appear to have condensed five centuries of capitalist development into the space of three years. In Year 1 'plunder capitalism' prevailed, with purchasers and providers seeking to exploit each other so rapaciously in the first round of contracting that they could not find anyone prepared to do business with them subsequently. By Year 3 however they seem to have discovered the attractions of the monopoly form of capitalism.

Just as the operation of the market entails transaction costs, it is clear that establishing it has entailed implementation costs, even if the difficulty of identifying and quantifying them means that estimates vary widely. Donald Light puts the eventual start up cost of the internal market at £2bn and recurring costs at £0.5bn annually (Light, 1991). The Government though has conceded only the following implementation costs:

	£m
1989-90	79
1990-91	306
1991-92(est)	383

(Hansard, 6 December 1991, c.245)

A total, in other words, of just over £0.75bn by the end of the first year. To this, though, would need to be added the following: the start up costs of the GPFH scheme:

	£m
1990-91	4.4
1991-92*	8.0

*first six months only

(Hansard, 30 January 1992, c.667)

We would also need to include the £11m estimated to be the cost of creating the asset registers needed for the calculation of capital charges (Mellett, 1991); and some part at least of the cost of the increase in the numbers of general and senior managers from 510 in 1986 to 13,200 in 1991 (Anonymous, 1992b, 1992c). Between 1987 and 1991 the general manager salary bill rose from £25.7m to £251.5m (Department of Health, 1992). Interpretation of these last statistics is, however, disputed as a result of disagreement about the extent to which the growth in general management is real or nominal. It is also necessary to see them in context. The salaries paid to general managers represent only 2.2 per cent of total wages and salaries in the NHS. Even if we add in the £1.2bn spent on other administrative and clerical staff as a crude proxy measure of the managerial and administrative 'overhead' it amounts still to just under 6 per cent of total NHS expenditure. This is in line with other estimates which have put NHS administrative expenditure at around 5 per cent (Harrison, S. 1991). The NHS has always been considered a 'good buy' in international comparisons, at least in terms of administrative costs, and although comparable data are not available it is clear that it remains so, certainly when compared with the 24.1 per cent calculated for the USA by Woolhandler and Himmelstein (1991). Nevertheless, the rate of increase in expenditure on senior management since 1987 is remarkable. In the US the rising costs of administration and regulation have in fact been identified as a major factor in the continuing escalation of health care costs experienced in the 1980s (Evans, 1986; Hadley and Langwell, 1991; Quam, 1991). It is estimated that the cost of health service administration in the US rose by 37 per cent between 1983 and 1987 (Woolhandler and Himmelstein, 1991).

Although it may ultimately be impossible to apportion the costs of implementation with any degree of certainty, a number of points seem clear. First, they are considerable and they have to be offset against any putative gains in efficiency brought about by the internal market. Second, it is apparent that, even on the basis of officially disclosed expenditure, they are running considerably in excess of the £220m budgetted for in the Financial Memorandum published with the NHS and Community Care Bill in 1989. Finally, they entail significant opportunity costs, since senior management is now consuming annually the equivalent of the running costs of four medium sized health authorities.

The state and the market: an American perspective

The influence of US health policy developments on the NHS reforms is well documented (e.g. Paton, 1992; Petchey, 1987, 1989; Rayner, 1988a, 1988b). Despite this, Ministers have consistently been quick to deny that it is the Government's intention to replace the NHS with anything like the USA model of health care provision. These denials must be respected and full recognition granted to the fundamental differences between the two health systems which complicate comparative analysis. Nevertheless, I still believe that consideration of USA experience may help us to identify some of the possible constraints on the evolution of the managed market.

In a suggestive analysis of US health policy, Ruggie (1992) has identified what she terms the 'paradox of liberal intervention'. Her argument may be summarised as follows. If we discount earlier small scale initiatives like the Veterans Administration programme, the origins of direct US federal government involvement in health care can be traced to the introduction of Medicare (the programme for the elderly) and Medicaid (the programme for welfare recipients) in 1965. (I would observe that indirect state involvement has a much longer history, of course - vide the tax and other exemptions granted to charity funded hospitals throughout this century, or the capital incentives offered for hospital construction in the 1950s). Ruggie (1992) terms Medicare and Medicaid liberal interventions since they are characterised by

> minimal interference in the essentially market based determination of access to and delivery of care, coupled with ad hoc, piecemeal intervention aimed at keeping the realm of public responsibility distinct from the private sphere and thereby limiting the extent of state intervention. (p. 924)

The significance of Ruggie's analysis resides not so much in the original intervention as in what has occurred since it. From its liberal minimalism, the state has been drawn into ever more intrusive and detailed management of the health care system. From being simply a source of funding for specific social categories otherwise unable to afford health care, the state has willy-nilly become the dominant third party in the previously private sphere of the doctor patient relationship. In Ruggie's words, the government has come to be involved not just in the management of health care, but in its 'micromanagement'.

What lessons can we draw from this analysis for the prospects of establishing a managed health care market on this side of the Atlantic? At the outset, crucial general differences must be recognised - in culture, history, social and political institutions - between the two countries even before the specific differences between the health systems are considered. Nevertheless, despite these differences I believe that consideration of the American experience can remain instructive. It suggests that once the state has acquired a role in health care, even if it is initially confined to financing part of its provision, the peculiarities of the product and, in particular, the difficulties of regulating the behaviour of its immediate producers mean that it is virtually inevitable that it will be drawn into the management of its delivery also. The fact that liberal administrations in the USA have experienced such difficulty in maintaining the boundary between the public and the private, between the state and the market in the sphere of health care provision suggests that, for the British state, disengagement from health care provision may be no easy task.

At precisely the same time that it has sought to withdraw from its traditional role as direct provider, the state here too has actually been becoming ever more firmly entrenched in the micromanagement of health care delivery. A whole array of policy initiatives since the early 1980s have reduced the 'secret garden of professional autonomy.. to the size of a window box' (Klein, 1989, p. 239). General management, clinical audit, clinical directorates, the Resource Management Initiative, and other such initiatives (culminating of course in the NHS and Community Care Act 1990) have resulted in the marked extension of direct and indirect state control over the NHS at the expense of clinical autonomy. It has also placed health care rationing firmly on the political agenda. Instead of treatment being allocated, as hitherto, largely covertly and by clinicians according to priorities that were either undisclosed or else justified by reference to generally unquestioned clinical criteria, in the internal market it will be purchasers rather than providers who will be responsible for deciding on what (and therefore effectively on whom) the limited health care budget will be spent. To elaborate Klein's metaphor, the important thing about window boxes is not just that they are small, but that they also offer nowhere to hide.

Inescapably, this assumption of the poisoned chalice of responsiblity for health care rationing by purchasers raises the issue of legitimacy - of decisions and decision makers alike. As we have seen already, purchasing authorities are bound to be confronted with the problem of justifying rationing decisions that are explicit rather than, as hitherto, concealed behind medical professional mystique. Moreover, as Sabin (1992) observes, their remit compels them towards the adoption of utilitarian values in determining their spending priorities. In an era of resource constraints, this implies that on occasion at least the good of an individual or of a minority even will have to be sacrificed for the greater good of the majority. This conflict between the utilitarian ethic and the right of the individual is, of course, not a new one but up until now it has remained largely obscured by the myth of unlimited and universal care distributed according to individual need. Nevertheless, the fact that it has been revealed rather than created by the reforms does not make it any the less controversial. Furthermore, it is worth noting that it has been accentuated (potentially at least) by the charter movement which uses the language not of collective, but individual, rights. Specifically, the patient's charter refers to the right of every citizen 'to receive health care on the basis of clinical need'. It is thus virtually inevitable that in coming months and years we will be confronted with a series of politically embarrassing cases where the utilitarian calculus of a purchasing authority has denied treatment to some real individual or individuals. As May (1992) shrewdly reminds us, it was the case of a child denied heart surgery that triggered the prime ministerial review of the NHS in January 1988 (not to mention the 'War of Jennifer's Ear' during the last election). By simultaneously raising the political profile of waiting lists as a 'vital sign' of the health of the NHS the Government may have restricted still further its room for manoeuvre by denying itself the use of the other traditional NHS rationing device - the queue. Finally, the fact that approximately 80 per cent of health care funding will still come from the Treasury is likely to mean that responsibility for unpopular rationing decisions will continue to be laid at the door of the Government rather than of purchasing authorities. If in the US we have been witnessing the paradox of liberal intervention, there is the possibility that here we may be observing the unfolding of a paradox of a rather different type. Namely, a political initiative that was designed to de-politicise the provision of health care by enlarging the scope of market forces but which had precisely the opposite effect. By placing health care rationing so firmly and explicitly on the agenda, I suspect that the government has ensured itself a continuing and much more central role in the management of health care delivery than perhaps it might otherwise have wished.

11 Thinking long in community care

Bleddyn Davies

From the ferment of ideas of the mid 1980s emerged Sir Roy Griffiths' masterful construction of a skeletal policy framework (Griffiths, 1988). Its time horizon was long, though it clearly showed why immediate action was necessary. Its range was broad. The report was widely welcomed in the policy world, though its philosophy was clearly of the second half of the 1980s, and some of its supporters must have had difficulty with some of its proposals since they quite clearly cut across some of the interests of powerful groups. A year later, the White Paper appeared (*Caring for People*, 1989). It accepted most of the features of the Griffiths agenda.

The discussion which followed reflects a characteristic of policy analysis everywhere, and of the UK of the last fifteen years in particular: a myopic sense of time preference in the definition of issues. It is understandable that SSDS living from hand to mouth should suffer from it. It is sad that the defective sense of time preference should be so widespread at the levels of government responsible for the long view, and surprising that it should dominate the arguments from most academic specialists.

First, consider the discussion of financing

The most obvious way in which the White Paper differed from the Griffiths proposal was in its failure to 'ring fence' long term care funds. The reaction to this rejection was immediate and prolonged. The Social Services Committee of the House of Commons attributed the most pungent of comments to Sir Roy[1]: 'I had provided a purposeful, effective and economic four wheel vehicle, but the White Paper has redesigned it as a three wheeler, leaving out the fourth wheel of ring fenced funding' (House of Commons, 1990a).

'Ring fencing' was a medium term, not a long term, issue, except in the sense that with inadequate levels of funding during the early years, SSDs would certainly be forced to make even more difficult choices if the most important of the potential benefits of the new policy were to be achieved -and perhaps be left with insufficient resources to achieve even those to a degree sufficient for the policy to look successful in retrospect[2]. It was primarily about the transfer of funds used by the National Health Service (NHS) to pay for persons in long stay hospital wards to support the development of services by the social services departments [SSDs] 'in the community'. At the rate of decline of persons in long term wards seen from the late 1980s, this was unlikely to be an issue for the new century. From the outset, the discussion was about the immediate future.

In the two years which followed, the attention turned more to the most immediate of issues: what the government would add to local authority grants to help pay for the additional costs of community care and particularly, to cover the care costs of the new responsibility to pay for persons in residential homes hitherto born from national social security votes.

So short termism ruled OK. What went almost unnoticed was that the White Paper had almost nothing to say about some of the longer run comments and recommendations which Sir Roy had made about financing mechanisms (Griffiths, 1988). The foci of the Select Committee continued to be the previous concerns of public financing. There was a report on funding for local authorities focused on ring fencing; a report on the funding of private and voluntary residential care focused on orders of magnitude and the immediate changes in funding mechanism; and reports on other matters of more immediate urgency. There was an equal dearth of long term academic thinking about financing in general, and about its implications for health and social security policies in particular. William Laing's pamphlet is an exception (Laing, 1990). The same charge rings less true of discussions of the supply side. On the one hand, the Department's *Policy Guidance* of 1990 and the unprecedented flow of (high quality) guidance from the Social Services Inspectorate also focused on the immediate tasks (Department of Health, 1990a). In these, there was a further narrowing of the conception of the regulative and promotional role of the 'enabling' community care authorities compared with the concept

201

advocated in the period leading to the Griffiths review. For instance, the DH guidance discussed only some of the variety of the 'trade and industry policies' discerned in attempts to apply American lessons to the UK (Davies, 1986a; Davies and Challis, 1986).

However, the Department of Health [DH] did engage the supply side better than financing. Many of those drafting guidance appreciated how big was the gap between current behaviour and the new policy ideals. Document after document declared the need for a 'profound cultural change' - though sometimes that appeared to be referring to making the best of a mixed economy, rather than to the ideals of consumer choice, consumer rights, the sensitive support of carers, and supply responsiveness generally. Much of the guidance went far to stipulating what a profound cultural change in the promotion of user responsive service meant, and to showing how such innovations of the new policy as the case management approach could be made to work in ways which would reinforce it[3].

So too much debate has reflected first, the hand to mouth economy of many British policy agencies, and secondly, a short view of the future.

Perhaps the most urgent appeal to think long was made in a daily newspaper. *The Guardian*'s article was of great interest because of the diverse backgrounds of its authors and the weight of their (justly deserved) reputations: David Hunter, Tessa Jowell, Huw Richards and Peter Westland (1992).

Their focus was the relationship between financing and structural mechanisms, and the attainment of some of the key objectives of the reform. Their argument was around some key aspects of the 'residualism' implicit in how the community care policy is evolving; 'fundamental assumptions' about the reduction in 'the role of the State as protector'. The particular cause of their anxiety was the move from what they call (perhaps misleadingly[4]) 'entitlement financing' to rationing on the basis of need. This they attribute to the shift in responsibility from health to local government financing, and so charging and means testing, without guarantees of minimum standards, and without sufficiently powerful mechanisms to ensure the enhancement of user choice and responsiveness to user needs and preferences. The problem, they suggest, is that under the new policy, the resources are to be 'rationed on the basis of need', with 'matching resources to needs' the 'task of local authority workers'. That, they seem to suggest, is what is 'at odds with the rhetoric of consumer choice and empowerment'. The risk, they argue is that we shall allow the central government 'virtually [to] opt out of its responsibility', 'at some later stage diffusing blame for failure by holding local government responsible.'[5] Hunter and his colleagues call for a shift to 'breakthrough politics' from 'technical politics'.

Hunter et al (1992) rightly imply the pervasive effects of large structural issues[6]. However British field agencies are not so much the creatures of these larger structures as to be able to accomplish nothing except when a myriad of stars are aligned. It may be more important as Hunter et al suggest to work at strategies to make the most of the 'technological advances' made possible by new micro structures created by the 'bottom up' strands of argument and evidence and build it into the new policy. This is the subject of Part 2.

This chapter can make only a few points about long run structures. It builds on the distinction between the 'top down' and 'bottom up' logics of the community care arguments. Part 1 raises issues about the major structures: about long term structures and financing. Part 2 discusses some of the issues which depend on the working of the 'bottom up' logic of the new community care. In particular, it asks whether case management will deliver the improved user influence, support of carers, balance between effectiveness with efficiency in the use of public funds.

1. Financing mechanisms and organisational structures

Here our task is to pose some unformulated dilemmas about the broad structures and mechanisms.

1.1 The sharply bounded domains of incompatible financing principles

In the past, we have complained about distortions due to the overlap of responsibilities between the SSDs and the NHS and the existence of distortions due to improvised mechanisms creating incentives which distorted. Now we shall have to live with the downside of much clearer boundaries.

Financing and price elasticities: The legal settlement of the 1940s embodied contrasting financing principles. The NHS was to be financed from the tax base. The consumption of local authority services by poor persons was to be subsidised, but not necessarily the consumption of others. At first, the local authorities could subsidise widely, supported by a buoyant tax base and the national priority of building up levels of service. As pressure on resources mounted from the mid 1970s, public

203

subsidisation was increasingly focused on the poor, greater use being made of user charging.

The White Paper stated that 'those able to meet all or part of the economic cost should be expected to do so'. It accompanied this with a proviso that 'ability to pay' should not in any way influence decisions on the services to be provided' (*Caring for People*, 1989, para 3.81). The actual words of the White Paper were that *provision decisions* should not be affected, not *actual consumption*. 'Provision decisions' implies what the case managers and other allocators decide that they would be willing to finance or provide. How far that splitting of a hair matters depends on 'elasticities of demand'.

Substantial charges would be compatible with 'secondary prevention' more specifically, front ended utilisation of the levels professionals think are necessary to prevent deterioration which would make the total lifetime costs to public funds much greater only if demand were price inelastic among those whose needs were judged high because of the potential for secondary prevention. That is so whether we mean responsiveness to charges in probability of consuming the smallest quantity, or the responsiveness for levels greater than that. The evidence about elasticities was ambiguous for the late 1980s[7]. However, the chances are that the elasticities will have risen since then. Nevertheless, the White Paper's statement did not cause much controversy because the behaviour it implied was much the same as the outcomes of current policy trends in most authorities.

Efficiency effects of incentives at the boundary: What the new community care arrangements have done is to create a straight, sharp boundary between the domains of the two contrasting financing principles. That affects decision making for those whose circumstances make them users. That has two consequences. First, it causes serious distortions of decisions about individual cases, creating disbenefits for them, their families, and the services. There are powerful perverse incentives to users which create ethical dilemmas for the field professionals, their managers, and ultimately their political masters; and the decisions which result diminishes equity and efficiency. This has equity and efficiency effects which are felt immediately: it undermines 'productive efficiency'. Secondly, it creates incentives which undermine the potential for innovation and change promoting worth while substitutions of ends and means. The equity and efficiency effects work through the loss of efficiency gains; more precisely, of X efficiency.

A dilemma facing geriatricians illustrates the first: the distortion of incentives affecting decisions about individual cases. In the UK, the

DH has ruled that 'no patient can be directed on discharge to either a residential or nursing home unless the patient or someone authorised to act on their behalf has applied to be admitted .. and a check should be made that the decision to apply for admittance was taken as a result of informed choice. The financial implications for the patient both in the short and long term will also need to have been fully considered' (Department of Health 1990b). (See also the less precise statement in the *Charter for NHS Patients*.) The DH has reacted to an immediate pressure in a way which creates a long run dilemma.

Importantly persons discharged in this way would become eligible to pay fees unless they had sufficiently low means to be eligible for social security benefits which would cover the charges levied by a residential home. Many geriatricians feel an ethical obligation both to inform patients and relatives of their right to refuse discharge and the financial consequences. However they also feel that the duty is exercised at the expense of fulfilling their duty to provide an efficient service for a community. That is, the financial interest of the individual patient may be completely at odds with that of the community which the geriatrician has the responsibility to serve.

The second consequence will matter quite as much in the long run. An important element of the new managerialism is its focus on responding entrepreneurially to opportunities and change. The community care argument of the 1980s illustrated the potential of greater resourcefulness and flexibility. Indeed, one strand of argument was that these had greater potential in community and long term care than in most other areas: the wide variety of need related circumstances which should affect what would be the best form of intervention in general, what tasks were performed when and in what way; the dominance in the lifetime costs of many of the tasks which could be undertaken in many ways using resources from many different sources, formal and informal. These implied great gains from responsive and resourceful substitutions, whether of ends or of means. (Davies and Challis, 1986).

The policy has created new boundaries of responsibility at which the opposing financing principles distort incentives. The policy drew the boundary of the SSD to include much but not all long term care. So long term community nursing was excluded. So were the hospital long stay beds used primarily for nursing and social care; and so, by extension in some areas, the nursing homes which since the late 1980s have been increasingly contracted by the NHS to provide this 'continuing care'.

However the potential for substitution across these areas is great. As long as the quality of life and care of so many long stay wards are anything but like St George's but per diem costs are high, substitutions between ends as well as means are desirable. Similar home care tasks in the USA are more expensive when performed by 'home health agencies' (nursing agencies), and that has been true here too.

Not only were there great practical difficulties in drawing the boundaries in such a way as to include them; for example, the diversity of organisation of continuing care and the role of the geriatrician in the medical care of elderly people, the sensitivities of the professions and the turf issues for organisations. There are clear limits to the degree to which potential substitutes and complements can be brought within the domain of one only of the opposing financing principles.

1.   There is a great variety in 'models of geriatric practice' (Brocklehurst, Davidson and Moore-Smith, 1989)[8], and that is matched by variety in the organisation of NHS financed continuing care. Local patterns should and do change. The variety is partly an efficiency - and effectiveness - increasing response to local endowments of physical and human capital, which are not easily adjusted in the short run. Partly, it reflects effectiveness -   increasing search behaviour.   It would be damaging to discourage such local adaptations.

2.   Advances in health technology will make demands for new mixes of inputs at the boundary between health and community care. The American experience illustrates how intensive higher technology nursing at home can save hospital costs.   This is spreading here (Marks, 1992). There are other developments in medical technology which allow the shortening of spells in hospitals; for instance, non invasive methods of investigation, trauma reducing surgical procedures. There are some who argue that the rate of reduction in the average length of stay of elderly persons in hospitals will diminish rapidly among the 5-10 per cent of elderly inpatients in acute beds who are 'ambiplex' (Zook and Moore, 1980) - with complex and ambiguous conditions, often involving progressive failure different bodily systems - which are at risk of post acute long term care and which are the focus of geriatricians.   This requires better support for the performance of social care tasks at home.   In this sense the medicalisation of home care whose downside has been so powerfully discussed by Carrolle Estes and others is something

which will come here, though it need not be pernicious if financed in a way which does not divert resources from the other purposes of community care (Estes, Swann and Associates, 1993).

3.   The largest savings in costs come from the substitution for acute beds, not from the substitution for residential or nursing home beds. So, for instance, it is efficiency in avoiding unnecessary utilization of acute beds which dominates the agency's economy in those American models - On Lok, PACE, the S/HMOs - which have financial responsibility for stays in acute beds as well as long term health and social care into the same agencies, and in which the agencies have strong financial incentives to operate efficiently as well as effectively.   Behaviour affecting it is therefore carefully managed, and there is a pervasive consciousness of the disastrous effects of excessive hospital stays (Yordi 1990; Abrahams et al 1989; Hennessy, C.H., 1989; Zawadski and Eng 1988; Kane, Illston and Millar, 1992; Newcomer, Harrington and Friedlob, 1990).

However, divisions of financing responsibility are fixed for long periods. Therefore they determine what substitutions agencies working within them seek much more continuously and pervasively than changing ideas about the potential for substitution affect the division of financing responsibility. So in the UK, there have been greater incentives (and it has been administratively easier) to set up models intended to substitute community based for residential care than on models for substituting residential or other modes for acute hospital beds, just as in the USA, there has been more effort to substitute community based care for nursing homes than nursing home inputs for acute beds (Davies, 1986a).

4.   The primary and community care policies gives them the NHS and SSD new obligations. The general practitioners have recovered some power of initiative. But even in the long run and in the absence of a dramatic change in policy, their response in the care of elderly people will differ greatly, and with it the degree to which they will become the focus of the new case management. (Authorities like Kent are moving fast towards attempting to base case management organisation on general practices to a degree which would have been unthinkable only a

few years ago).

To conclude:

- Any definition which covered all substitutes and complements in community- and long term care would also cover groups whose main functions are quite unrelated to long term care, and no one definition of the domains for each financing principle would suit all areas of the country in a system whose local organisations allowed responsiveness to local endowments of physical and human capital and variations in ideas about what organisational models yield most benefits.
- Nevertheless, there should be redefinitions of the boundaries to remove some of the anomalies. An important feature of the new community care argument is its emphasis on the 'investment opportunity': putting in resources early to reduce costs and/or improve outcomes over the remainder of the life span. Identifying these will need more insight into disease and treatment possibilities than possessed by most social care personnel who see many ambiplex patients early. Putting together new teams at the field level will be important for taking the investment opportunities. It is interesting how as DH guidance has been worked through with ever greater focus on field realities and potential, the emphasis has increasingly switched to coordination across the boundaries of responsibility written into the White Paper and the Act. It is the boundaries which have created the major incentives. But as they now are, they will have to be crossed by many of the local initiatives around particular opportunities which it is the aim of the new managerialism to stimulate.

1.2 A new benefit required?

The issue: If the conclusions of section 1.1. are correct, there is no easy organisational escape from this downside of the greater clarity of responsibilities which the new arrangements have brought. The new clarity has put into sharper relief a gap which has always been there in the British system: we lack a suitable financing mechanism which allows persons not poor enough to be eligible for complete coverage by the State to meet the high costs of long periods of care.

Viewed thus, our problem is more like that of France or the United States. In the United States, the Pepper Commission Final Report (1990) provided a new focus for the discussion of financing mechanisms for long term care. To remove the bias towards the nursing home, it proposed a home care benefit for persons with a high level of disability.

The discussion around it provides a rich source for ingenious ideas about financing mechanisms in an increasingly mixed financing and supply economy. The two French reports of 1991, Boulard (1991) and Schopflin (1991), proposed an *'allocation autonomie et dépendance'*, merging into it various other allowances, particularly the *allocation compensatrice*, and removing the funding bias towards residential care modes[9].

Characteristics of the benefit: The precise form of the benefit would require careful and expert discussion. However, some features should be considered.

- It should be tailored to the needs for long term social and nursing care, and so be separated from general funding for health services. The point is partly about the integrity of the aims and values of long term care: there are mutual benefits in alliances between acute medical and long term care, but little case for allowing the values of the former to dominate those of the latter, with the inevitable redistribution of resources from truly long-term care - in other words, there is little case for importing some vices which are more powerful in some other countries than here (Estes, Swan and Associates, 1993). It is partly about creating a hybrid which would combine some of the features of the two main financing mechanisms at the margins where their incompatibility most interferes with equity and efficiency.

- A main aim would be to remove the risk of pauperisation by long term care need among those most at risk of it. It should not be restricted to the poor, though ways could be found to taper its net benefit. Doing so, it would limit the damage caused by the growth of a new political minefield: attempting to chase divested assets. The definition of the beneficiaries should cover citizens against the minority risk of having to spend on at a high weekly rate for long enough for a high proportion of elderly people to be pauperised, softening the impact of SSD variations and perverse incentives to users to block acute beds, and freeing SSDS from the devastating financial consequences of unpredicted variations in the prevalence of the heaviest cases[10].

- Though assessed by a brokerage agency, how the money is used should be responsive to user wishes - and indeed, handled by them to the maximum degree compatible with the protection of interests of clients. The aim would be to strike a good balance between user empowerment and equity and efficiency in the use of public resources[11]. Neither one nor the other can have an absolute precedence. The effort must be to achieve as much of all three as ingenuity allows. The circumstances in which this would reduce equity and efficiency are too many and complex to define in other than generalities at a level which would cause waste and exclusion however carefully they are worded by well informed persons. So there must be at least optional brokerage support for all [12]. So the benefit would achieve its purposes best if it were supported with, and integrated into, brokerage of the kind reflected in the best case management practice. However that merges into arrangements which combine features of entitlement with discretionary benefits. For instance, the Schopflin Report (1991) advocates assessment of eligibility and brokerage by multidisciplinary teams in ways which makes it close to case management. The Israeli CLTCI likewise requires full and rigorous assessment by a nurse.

- There should be a copayment from most users large enough to create incentives to countervail the tendency of providers and others to seek to escalate costs, either because they want standards which are higher or because they sought excessively comfortable budgetary slack[13]. (For the poor, the SSD would be the main copayer.)

- It should be targeted at persons of high disability: persons who in the past would have received continuing care in hospitals and nursing homes, and who might consume high cost packages for substantial periods. Numbers at risk are in fact extremely sensitive to the stringency of the eligibility criteria. Table 12.1, based on a reanalysis of the 1985 Disability Survey, shows the effects on numbers eligible of different numbers of persons of varying disability levels, ability to perform activities of daily living [adls], cognitive impairment and behavioral disorder due to dementia related conditions, and income. The sensitivity both to the adl level and to income is striking.

So perhaps it is not surprising that as far as I am aware, none of the countries whose governments have recently made or proposed changes have been prepared to consider the entitlement solution for other than the most disabled. The Pepper Commission (1990) suggested that the minimum level should be incapacity to perform three of the five tasks of daily living commonly used in the discussion of the implications of American targeting. This excludes all but a low proportion of persons living in the community, and a low proportion of those currently receiving community-based long term care. The Schopflin Report (1991) likewise proposed an equivalent level of disability as its eligibility criterion. The Israeli CLCTI too provides an entitlement only for those with two ADLs or the need for constant attendance, and who also have incomes no greater than some multiple of the national wage (Factor, Morginstin, and Naon, 1991). In effect, such entitlement programmes are conceived only for the most disabled, and are accompanied by other programmes for those of lesser disability based on discretionary allocations. A comparison of these criteria with Table 12.1, and with data on the incapacities of recipients of British community based services, shows that a benefit based on such stringent conditions would be of little relevance to most current users. The group for whom such a benefit would be greatest would be those in continuing hospital (Millard, 1992) or nursing home care, together with some in residential care and cared for at home by relatives.

The need for a review of financing mechanisms: The flows of funds are complex. There is now a need to review the whole range of financing mechanisms. This should cover social security and taxation, charging policies, as well as intersectoral flows between health, SSDs, and housing agencies. Starting with a system mixing insurance funds with social assistance, the French have linked the establishment of the *allocation autonomie and dépendance* with the abolition of the *allocation compensatrice*.

The orders of magnitude are large. Applying the rates coming into force in April 1991 to the number of Attendance Allowances received by persons aged 65 and over current at the end of March that year suggests an annual expenditure of more than one billion pounds. By 1991 the number of 'current' allowances to persons aged 65 and over rose to 4.8 times it 1977 level, and the value of the benefits paid rose 13.9 times (at current prices[14]. The total number of 'current' Invalid Care Allowances rose thirty fold over the same period (Department of Social Security, 1993).

The Attendance Allowance has only recently been clearly used to support community and long term care, and still in few areas and for persons who receive certain kinds of services. It has uptake and other problems. The authorities who attempt to tap it are within the law, but not within the spirit of the vague assumptions which most users have come to have of it. One would imagine that those who most describe and defend the interests of family carers disapprove of the authorities' attempts. It is certainly the case that the literature on the costs of caring show many costs quite unrelated to care (Glendinning, 1992a). The Invalid Care Allowance is low. However its principles are different from the other financing mechanisms and so that too creates perverse incentives.

To work these things out will require the despised 'technical policy and politics', indeed technical policy at the most micro level as well as 'breakthrough politics'[15].

Table 12.1
Sensitivity to low income component of targeting definition

Floor level of Target Group Definition		Living Arrangement			
		Alone	With Spouse	With other	All
Household shopping	All incomes	100.0	100.0	100.0	100.0
	Low incomes**	86.0	84.1	68.1	80.6
Snacks or vacuum cleaning	All incomes	71.5	63.9	75.8	69.6
	Low incomes**	59.8	50.9	48.1	53.3
At least 1 of 5 ADLs*	All incomes*	34.4	56.4	59.5	49.4
	Low incomes**	27.4	44.7	34.9	36.0
At least 2 of 5 ADLs*	All incomes	14.5	37.2	41.7	30.3
	Low incomes**	10.4	28.1	22.5	20.5
Cognitive Impairment with 1 of 7 IADLs*** or					
Household shopping	All incomes	101.3	100.5	100.9	100.8
	Low incomes**	87.4	84.2	68.8	81.4
Snacks or vacuum cleaning	All incomes	73.8	72.3	77.6	71.8
	Low incomes**	61.9	52.8	49.9	55.3
At least 1 of 5 ADLs*	All incomes*	38.5	58.5	64.1	53.0
	Low incomes**	31.6	46.5	38.3	39.1
At least 2 of 5 ADLs*	All incomes	20.7	40.9	48.4	35.7
	Low incomes**	16.1	31.0	27.4	24.8
Cognitive Impairment with 1 of 7 IADLs or					
Behavioural Disturbance with 1 of 7 ADLs or					
Household shopping	All incomes	101.8	100.9	101.3	101.3
	Low incomes**	87.6	84.9	68.5	81.8
Snacks or vacuum cleaning	All incomes	74.7	68.3	79.2	73.4
	Low incomes**	62.9	54.8	50.1	56.7
At least 1 of 5 ADLs*	All incomes*	40.8	60.9	64.8	55.0
	Low incomes**	33.3	48.7	37.7	40.8
At least 2 of 5 ADLs*	All incomes	22.6	45.0	50.0	38.5
	Low incomes**	17.8	34.8	26.6	27.3

Notes:
* The 5 types of ADL are 'washing yourself all over', 'dressing', 'getting to and using the toilet', 'getting in and out of bed', and 'feeding'.
** Low income is an income below the ninth decile of household equivalent income in ascending order.
*** The 7 types of IADL are 'household shopping', 'preparing a snack', 'using a vacuum cleaner', 'making a cup of tea', 'preparing a hot meal', 'washing and drying dishes', and 'dealing with paperwork'.

Source: Reanalysis of the OPCS Disability Survey in Davies and Kheradmandia, (1992).

Financing the lower cost care packages of the non poor: If the most which we can hope for is a tax and copayment funded programme for the most costly, how do we overcome the gap in the financing mechanisms for those whose care costs are lower? We should not neglect the potential of mechanisms developed for risk pooling independently of the State: the funded group benefits and social care maintenance organisations on which further work was recommended by Griffiths. We do not seem to be going back to Beveridge. Financial structures of the 1990s lead to quite different organisational forms. The policy system having left a vacuum, Schumpeterian capitalism in its late twentieth century form is fast moving in. There has been a rapid increase in the range of insurance related 'products' now on offer. They are being designed for persons with different needs, facing issues at different stages of life. In that way, they are able to offer variety to match needs, an argument with analogous limitations to the similar one used in support of relying on independent pension arrangements. They are building on the experience of the Americans and others.

One must not oversell their relevance. For reasons which are well known, they are currently affordable only by the well off. But if we are to have funded schemes, we must think as far ahead as the second quarter of the next century.

Their potential can be enhanced. More appropriate precedents could be taken for tax treatment). They require regulatory frameworks which balance security, adequate benefit structures, and ethical selling practices. The State - the SSDs, if one takes the BRITSMO or BRITSBRO models (Davies and Goddard, 1987a; 1987b; Davies and Challis, 1986) - could negotiate arrangements to share the risk for these to a degree which would not increase its total commitment of public funds in return for setting lower limits to benefit structures, upper limits on risk ratios, and codes for ethical practice. Experiments in various American states and the technical discussions prepared for the Pepper Commission (1990) have shown possibilities. Affordability should not be a key constraint if contributions can be paid over a long time: what would have to be covered would be packages of moderate unit cost albeit over a mean period of some years[16].

So we need some breakthrough political imagination first in assessing the need for an entitlement benefit for persons requiring the most expensive care packages, and secondly in considering public policy and public private partnerships for independent mechanisms based on insurance.

213

1.3 Structures

Financing mechanisms are only part of the problem of achieving equity and efficiency at the interface between health and social care. The system of governance of the two kinds of authority is incompatible. Local authority policy is sensitive to council ethos and the local ballot box. That sometimes causes clashes between political and technocratic cultures.

There is a large and well known literature on the differences which have emerged in joint coordination and planning, from the pioneering work of Webb and Wistow (1986) on. During the 1980s, the problems became more serious with the emergence of hung councils and greater instability of control between and within parties. For instance, the four Scottish health boards distrust social service authorities and so have made contracts with nursing homes for the placement of persons who would otherwise block beds, the health boards meeting the costs. Others are directly contracting with housing associations to provide what amounts to nursing home care, thereby obtaining social security funding for living expenses and rent to which they add the care costs. That mechanism, pioneered in projects launched in response to the Care in the Community programme, has been in widespread use by social services departments in the development of their policies for elderly persons.

Bebbington and Kelly (1992) describe how some of the most fiscally stressed London authorities with the highest unit costs have increased their unit costs absolutely and in relation to other authorities, coping with the fiscal stress by reducing the volume of services[17].

It is possible that there may be a correlation between higher spending in relation to need with pressures making progressively greater relative inefficiency inevitable. If so, the grant system cannot compensate for territorial variations in needs for spending without reinforcing inefficiency. During the managerialist 1980s, from the launch of the Financial Management Initiative on, the central government clearly committed itself to a priority of improving efficiency. A financing system which condones inefficiency in the pursuit of equity can not long survive with this new priority. Moreover, health and social services are interdependent. The success of some such overdue reform of London health services as that proposed by the Tomlinson Committee depends on the community care authorities adjusting to the consequences with flexibility (Tomlinson, 1992). Moreover, all the trends of the last few years in medical technology and management have suggested that the London authorities should be increasing not reducing volumes, not reducing them in order to maintain unit costs.

Political instability and hung councils may be simply a correlate of political values and cultures which are the true cause of the 'inefficiency': the pre Herbert borough of Southwark had as its uncompromising motto, 'the health of the people is the highest law'. In that case, the problem is too fundamental to be tackled by redrawing boundaries, introducing a form of proportional representation giving weight to the median voter, having annual elections for a proportion of the seats[18].

Perhaps the only way in which it could be tackled would be to shift the balance of authorities' functions between the technocratic and the political. (Crossman posed a dilemma in establishing the Royal Commission on Local Government: between scale and democracy and scale and efficiency.) The argument of the 1960s embodied in the Heath administration's arrangements of 1974 put a heavy emphasis on the technocratic, the provision of services within the framework of more sophisticated local service policy. The arrangements produced large local authorities, the largest multi purpose in the world. Michael Heseltine later argued that a better balance would put more emphasis on the political, the reflection of local citizens' values and conflicting interest group pressures in policy guidelines. Reforms reflecting that would remove the new form of the old paradox long noted by John Stewart (1986): local government is not organised around the mediation of conflicting interests among the populations of local territories winning citizen interest and loyalty, but around the commissioning and provision of services, a much narrower role.

That remains a key dilemma for policy areas like community care. It is the fundamental reason why technocratic health commissioning will never fit well with enabling local authorities. The Heseltine resolution would result in smaller authorities in many areas[19]; authorities which would press politically based argument and pressure on commissioning-cum-trade and industry policy (CTIP) agencies. They might well be at arm's length from the local authorities, whose influence would be enhanced by their power to use local taxes to provide incentives for the commissioning agencies to respond. Many of the CTIP agencies would have wider geographical territories. Such CTIP agencies, not being directly governed by local politicians, could be financed with similar grant arrangements to those now in existence. The CTIP agencies might create a hybrid culture appropriate for long term care, and employ geriatricians, professions allied to medicine, and professions associated with social care. The incorporation of geriatricians would put them into key roles in selective assessment.

An alternative might be the eventual organisational separation of the political from the CTIP functions; perhaps health/social care agencies such as were floated by the Audit Commission (1986) and academics (Ferlie Challis and Davies, 1985). A third possibility might be to shift the responsibility for the more costly forms of community care to health services.

2. What mileage from implementing the present policy: new evidence about care management

The redrawing of the boundaries between the NHS and the SSD, far less the introduction of a new benefit, the extension of public policy to cover insurance related financing mechanisms for those ineligible for free service, or in some areas, a reform of local government which is more fundamental than now on the agenda, are nothing if not the stuff of 'breakthrough politics', as Hunter et al (1992) called it. So it is useful to ask whether the enhancement of user choice and responsiveness to user needs and preferences, the better selection of ends, matching of tasks to needs, and the more efficient mixing of inputs, and the improvement in the content of care can occur without them. That is, one should ask whether the implementation of elements of existing policy in ways which try to achieve most in the long, not medium or short, run.

Most of the concerns are about the matching of resources to needs, about achieving better performance of the core case management tasks. In this section, we present new evidence about two issues: whether there are case management models which have improved outcomes sufficiently consistently to suggest that progress with respect to the equity and effectiveness concerns expressed, for instance, by Hunter et al, (1992) is possible given the successful implementation of policy as it is (section 2.1); and whether there is evidence which supports the central - but previously untested - proposition of case[20] management theory, that there is a range of variation over which increased input into case management improves the impact of other home care services.

2.1 Case management experiments: do they show improved outcomes?

There has been much British evidence from special British projects that case management can achieve considerable gains in these respects, although operating within systems which have all these problems. There are whole programmes of case management projects whose evaluations suggest such improvements. A notable example is the Australian programme of 48 Community Options Projects, implementing variants of a model based on the Kent Community Care Project and the Wisconsin Community Options Programme (Australia: Department of Health, Housing and Community Services, 1992). I have argued that the Americans may have underestimated the success of some of the most conspicuous of the case management experiments (Davies, 1992a; Davies, 1992b; Davies et al, 1990). The Neighbourhood Team model in the ACCESS programme, again based on the Kent Community Care Project, was highly successful in Up-State New York (Eggert et al, 1991). Table 12.2 summarises results from the PSSRU projects whose evaluations have been completed so far. I have argued that it is unsurprising that they have been so successful by most criteria.

However, the evidence from the PSSRU studies present one major problem of inference: they might suffer Hawthorne effects. All were to some degree showpieces; some often visited during their implementation, with the leading case managers themselves touring the country telling the world about the work. They were all to varying degrees actively kept in line by an anxious PSSRU management.

However, two (the Sheppey and Tonbridge programmes) enjoyed only the same attention as another 35 programmes in the Kent of their period, and only the support which Kent provided as a case-management-cum-provider agency: a short induction course; a period of observation in the Thanet project; the documentation and data system established in the Thanet project; monthly meetings of community care workers for training sessions provided by outside experts and the presentation of cases, and the discussion of common interests; quarterly meetings attended by care managers, headquarters management, and PSSRU members for care managers views to be put to management and for management to transmit information and for the discussion of analyses prepared by my colleague John Chesterman comparing case management team data were presented; and case presentations by case managers[21]. In other words, Kent certainly had some of the support features provided by a care management agency -though not all, for instance, adequate arrangements for local case supervision by senior personnel with case management experience[22].

The same data for the evaluation of outcomes was collected for them as for the Thanet experiment and its replications[23]. So their results[24] have a special place in the PSSRU catalogue: they are the main source of rigorous evaluation information about PSSRU style case management left to fend for itself in the kind of alien environment and with the

217

Table 12.2
Results over one year in PSSRU community care experiments

Outcome	Social Care Models				Health/social care models	
	Thanet	Gateshead	Sheppey	Tonbridge	Gateshead	Darlington[a]
Location						
Difference in per cent in own home (E-C)	+35	+27	+18	+15	+35	+54
Difference in per cent in institutions (C-E)	+16	+35	+10	+15	+46	+85
Client morale: probability of difference in group means arising by chance						
Overall morale	.001	.08	ns	ns	na	.04
Satisfaction with life development	.002	.05	ns	.06	na	ns
Depressed mood	.007	.01	.01	.05	na	.006
Quality of client care						
Need for extra care	.025[b]	.001	.01[g]	.001[g]	na	.001
Burden on carers						
Expressed burden	.03	.05	ns	.07	na	c
Strain	.09	.001	ns	ns	na	c
Mental health problems	.09	.001	ns	ns	na	c
Costs of SSD and NHS over period						
Cost saving (per cent)	+3[dh]	-68[deh]	-18[ch]	+20[dh]	+4[d]	+6[cd]
		+3[df]	0[dh]	+36[d]		

Sources: Davies, et al (1990), Davies and Challis (1986): Challis et al (1988, 1989).

Notes:

a	Over 6 months not 1 year	e	Inner city
b	Lowest significance level for any aspect	f	Other areas
c	Indicator differences complicate comparisons	g	Costs over the year
d	Opportunity costs with 5 per cent discount rate in Thanet, revenue costs with capital allowance for hospitals in Gateshead, and revenue costs in Darlington	h	Costs per week in the scheme
		na	Not available

218

small amount of protection and support which we can expect to be typical of standard implementations in the mid1990s. Despite small numbers, Table 12.2 shows them to have been successful[25].

So the PSSRU social care model worked with beneficial results when introduced as part of the standard range of services.

1. The kinds of improvement give the clients the most important of choices - to be cared for at home in circumstances in which they would otherwise be admitted to institutions although not wishing it, and, indeed, of remaining at home until death or shortly before.

2. In most projects and programmes, principal informal carers in the case managed contexts expressed views which implied that in most ways they felt better off though they undertook the caring tasks for longer, and in hardly any respects did their statements imply that they felt themselves to be worse off.

3. These effects were evident in the standard programmes in Sheppey and Tonbridge as well as the more protected experiments. The circumstances of these standard programmes were less auspicious than most of the pilot/demonstration projects now being launched; and arguably less auspicious than attempts to apply similar models over entire authorities.

2.2 Case management input and the impacts of home care services

Evaluations have not assessed the impact of case management itself, but the impact of programmes which embody case management[26]. What therefore can we make of the contribution of the case management itself[27]?

To separate out the contribution of case management, we must return to basic theory. Exactly how does case management with the authority and influence to secure more subtle, equitable and efficient responses to clients needs and wishes work?

2.2.1 Theory

The starting point is that 'marginal productivities' of case management and other inputs vary. Therefore, reflecting the first order conditions for optimisation, managers must seek to equalise the ratios of inputs of case management and other inputs to their relative prices if they are to make the best use of resources (Henderson and Quandt, 1980, p. 76).

The most general postulate of case management argument is that there are ranges of case management inputs and inputs of the other resources consumed by community based care, over which an increase in the inputs of case management can decrease the costs of beneficial outcomes enough to make increasing inputs of home care worth while. It follows that under some circumstances, the inputs of case management reduces the costs of outcomes obtained from other community based services.

The argument is slightly more complicated.

1. Case management is not primarily an input which by itself produces outcomes, though there are some which are possibly produced more by it than by other inputs[28]. Case management works mainly by influencing and mixing other inputs in ways which reduce the costs of outcomes to public funds, though the marginal productivity of other home care services also reflects factors outside the control of the case managers.

2. The marginal productivity curves for case management inputs and for other home care services depend on one another.

Diagram 12a shows the postulated shapes of the productivity curves for case management inputs (given the level of other inputs) and other community service inputs (given the level of case management inputs)[29].

Community: postulated relationships

The first part of Diagram 12a suggests a likely shape for the relationship between the level of inputs of case management and the highest common factor of nearly all case management evaluations, the duration of stay at home ('HOMEDUR') rather than in some form of residential care. At very low levels of input of case management, additions might increase the probability of admission to institutions for long term care for some user groups. The reason is that at extremely low levels, it is often the case that no one manages the careful work needed in some contexts to help persons to make an appropriate choice to enter a home, and to help in subsequent processes. But in general, the greater the case management input, the more the impact of the home care services on duration of stay at home. It is not necessary to

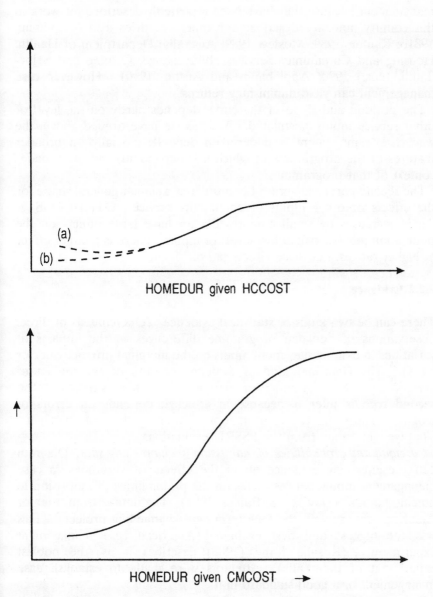

Diagram 12a: Care management inputs, other costs of community based social and community health services, and average duration of stay in the community: postulated relationships

describe the processes in entrepreneurial and user focused case management because they have been repeatedly described for work in this country, and are described for other countries also (Goodman, 1981b; Kanter, 1989; Moxley, 1989; Australia: Department of Health, Housing and Community Services, 1992; Howe, Ozanne and Selby-Smith, (eds.) 1990; Applebaum and Austin, 1990). However case management can yield diminishing returns.

The position and slope of the curve depends partly on the level of other service inputs postulated. Also, as we have argued above, the way case management is undertaken depends crucially on broader features of the programme of which it is dependent, and the broader context of that programme.

The second part of Diagram 12a postulates a similar general shape for the effects of other inputs of community services, OTHHCCOSTS. Again increases by small amounts do not have large effects on the population most at risk at low levels of inputs. There is a larger effect at higher ranges, but these effects tail off[30].

2.2.2 Evidence

There can be two kinds of statistical evidence. (One consists of direct observations of between programme differences in the impacts of variations in case management inputs on the marginal productivities or costs). The (inferior) kind of evidence consists of the impact of variations within programmes on marginal productivities or costs. The second type is inferior because in effect it depends on errors of judgment and other causes of suboptimisation by the case managers. That we can obtain from the PSSRU evaluations.

Caseload and probabilities of admission in channelling sites. Diagram 12b presents new evidence about the effects of variations in case management inputs between sites on the probabilities of admission to nursing homes[31] (Davies and Baines, 1993). The data is from a major American experiment, the long term care channelling project[32]. This was the biggest and best evaluated American case management experiment. (Rosalie Kane (1988) describes it as 'the noblest experiment of them all'.) Attempts were made to establish case management of a good standard in it.

Diagram 12b shows the results of an analysis to test the hypothesis that the more successful sites would have lower average case management inputs; that is, higher case management case loads. The criterion of success taken was based on differences between actual monthly admissions to nursing home case and the probabilities in each

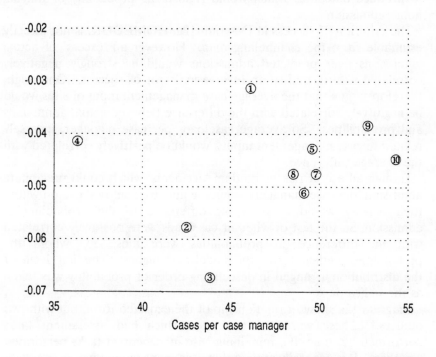

Notes
Key to sites:

1	Miami	2	Eastern Kentucky	3	Southern Maine
4	Baltimore	5	Greater Lynn	6	Middlesex County
7	Rensselaar County	8	Cleveland	9	Philadelphia
10	Houston				

Indicator = $-0.128 + (0.002 \times caseload) + (0.026 \times site\ dummy)$
Standard error: $\{0.016\}$ $\{0.0003\}$ $\{0.004\}$
adj. $R^2 = .80$ $p = < .005$ $df = 7$

Diagram 12b: Nursing home admission and caseload size for channelling sites

month of admission predicted from a model estimated from the channeling set by Davies and Baines (1993). The criterion focused on those for whom one would expect the case manager to be working in to produce outcomes which would reduce the probability of nursing home admission.

The criterion of success in Diagram 12a, HOMEDUR, is not directly estimable from the channelling data. However an 'excess' of actual admissions over predicted admissions would be strongly negatively correlated with it, and so an **inverse** indicator of success. One might therefore argue that the average case management input of sites would be **negatively** correlated with the difference between actual admissions and probabilities. So average caseloads per case manager, inversely related to case management inputs, would be **positively** correlated with the average difference.

Though all are at risk of random 'accidents' which could precipitate admission, the case managers would be able to identify those on whom their activity would make a big difference to the probability of admission. So the test of whether caseloads were positively correlated with the difference in probabilities were those for whom the probabilities predicted from the model were highest. The first decile of the distribution arranged in descending order of probability was taken as the indicator.

Diagram 12a shows a relationship of the expected form, but with two outliers. These were the two sites which had assessment tasks performed by some, the remaining case management tasks performed by others. It is generally argued that case management works best with continuity in case management responsibility. Case management theory stresses the interdependence of assessment and care planning, assessment as a continually repeated - if not continuous - process (Davies, 1992c, inset 1). So a model was estimated with the first decile difference between outcome and the estimated probability for the first decile case in the site as dependent variable, and site case management caseloads and a dummy variable denoting either Baltimore or Miami as the independent variables. The predictions were strongly supported by the model, which fitted well and yielded high significance for each coefficient.

Case management costs and the costs of outputs of other home care services in Sheppey: The postulated relationship may be more weakly seen in relationships within projects. Decisions about the allocations of resources are made in circumstances of uncertainty. Even when there are the incentives to optimise that are built into the PSSRU models, there will be considerable random errors. These random errors cause some to have more case management input than would make the best use of resources, some less. So we may be able to see the relationships we seek within projects. However, the more successful the response to the incentives to optimise, the weaker the effects are likely to be.

The models have so far been computed only for the Sheppey programme[33]. Consider the results of the model in Table 12.3[34].

The model forms predict the three forms of costs of case managed services. Two are elements of case management costs (CMCOSTS): those due to the number of 'transactions' undertaken (visits to the client, meetings with other kinds of worker, 'Transactional CMC'), and those due to instability and change in the client's circumstances ('Volatility and Change CMC'). The third is 'OTHHCCOSTS', the costs of other community based services. Each of these endogenous variables is predicted in its own equation. The two case management cost variables are predictors in the equation for other home care costs[35]. 2SLS was used to remove correlations among residuals, and the equations appropriately 'identified'.

The most important result is that one of the case management costs does have clear negative effect on other costs of community based care. The analysis shows that it is some forms of case management activity - in Sheppey, activity in response to the volatility and change in needs related circumstances - which most clearly reduce the inputs from other home care services required to produce the outcomes. Both the number of case management transactions and much of the other home care service costs were to some degree mutually determined by client characteristics.

The table shows other interesting relationships:

- There are clear and straightforward relationships between spending on community services and some important outcomes: the greater the expenditure, the better the outcomes, given other influences. When case managers accidentally breach the principle of equity with respect to outcomes at a given need by relatively over- or under providing resources to cases, the additional resources improved important outcomes for the lucky clients[36].
- Likewise the equations for case management costs make good sense. For instance, the inputs affect morale of clients, and affect clients perceptions of the practical effects of caring.

So from this test, too, there is evidence that there are ranges over which increased case management inputs improves the benefits from other home care expenditures.

Table 12.3
The effects of case management on the costs of outcomes in Sheppey

Predictors	Transactional CMC	Volatility and change CMC	OTHHCCOSTS
Endogenous CMC			
Transactional	–	–	2.30***
Volatility & Change CMC	–	–	-4.69****
Output			
Morale	.0141**	.00569*	.163****
Quality of care (General Health)[2]		.428****	3.90.10**
Decreased confusion/disorientation			
HOMEDUR		.0157***	.102****
Practical and social effects of caring			.142***
Quasi-inputs			
Severe arthritis			16.21***
Giddiness		-1.38****	
Urinary incontinence	1.45****	.785***	
Confusion		-.361**	
Depressed mood			-8.87**
Female	1.79****		
Age		.0337**	
Lives alone	3.49****	-.702*	
Recent Bereavement	.435****	-.164***	
Initial quality of care		-.0337**	
Total weekly contacts		-1.15****	
Practical and social effects of caring			
Constant	-14.75***	3.47****	-39.41***
Adjusted R^2	.73	.73	.89
Significance of R^2	<.000	<.000	<.000

Significance levels * 10% level ** 5% level *** 1% level **** .1% level

226

3. Conclusions

David Hunter and his colleagues (1992) concluded their article by arguing that it is necessary to suspend 'technical politics', the application of policies already operating: 'breakthrough politics' in the form of a 'major new initiative' presaging substantial change are necessary. The evidence presented above suggests rather that it is necessary to add breakthrough to technical politics.

The first part of the chapter showed ways in which what the breakthrough politics should deliver would have to go beyond what Hunter et al had in mind: a new mechanism for financing the needs of persons trapped in the chasm between the incompatible principles of health and community financing; the extension of policy to cover independent insurance related mechanisms for persons not eligible for state benefits on the grounds of poverty; the encouragement of public private partnership in the development of mechanisms for financing the lower unit cost but extended consumption of home care; and perhaps more radical and widespread reform of local government in some areas than the Boundary Commission is now undertaking.

Evidence in the second part of the chapter suggests that there is much mileage left in technical politics, if by that we mean the careful working through of policies which are already articulated. The ultimate criteria of success are about the quality of life and care, equity, choice and the like, and the need to get every ounce of welfare from public funds. The performance of core tasks of case management greatly influences success by these criteria. Therefore we have presented new evidence that within existing structures, models for achieving the better performance of the tasks hold real promise. The evidence is in one way more encouraging than what has hitherto been published, because it draws on programmes whose contexts were less auspicious than the good implementation of current policy could expect.

However we can all agree that the implementation of the new policy has hardly started, and that the changes which will flow from that implementation itself will be pervasive. But most important, we can agree that there are more fundamental policy changes necessary if we are to work through the full implications for the long run of the ideas of the 1980s. This is not the time for academics to lose themselves in making the best of existing policies. Above all, in technical as in breakthrough politics, in making something of existing frameworks as well as in making big changes in those frameworks themselves, we shall have to think long.

Notes

1. Unfortunately, what is no doubt a printing error in the Committee's report caused the reference not to be printed, depriving the reader of the chance to read Sir Roy's comments in full.

2. The problem is the old one. We can describe service shortfalls by current expectations and obvious failures to provide services to cases in dire need. We can estimate numbers with various characteristics and the amounts of service they get, though even in principle it is trickier to measure underconsumption than we used to think (Duclos, 1992). What we cannot yet do is definitively to state that the total flow of funds is adequate were one to assume the most efficient choice of means in achieving adequate care defined in terms of equity and outcomes. Hence the importance of working towards concrete, measurable, and monitored standards of performance covering access and care character (Statham and Harding, 1993).

3. Of course, there are reservations about features of the drafting. And of course, there are useful things there in the academic literature whose implications were not incorporated where they might have been useful. However the quantity and intellectual quality of DH comment and guidance was transformed compared with earlier periods. The DH appeared to have acquired a quite new sense of purpose. At that time, the quantity, focus, innovativeness and quality of the flow overtook any other country whose long-term care policy-making I have been following.

4. Misleadingly, because one of the mechanisms whose departure they lament provided cash or service only on the basis of professional (and partly subjective) assessments of need. What they are lamenting is not the loss of an entitlement but full funding from national taxes.

5. It is of course unfair to nit-pick about the precise formulation of a brief article put together by persons with quite different perspectives, whose aims are to raise disquieting issues with a wider public. But they do suggest the problem to be that the system will be 'rationed on the basis of need, with matching resources to needs' the task of local authority workers. That, a

reader might infer they are suggesting, is what is 'at odds with the rhetoric of consumer choice and empowerment'.

Indeed, the reader might infer two more propositions: (i) that they regret the end of two of the powerful entitlement elements of our current arrangements for long-term care financing, and (ii) that there are no other entitlement elements in these arrangements.

I do not believe that those authors would seriously argue in favour of either proposition.

(i) The Attendance Allowance is still an important cash benefit if not fully a non-discretionary entitlement element in the system. There are others like the ICA.

(ii) The replaced social security entitlement is the benefit which allowed persons to enter residential care without so much as access to brokerage help and advice based on expert assessment. Although it provided a safety valve, it caused gross distortions about which we all know. The health finance was above all used to pay for accommodation in long-stay hospitals. The accommodation may have been free of charge, but it generally provided an unsatisfactory way of life despite its high cost. Of course, health authorities are replacing long-stay hospital with nursing home care, and better matching and quality control might be improved. But can one imagine that there could be other than more of the problems of cost-shifting with two types of agency commissioning long-term residential care for persons of low income, each with financing mechanisms based on incompatible principles?

6. One has only to look at the way in which so much of the effort and frustration of the American system of long-term care simply reflects the basic structure of the Medicaid programme: a basic framework which historians tell us was almost an afterthought, the donkey's tail in Bruce Vladeck's metaphor (Feder, 1977; Vladeck, 1979). The distorting effects of Medicaid are surely a reason why much American case management systems so often act in ways which do not further the achievement of the higher goals of long-term care policy; why in practice it turns out to be mainly a device for making the best of a structure without a universal home care benefit in a system whose fragmentation has

.been reinforced by the insurance assumptions which carried over from Medicare in the early design of Medicaid.

However, organisations seem to have extraordinary cultural entropy, even when, viewed from close to, they seem to be changing with extraordinary speed. What was observed about the British SSD services for elderly persons of the mid/late eighties were the stubborn continuities (Davies, et al, 1990) observations confirmed by more recent observation. This entropy can also be seen if one compares not the same organisations over a decade, but similar organisations in different countries over that period. The magnitude of differences between organisations almost always swamp magnitudes of changes in them.

The values, expectations and modus operandi of the British field professions were a product of the idealistic 1960s, and were formed in one of the world's better financed and most consolidated systems. The expectations and modus operandi of those who work in American long-term care were the product of the extraordinarily fragmented and Medicaid-dominated system. So organisational entropy in the UK will reduce the risks of excessively sacrificing access and prevention for excessive concentration as much as it makes the adoption of more flexible and responsive methods slower. Organisational entropy in the US builds in much more serious vices.

For these reasons, we can hope for more from our reforms here than in countries with worse long-term care histories. In particular, we can hope more from intelligent arrangements for case management.

7.   Evandrou et al (1992) estimated modest price elasticities of uptake by making ingenious use of the GHS. That was a cross-section analysis. The data source made it necessary to depend on a narrow range of variables and crude indicators of need-related and other consumption-influencing. Davies et al, (1990) tested hypotheses about the effects of price on the variations in the quantity of services consumed by persons of different types and degrees of need. They did not estimate the price responsiveness of the decision whether to consume at all. The data were for a cohort followed through time, and was more extensive. Paradoxically, Davies et al, (1990) did not find price responsiveness of the quantity consumed among those consuming

some service among any need groups. The clue to the paradox was the negative income elasticity found. That and the study of the services in action suggested that allocations were primarily supplier-determined - that the user's responsiveness to price among those who continued to consume was overshadowed by the supplier's response to need-related circumstances. What inference can be made from the literature is discussed in Davies et al (1990).

8. See for contrasting models, Evans and Graham (1984) and Horrocks (1986). At one extreme, some have the substantial separation of elderly patients as the responsibility of geriatric departments, on the grounds that this helps to establish the methods and values of geriatric medicine in a protected enclave. In the Newcastle model, the geriatrician is one member of an intake team of physicians for elderly persons likely to be ambiplex. There appears to be a trend in some places towards specialisation by geriatricians in certain disease areas, and a reduction in their efforts to coordinate across medical specialities and the health/social care boundaries - though in some of the areas, there has been an attempt to countervail the problems of such a policy by appointing other generalists to achieve the required coordination. Chronological age seems to affect the reaction to many procedures only for a minority of elderly persons. The less invasive become the procedures, and the more surgery is made unnecessary, the smaller that minority is likely to be. The contrasts in models of geriatric practice is paralleled by contrasting models for the organisation of hospital psychiatry for elderly persons.

9. The long-awaited proposal by the government was put to the National Assembly on December 10, 1992 with the bill on the *fonds de solidarité vieillesse*.

It was considered again by the National Assembly on December 21, 1992 it then being in the form of amendments to the *diverses mésures d'ordre social*. The chair of the senate commission there objected to voting on it in that context. For instance, it leaned away from the creation of the multi-disciplinary field teams setting the allocation and offering case management service proposed in the Schopfin Report (1991), instead leaning on the higher level coordinating committee discussed by Boulard (1991). Until a month before, it is reported, consensus had reigned: *'il fallait saisir à bras le corps le dossier sur la prise en charge des personnes agées dépendantes'*. The Secretary of State for the Family and Elderly Persons held ready a white paper based on the Boulard and Schopflin reports, and made long-run proposals covering the whole field. However the Prime Minister was prepared to accept the proposal only with a smaller commitment of public funds. The proposal then made did not raise great enthusiasm among the deputies and interest groups. However the measure was approved as part of a bill which was held to be a vote of confidence in the government, though it could fail to go to the Senate and become law before the March elections. During the previous year, the government had raised expectations that there would be a major reform, so that the modest proposals actually made were rejected. *Le Monde* commented: *'La montagne semble avoir accouché d'une souris'*. It was feared that there would be months of conflict between the government and the departments. Nevertheless, the proposals did include the *'prestation autonomie et dépendance'*, a means-tested benefit varying with the disability of the person, not exceeding 80 per cent of the *majoration tièrce personne*, with a limitation of *récuperation pour succession* and of the *obligation alimentaire* to children and parents. (Chombeau, 1992).

10. The distribution of persons consuming mixes of social care services with high weekly costs has a powerful positive skew. That helps to make risk pooling worth while however financed.

11. There are some for whom William Laing's proposal (1990) would be completely compatible with equity and efficiency in the use of public money. The problem is that unless the multidisciplinary care management team has a presumptive right to choose the degree of care management intervention, there could be a substantial number of disastrous outcomes. It is unrealistic to deny that a substantial number of persons with the relevant need-related circumstances need this help and protection.

12. For some this should be a required condition for benefit, partly to help to define complex issues in volatile circumstances requiring continuing monitoring, partly to match resources flexibly and make possible solutions which are more equitable and efficient, partly to protect those who would otherwise be exploited. In such circumstances, assessment with the offer of

232

brokerage assistance to client decision-making which is sufficiently frequent could become indistinguishable from user-responsive case management, since case managers who face sensible caseloads have a strong incentive to use clients and carers as the case managers to the degree that the relationships and complexity of the situation allows, irrespective of the formal definition of responsibility. However, that requires a clear evidence that users could not bear it, and the willingness to accept the risk entailed.

13. Copayment would contribute to preventing the escalation of costs as long as there were far from complete coverage of the 'non-poor' by long-term care insurance, or the insurance benefits included copayment. What is important is the incentive at the margin. That requires some copayment formulae rather than others.

14. Estimated crudely by comparing the products of the number of allowances current and the benefit level. The benefit level taken to correspond with the number of allowances at the 31 March 1991 was that for the 8th April of that year.

15. Success would to a great degree depend on such fine-grained aspects as what assessment procedures are adopted and how the multidisciplinary teams are organised and led. The variety in the behaviour and outcomes of Australian Geriatric Assessment Teams is instructive (Australia: Department of Health, Housing and Community Services 1992; Brown and McCullum 1991). Examples of important matters are, for instance, issues of subjectivity, unreliability in judgements, and the response of assessment judgements to incentives in the same ways as occur in discretionary programmes. Demands for Israel's CLCTI outran the estimates of persons eligible in a way which suggests the exaggeration of need by assessors (Morginstin and Shamai, 1988). The cost escalation caused is one of the main reasons for bringing authority, responsibility and accountability for decisions about the matching of resources to needs to the client/fieldworker level in order to create good incentive structures at that level.

16. Wiener's American models illustrate the importance of funding for affordability.

17.   The increase in unit costs is greater than can be explained by trends to concentrate services on those with the most costly problems to tackle. And whereas during the 1960s, party control appeared to be the powerful determinant of variations in spending, and the variations in spending were due primarily to variations in volumes of service (Davies et al, 1971; 1972), the stability of authority control now seems to be more important and variation between areas seems to be greater with respect to unit costs than volume of service (Bebbington and Kelly, 1992). Such authorities were engaging such painful processes as changing the terms and conditions of employment by the early 1990s (Bebbington and Kelly, 1993). However, this response to the growing fiscal stringency throughout the 1980s was late, and authorities with these characteristics may find it difficult to resist the pressure to reinstate some of them when the depression ends. To evaluate that argument we should need to understand the policy and executive processes lieing behind the recent reductions in unit costs, particularly the assumptive worlds of the groups involved.

18.   To achieve a mix of voters more representative of the country as a whole might require in some areas very large authorities with conflicting interests between each of its constituent areas. In others, it may be impossible to so draw the boundaries as to achieve a more nationally representative mix.

19.   In this respect, the changes being considered in Wales are of great interest. The replacement of counties and some 30 districts by perhaps between two dozen and thirty unitary authorities might make more sense politically. However, that would yield an average size of perhaps 70 thousand persons; too small to meet the requirements of an increasingly technical CTIP agency for community care.

One consequence might be to make local authorities front-line commissioners, leaving the broader policy-making and trade and industry policy functions to the Welsh Office. (Local health and social services authorities are increasingly described by the central government as 'field agencies'.)

The machinery for that outcome could exist in England only with an unlikely outcome of British politics in the context of an EEC-encouraged move to a 'Europe of regions'. Ironically, local government with greater emphasis on government rather than the management and regulation of technocratic areas of policy might thereby have a broad enough focus to develop as a broader counterweight to the centre through the power and connections of its leading politicians, and so become more like local government in France and some other countries.

20. It is called 'case' not 'care' management here only because that is the term used in most countries.

21. The style of management was therefore more collegial than typical in social services. The case presentations, modelled on those in medical settings, were one move towards a more elaborate peer review system which it was argued in *Matching Resources to Needs* should include periodic on-site reviews by senior care managers and case visits, following and in some respects going beyond the American examples there discussed. The sessions reflected the common dilemmas of case management the world over, as reflected for instance in the research of Rosalie Kane and her associates (Kane and Illston, 1991). Another move towards that was the establishment of a group of the more esteemed case managers nicknamed 'the good and the great'. The good and the great worked with the PSSRU to develop guidance on matters like the criteria for fixing payments for helpers. The collegiality was reflected also in the training sessions to which were invited experts on areas where the case managers felt a need for greater understanding and competence. Examples of the subjects were alcoholism and paraphrenia.

These arrangements disappeared in the change which followed the adoption of the policy to develop Kent Home Care.

22. Kent was simultaneously trying to further area devolution and to develop the case management idea, and indeed, to spread it to other client groups. See for instance, the Maidstone community care project for persons with learning disabilities, and intended to incorporate the main features of the Thanet model (Haycox and Brand, 1991; Knapp et alia, 1992). It was therefore not prepared to develop the full central machinery needed to perform all the functions of a case management agency well. Most of the area managers did not show great understanding of (or enthusiasm for) the principles of the new case-managed

community care. They were content to apply for the posts provided from top-sliced headquarters funding, but to provide little support in implementing a radical reform.

23.   Others can be expected to be more useful as exemplars of excellence, laboratories whose observations can help to show how care management arrangements, knowhow, commitments and practice can be most effectively developed in the new community care. The case managers in the Thanet project not only had a period of six months based at the PSSRU, but they suffered weekly meetings in which they were interrogated and harangued by their area director, a representative of the Director of Social Services from headquarters and the principal evaluator. Additionally, they took active part in presentations on the work in various parts of the country and elsewhere. The Gateshead team were supervised by a monthly meeting involving my colleague David Challis, a quarterly review by the steering committee chaired by the author and attended by the Director of Social Services and representatives of the sponsoring agencies. Again they played a large part in the dissemination of the approach to other authorities and in national conference presentations.

24.   Analysed and written by John Chesterman and I. See Chesterman, Challis, and Davies (1993).

25.   An important difference between these two experiments and the others is the small number of cases. The other two social care models of direct case management with budgetary devolution, Gateshead and Thanet, both had substantially more cases: 32 matched pairs in Sheppey, 23 in Tonbridge, 74 in Thanet, and 90 in Gateshead. Clearly the analysis of the Sheppey and Tonbridge data can not expect to achieve statistically significant differences for any but large effects.

26.   See the detailed discussion of the nature of the evaluations of case management projects around the world in Davies (1992a), and the summary comments on the American evaluations in Davies (1992b).

27.   The answers to this question in the literature are based on observing process: the summaries of the views of the evaluation consultants in the Australian national report on the evaluation

of Community Options projects, the examples scattered through the process report of the channelling experiments, the large number of articles by those who describe features of case management practice (Applebaum and Austin, 1989; Challis and Davies, 1986a, chaps 3-6 and Davies and Challis, 1986, chaps 6-8). But these are low level generalisations. They leave us without a quantitative sense of the scale of the contribution.

28.   This is illustrated by the way in which users of the CMP appreciated the style of their treatment by advocates (misleadingly named case managers) with little influence on resources, though the users had strong reservations about the degree to which the 'case managers' actually influenced the supply of resources, as Dora Pilling (1988a, pp 3-4) showed. (The results of this and other projects in which case managers have weak authority over resources is discussed in Davies, et al, 1990, p. 335-6).

29.   Diagram 12b is the core of the formal model described in Appendix 2 of Davies (1992c). The south-east quadrant of the diagram in that appendix hypothesises the implications of two levels of case management inputs (traced through from case management loads given casemix to the costs of case management, CMCOST) for the effects of different levels of other home care costs for duration of stay at home. (The diagram is a summary of the logic connecting case management arrangements and home care costs to residential utilisation, and so back to the level of home care costs beyond which equivalent outcomes are more cost-effectively obtained. To express the logic diagrammatically, it has been necessary to reverse directions on some axes including the axes in the south-east quadrant.)

The southeast quadrant therefore has two curves corresponding to the second part of Diagram 12a. It asserts that comparing low CMCOST (for instance, as low as in standard British home care) with higher CMCOST (say at the level of the PSSRU experiments), (i) the **average** HCCOST of a level of HOMEDUR will be higher, and (ii) that the cost of an **increase of one unit** of HOMEDUR will also be higher. That is, the both the average and marginal costs of HOMEDUR will be greater with very low than with moderately high CMCOST.

The argument on which Diagram 12a is based makes some of the other assumptions made in that appendix also. Therefore the appendix should be consulted for the list of the assumptions made.

30. The relative positions and slopes of the two curves in Diagram 12a are too dependent on the case mix postulated for the geometry of the parts of the diagram to be finely drawn. However, it has been attempted to draw the diagram in such a way that with medium-high CMCOST and HCCOSTS, the relative spending on case management and other community-based services broadly correspond to the experience in the Sheppey community care programme.

31. The Davies-Baines analysis was based on a model with a general form developed by Greene, who on the basis of extensive preliminary analysis, Greene, et al, (1992) produced a model which predicted this probability from service inputs and need-related circumstances of clients (as part of an analysis of how much better the outcomes might have been had the impact mix been optimal). The Davies-Baines model was computed for experimental cases only.

The results were higher estimates of the coefficients reflecting the marginal productivities of the main home care services than yielded by Greene, implying that the additive forms used by Greene (and all the other modelling analyses and reanalyses of the channelling data known to the author) may underestimate impacts because - as is implicit in case management theory outlined above, and the argument of pp. 291-3 of Davies et al (1990) - case management works by affecting the influence of each unit of home care care resource by targeting it better and by other means.

The equation was used to predict probabilities for the experimental cases (i) assuming that the direct and indirect effects of case management were the same in all sites, and (ii) standardising for the effects on probabilities of those need-related circumstances which affected cases' probabilities. Then the average of the differences between the actual predicted probabilities were compared across the ten sites. The more effective the case management in each site either directly or indirectly (by improving the productivities of services), the lower the average difference between actual and predicted probabilities for the cases in the sites. (The standardisation procedure removed the effects of differences in the need-related circumstances of site caseloads.)

32.   There is as yet an insufficient number of case management evaluations with the requisite data for comparable programmes yet available to undertake the analysis with British data.

33.   The UK evidence so far published has been focused on the questions tackled in *Matching Resources to Needs in Community Care*, the main book about the Thanet Community Care project, not questions like that posed here.

      Similarly, the effects of case management inputs on HOMEDUR -or variables which would measure it -have not been tested in the USA, despite the range of case management programmes and the evaluation data for some of them. The reason is that the American case management evaluations were insufficiently rooted in theory about exactly how their arrangements were to impact on outcomes, resulting in designs for data collections in which case management inputs have not been carefully measured for individuals. This was so even for the long-term care channelling project, the $40m evaluation of the impact with a large collection of data about the impact of participation in the programme over one year on 4,900 cases and informal carers in ten sites from Florida and Texas to Up-State New York, Massachusetts and Maine (Carcagno et al; 1986, p. 26).

34.   See Chesterman, Challis and Davies (1993) for the definition and derivation of the variables.

35.   Various alternative forms of simultaneity were tested before this one was selected.

36.   That this was associated with a failure to optimise is no paradox. The improvements for the lucky cases reflected **technological** relationships. The suboptimisation was a failure to apply the equity principle without error or bias given the technological relationships.

Bibliography

Abel-Smith, B. and Titmuss, K. (eds.) (1987), *The Philosophy of Welfare, Selected Writings of Richard M.Titmuss*, Allen and Unwin, London.

Abrahams, R., Capitman, J., Leutz, W. and Macko, P. (1989), 'Variations in care planning practice in the Social\HMO: an exploratory study', *The Gerontologist*, 29, 6, pp. 725-736.

Adler, M. and Raab, G. (1988), 'Exit, choice and loyalty: the impact of parental choice on admission to secondary schools in Edinburgh and Dundee', *Journal of Educational Policy*, 3, pp. 155-79.

Adler, M. and Sainsbury. R. (1990), *Putting the Whole Person Concept into Practice (Parts 1 and 2)*, Department of Social Policy and Social Work, Edinburgh.

Adler, M. and Williams, R. (eds.) (1991), *The Social Implications of the Operational Strategy*, New Waverley Papers, Social Policy Series No.4, Department of Social Policy and Social Work, Edinburgh.

Age Concern (1991), *Organisation and Administration of the DSS*, mimeo.

Aglietta, M. (1979), *A Theory of Capitalist Regulation: the US Experience*, Verso, London.

Alcock, P. (1990/1991), 'The end of the line for social security: the Thatcherite restructuring of welfare', *Critical Social Policy*, Winter, pp. 88-105.

Allen, I., Hogg, D. and Peace, S. (1992), *Elderly People: Choice, Participation and Satisfaction*, PSI, London.

Andrews, K. and Jacobs, J. (1990), *Punishing the Poor*, Macmillan, London.

Anonymous. (1992a), 'Fundholders' savings expose errors', *BMA News Review*, 18, 12, p. 28.

240

Anonymous. (1992b) Headlines. *British Medical Journal,* 304 p. 400.

Anonymous. (1992c) Headlines. *British Medical Journal,* 304 p. 602.

Applebaum, R.A. and Austin, C.D. (1989), *Long-term Care Case Management,* Springer, New York.

Applebaum, R.A. and Austin, C.D. (1990), *Long Term Care Management: Design and Evaluation,* Springer, New York.

Appleby, J., Little, V., Ranade, W., Robinson, R. and McCracken, M. (1991a), *How Do We Measure Competition?* Monitoring Managed Competition Project Paper No. 2, NAHAT, Birmingham.

Appleby, J., Little, V., Ranade, W., Robinson, R. and McCracken, M. (1991b), *Implementing the Reforms: A Survey of Unit General Managers in the West Midlands Region,* Monitoring Managed Competition, Project Paper No. 5, NAHAT, Birmingham.

Association of Metropolitan Authorities (1991), *Too High a Price?* Association of Metropolitan Authorities/Local Government Information Unit, London.

Audit Commission (1986), *Making a Reality of Community Care,* HMSO, London.

Audit Commission (1992), *Community Care: Monitoring the Cascade of Change,* HMSO, London.

Australia: Department of Health, Housing and Community Services, Aged and Community Care Division (1992), 'It's your choice: national evaluation of community options projects', *Aged and Community Care Service Development and Evaluation,* Series No. 2, Australian Government Publishing Service, Canberra.

Bacon, R. and Eltis, W. (1976), *Britain's Economic Problem: Too Few Producers,* Macmillan, London.

Balbo, L. (1987), 'Crazy quilts: rethinking the welfare state debate from a woman's point of view' in Showstack Sassoon, A. (ed.), *Women and the State: the Shifting Boundaries of Public and Private,* Hutchinson, London.

Baldock, J. and Ungerson, C. (1991), '"What d'ya want if you don' want money?": a feminist critique of paid volunteering' in Maclean, M. and Groves, D. (eds.) op.cit, ch. 8.

Baldwin, S. (1985), *The Costs of Caring,* Routledge and Kegan Paul, London.

Barnett, J. (1982), *Inside the Treasury,* Andre Deutsch, London.

Barr, N. (1992), 'Economic theory and the welfare state: an interpretation', *Journal of Economic Literature,* 30, June pp. 741-803.

Barr, N. and Coulter, F. (1990), 'Social security: solution or problem?' in Hills, J. (ed.), op.cit, ch. 7.

Barr, N., Glennerster, H. and Le Grand, J. (1989), 'Working for patients - the right approach?', *Social Science and Administration*, 23, pp. 117-27.

Bartlett, W. (1991), 'Quasi-markets and contracts: a markets and hierarchies perspective on NHS reform', *Public Money and Management*, Autumn, pp. 53-61.

Bartlett, W. (1992), *Quasi-markets and Educational Reforms*, Studies in Decentralisation and Quasi-Markets working paper No. 12, SAUS, Bristol.

Bartlett, W. and Le Grand, J. (1992), *The Impact of NHS Reforms on Hospital Costs*, Studies in Decentralisation and Quasi-Markets working paper No. 8, SAUS, Bristol.

Baumol, W. (1967), 'Macroeconomics of unbalanced growth: anatomy of urban crisis', *American Economic Review*, 57, 3, pp. 415-26.

Bebbington, A.C. and Kelly, A. (1992), *Unit Costs, Policy Drift and Territorial Justice for Local Authority Personal Social Services*, Discussion Paper 799, February, PSSRU, Canterbury.

Bebbington, A.C. and Kelly, A. (1993), *Area Differences in the Cost of PSS Staff and their Relevance to Standard Spending Assessments*, Discussion Paper 898/3, PSSRU, Canterbury.

Beecham, L. (1991), 'Singlehanded GP becomes fundholder', *British Medical Journal*, 303, p. 860.

Beilharz, P. (1992), *Labour's Utopias*, Routledge, London.

Benefits Agency (1991), *Framework Document and Business Plan*.

Benefits Agency (1992), The Benefits Agency 6th July Conference Report, mimeo.

Bennett, F. and Oppenheim, C., (1991) 'A window of opportunity', unpublished paper, CPAG, London.

Berry, L. (1988), 'The rhetoric of consumerism and the exclusion of community', *Community Development Journal*, 24, 4, pp. 266-72.

Berthoud, R. and Horton, C. (1990), *The Attendance Allowance and the Costs of Caring*, Policy Studies Institute, London.

Berthoud, R., and Kempson, E. (1992), *Credit and Debt: the PSI Report*, Policy Studies Institute, London.

Bewley, C. and Glendinning, G. (1992), *Involving Disabled People in Community Care Planning*, Social Care Research Findings, No. 27, Joseph Rowntree Foundation, York.

Bosenquet, N. and Propper, C. (1991), 'Charting the grey economy in the 1990s', *Policy and Politics*, 19, 4, pp. 269-82.

Boulard, J.C. (1991), *Vivre Ensemble*, Assemble Nationale, Rapport D'Informational Depose, par la Commission des Affaires Culturelles Familiales et Sociales, France.

Bradshaw, J., and Holmes, H., (1989), *Living on the Edge - A Study of the Living Standards of Families on Benefit in Tyne and Wear*, CPAG, London.

Bradshaw, J. and Lawton, D. (1980), 'An examination of equity in the administration of the Attendance Allowance', *Policy and Politics*, 8, pp. 39-54.

Brady, J. (1987), *Living in Debt*, Birmingham Settlement Money Advice Centre, Birmingham.

Brindle, D. (1992), 'Increase in NHS funding cancelled by demands on budgets', *The Guardian*, 7 May 1992, p. 11.

Brocklehurst, J.C., Davidson, C. Moore-Smith, B. (1989), 'Interface between geriatric and general medicine' *Health Trends*, 21, pp. 48-50.

Brown, J. and McCallum, J. (1991), *Geriatric Assessment and Community Care: A Follow Up Study*, Aged Care Service Development and Evaluation Reports, 1, Department of Health, Housing and Community Services, Canberra, ACT, Australia.

Browne, L. (1990), *Survey of Local Authorities Direct Payments*, RADAR, Mimeo.

Bruce-Gardyne, Jock (1986), *Ministers and Mandarins*, Sidgwick and Jackson, London.

Bryson, A. (1989a), 'The enterprise culture and the welfare state', in Burrows, R. (ed.), (1991), *Deciphering the Enterprise Culture*, Routledge London.

Bryson, A. (1989b), 'The 80's: Decade of Poverty', *Low Pay Unit Review*, No. 1, pp. 11-14.

Buckle, J. (1986), 'A case for review: problems with Attendance Allowance procedures', *Progress*, 10, pp. 4-12.

Butler, P. (1992a), 'The hunting of the snark', *Health Service Journal*, 102, 27 August, p. 10.

Butler. P. (1992b), 'London hospitals fear cash will not prevent market chaos', *Health Service Journal*, 102, 4 June, p. 6.

Bynoe, I., Oliver, M. and Barnes, C. (1991), *Equal Rights for Disabled People: The Case for A New Law*, IPPR, London.

Byrne, D. (1987), 'Rich and Poor: The Growing Divide', in Walker, A. and Walker, C., (eds.) op.cit., ch. 4.

Carcagno, G.J., Applebaum, R., Christianson, J., Phillips, B., Thornton, C., and Will, J. (1986), *The Evaluation of the National Long-term Care Demonstration: The Planning and Operational Experience of the Channelling Projects: Volume 1* Mathematica Policy Research Inc., Princeton, New Jersey.

Caring Costs (1991), *Taking Care, Making Do*, Caring Costs.

Caring for People: Community Care in the Next Decade and Beyond, (1989), Cm 849, HMSO, London.

Caring for Quality, (1990), Department of Health, SSI Conference II, 12-13 February.

Carter N., Klein, R. and Day, P. (1992), *How Organisations Measure Success*, Routledge, London.

Challis, D. and Davies, B.P. (1986a), *Case Management in Community Care*, Gower, Aldershot.

Challis, D. and Davies, B.P. (1986b), *Case Management in Social and Health Care*, PSSRU, Canterbury.

Challis, D., Chessum, R., Chesterman, T., Luckett, R. and Woods, R. (1988), 'Community care for the frail elderly: an urban experiment', *The British Journal of Social Work*, 18, Supplement, pp. 43-54.

Challis, D., Darton, R., Johnson, L., Stone, M., Traske, K. and Wall, B. (1989), *Supporting Frail Elderly people at Home: The Darlington Community Care Project*, PSSRU, Canterbury.

Charities Aid Foundation (1990), *Charity Trends 1990*, CAF, Tonbridge.

Chesterman, J., Challis, D. and Davies, B.P. (1993), *The Costs and Welfare Outcomes of Case-Managed Community Care for the Frail Elderly in Two Routine Programmes*, PSSRU, Canterbury.

Child Poverty Action Group, (1988), *Poverty: The Facts*, CPAG, London.

Chombeau, C. (1992), 'Le projet du gouvernement sur les personnes agées dépendantes', *Le Monde*, 22 Decembre, p. 10.

Clarke, A. and McKee, M. (1992), 'The Consultant episode: an unhelpful measure', *The British Medical Journal*, 305, pp. 1307-8.

Clarke, J. (1991), *New Times and Old Enemies: Essays on Cultural Studies and America*, Harper Collins, London.

Clarke, J. and Langan, M. (1993), 'Restructuring welfare: the British welfare regime in the 1980s.' in Cochrane, A. and Clarke, J. (eds.) *Comparing Welfare States: Britain in international context*, Sage, London.

Clarke, J. and Newman, J. (1993), 'The right to manage: a second managerial revolution?' *Cultural Studies*, (forthcoming).

Clarke, J.S. (1943), 'The staff problem.' in Robson, W.A. (ed.) *Social Security*, Allen and Unwin, London.

Cm 1514 (1991) *Social Security: The Government's Expenditure Plans 1991-92 to 1993-94*, HMSO, London.

Cm 1914 (1992) *Social Security: The Government's Expenditure Plans 1992-93 to 1994-95*, HMSO, London.

Cochrane, A. (1989), 'Restructuring the state: the case of local government.' in Cochrane, A. and Anderson, J. (eds.) *Politics in Transition*, Hodder and Stoughton, London.

Cochrane, A. (1991), 'The changing state of local government: restructuring for the 1990s.' *Public Administration*, 69, pp. 281-302.

Cochrane, M., Ham, C., Heginbotham, C. and Smith, R. (1991), 'Rationing: at the cutting edge', *British Medical Journal*, 303, 6809, pp. 1039-42.

Cockburn, C. (1991), *In the Way of Women: Men's Resistance to Sex Equality in Organisations*, Macmillan, Basingstoke.

Collini, S. (1993), 'Arnold' in Thomas, K (ed.), *Victorian Thinkers*, Oxford University Press, Oxford.

Competing for Quality: Buying Better Public Services, (1991), Cm 1730, HMSO, London.

Cook, D. (1989), *Rich Law Poor Law*, Open University Press, Milton Keynes.

Cooke, A., Hirst, M. and Bradshaw, J. (1987), 'Attendance Allowance at age 16: time for review', *Child Care, Health and Development*, 13, pp. 169-80.

Cousins, C. (1990), 'The restructuring of welfare work: the introduction of general management and the contracting out of ancillary services in the NHS.' *Work, Employment and Society*, 2 June, pp. 210-228.

Coyle, D. (1992), 'Inside a crystal ball', *Independent on Sunday*, 15 November, pp. 12-14.

Craig, G. (1992a), 'Passing the buck', *Social Work Today*, 14.5.92, pp. 16-18.

Craig, G. (1992b), *Cash or Care: A Question of Choice? Cash, Community Care and User Participation*, SPRU, York.

Craig, G. (1992c), 'Managing the poorest - the Social Fund in context' in Carter, P., Jeffs, T. and Smith, M.K., (eds.) *Changing Social Work and Welfare*, Open University Press, Milton Keynes, pp. 65-80.

Craig, G. (1992d), *Replacing the Social Fund*, Joseph Rowntree Foundation/SPRU, York.

Culyer, A., Maynard, A. and Posnett, J. (eds.) (1990), *Competition in healthcare: reforming the NHS,* Macmillan, London.

Dalley, G. (ed.) (1991), *Disability and Social Policy*, Policy Studies Institute, London.

Davies, A. and Willman, J. (1991), *What next? Agencies, Departments and the Civil Service*, Constitution Paper No 5, IPPR, London.

Davies, B.P. in association with Reddin, M. (1978), *Universality, Selectivity and Effectiveness in Social Policy*, Heinemann, London.

Davies, B.P. (1986a), *American Lessons for British Policy and Research on the Long-term Elderly*, Discussion Paper 420, PSSRU, Canterbury.

Davies, B.P. (1992a), 'Case management and the social services: on breeding the best chameleons', *Generations Review*, 2, pp. 18-22.

Davies, B.P. (1992b), *Case Management, Equity & Efficiency, The International Experience*, PSSRU, Canterbury.

Davies, B.P. (1992c), *Case Management: Potential for Improving Effectiveness and Efficiency of Care to Frail Elderly Persons*, PSSRU, Canterbury.

Davies, B.P. and Baines, B. (1993), *The Effects of Case Management Inputs on the Productivities of Home Care Services*, Discussion Paper 917, PSSRU, Canterbury.

Davies, B.P. and Challis, D. (1986), *Matching Resources to Needs in Community Care*, PSSRU, Canterbury.

Davies, B.P and Goddard, M. (1987a), *The Brokerage-Only BRITSMO; The BRITSMO Concept*, Discussion Paper 554, PSSRU, Canterbury.

Davies, B.P. and Goddard, M. (1987b) *The, Insurability of the Risk of Long-Term Care*, Discussion paper 555, PSSRU, Canterbury.

Davies, B.P. and Kheradmandia, M. (1992), *On the Sensitivity of Needs Estimates to Targeting Criteria*, Discussion paper 791, PSSRU, Canterbury.

Davies, B.P., Barton, A.J., McMillan, I.S. and Williamson, V.K. (1971), *Variations in Services for the Aged*, Bell, London.

Davies, B.P., Barton, A. and McMillan, I. (1972), *Variations in Children's Services Among British Urban Authorities*, Bell, London.

Davies, B.P., Bebbington, A.C., Charnley H. and Colleagues (1990), *Resources, Needs and Outcomes in Community-Based Care: A Comparative Study of the Production of Welfare in Ten Local Authorities in England and Wales*, PSSRU Studies, Avebury, Aldershot.

Davis, K. (1986), *Developing Our Own Definitions*, British Council of Organisations of Disabled People, Mimeo.

Dawson, P. and Webb, J. (1989), 'New production arrangements: the totally flexible cage?' *Work, Employment and Society*, 3, 2, pp. 221-238.

Day, P. and Klein, R. (1991), 'Variations in budgets of fundholding practices', *British Medical Journal*, 303, pp. 168-70.

Deacon, A. (1990), 'Moral dilemmas in an age of consent', *Poverty*, 76, pp. 7-10.

Deacon, A. and Bradshaw, J. (1983), *Reserved for the Poor*, Blackwell and Robertson, Oxford.

Deakin, N. (1993), 'A future for collectivism?' in Page, R. and Baldock, J., (eds.) op.cit, ch. 2.

Department of the Environment, (1991), *Competing for Quality*, HMSO, London.

246

Department of Health (1990a), *Caring for People: Community Care in the Next Decade and Beyond, Policy Guidance*, HMSO, London.

Department of Health (1990b), *Circular (90) 1: Discharge of Patients from Hospitals*, Department of Health, London.

Department of Health/SSI (1991), *Care Management and Assessment: Summary of Practice Guidance*, HMSO, London.

Department of Health (1992), *Health and Personal Social Service Statistics for England*, HMSO, London.

Department of Social Security (1990), *The Way Ahead*, Cm 917, HMSO, London.

Department of Social Security (1993), *Social Security Statistics 1993*, HMSO, London.

DHSS (1974), *Social Security Provision for Chronically Sick and Disabled People*, HC 276, HMSO, London.

DHSS (1985), *The Reform of Social Security*, HMSO, London.

Disability Alliance (1987), *Poverty and Disability: Breaking the Link*, Disability Alliance, London.

Disability Manifesto, (1991), *An Agenda for the 1990s*, Disability Manifesto Group, London.

Donnison, D. (1982), *The Politics of Poverty*, Robertson, Oxford.

Duclos, J.Y. (1992), *The Take-up of State Benefits: An Application to Supplementary Benefits in Britain Using the FES*, STICERD, 71, LSE, London.

Dunleavy, P. (1991), *Democracy, Bureaucracy and Public Choice*, Harvester/Wheatsheaf, Hemel Hempstead.

Efficiency Unit (1988), *Improving Management in Government: The Next Steps*, HMSO, London.

Efficiency Unit (1991), *Making the Most of Next Steps: The Management of Ministers' Departments and their Executive Agencies*, HMSO, London.

Eggert, G.M., Zimmer, J.G., Jackson Hall, W. and Friedman, B. (1991), 'Case Management: A Randomized Controlled Study Comparing a Neighbourhood Team and a Centralized Individual Model', *Health Services Research*, 26 p. 4.

Ehrenreich, B. (1987), 'The new right attack on social welfare' in Block, F. et al. *The Mean Season: The Attack on the Welfare State*. Pantheon Books, New York.

Elam, G. (1991), *Consumer Research in the Department of Social Security*, Social Security Research Yearbook, Department of Social Security, HMSO, London.

Esping-Anderson, G. (1990), *The Three Worlds of Welfare Capitalism*, Polity, Cambridge.

Estes, C.L. Swann, J.H. and Associates (1993), *The Long Term Care Crisis: Elders Trapped in the No-Care Zone*, Sage, California.

Evandrou, M. (1990), *Challenging the Invisibility of Carers: Mapping Informal Care Nationally*, Working Paper WSP/49, STICERD, LSE, London.

Evandrou, M., Falkingham, J. and Glennerster, H. (1990), 'The personal social services: everyone's poor relation but nobody's baby' in Hills, J. (ed.), op.cit, ch. 6.

Evandrou, M., Falkingham, J., Le Grand, J. and Winter, D. (1992), 'Equity in health and social care', *Journal of Social Policy*, 21, pp. 489-524.

Evans, J.G. and Graham, J.M. (1984), 'Medical care of the elderly: five years on', *Journal of the Royal College of Physicians of London*, 18, pp. 18-24.

Evans, R. (1986), 'Finding the levers, finding the courage: lessons from cost containment in North America', *Journal of Health Politics, Policy and Law*, 11, 4, pp. 585-615.

Factor, H., Morgenstin, B. and Naon, D. (1991), 'Home Care Services in Israel'. in Jamieson, A. (ed.), *Home Care for Older People in Europe: A Comparison of Policies and Practices*, Oxford University Press, Oxford.

Falkingham, J., Hills, J. and Lessof, C. (1992), *William Beveridge versus Robin Hood: Redistribution Over the Life Cycle*, paper given at, 50 Years After Beveridge Conference, University of York.

Family Policy Studies Centre (1989) *Family Policy Bulletin*, Winter, FPSC, London.

Feder, J.M. (1977), *Medicare: The Politics of Federal Hospital Insurance*, Lexington Books, Lexington, Massachusetts.

Ferlie, E., Challis, D.J. and Davies, B.P. (1985), 'Innovation in the care of the elderly: the role of joint finance', in Butler, A. (ed.) *Ageing: Recent Advances and Creative Responses*, Croom Helm, London.

Finch, J. (1989), *Family Obligations and Social Change*, Polity, Oxford.

Finch, J and Groves, D (eds.) (1983), *A Labour of Love: Women, Work and Caring*, Routledge and Kegan Paul, London.

Flynn, N. (1989), 'The New Right and social policy', *Policy and Politics*, 17, 2, pp. 97-109.

Ford, J. (1990), 'Households, housing and debt', *Social Studies Review*, May.

Ford, J. (1991), *Consuming Credit, Debt and Poverty in the UK*, CPAG, London.

Forrest, R. and Murie, A. (1991), *Selling the welfare state*, Routledge, London

Fowler, N. (1991), *Ministers Decide*, Chapman, London.

Friedman, M. (1962), *Capitalism and Freedom*, Chicago University Press, Chicago.

Friedman, M. and Friedman, R. (1985), *Free to Choose*, Penguin, Harmondsworth.

Fulton Report (1968), *The Reform of the Civil Service*, HMSO, London.

Galbraith, J.K. (1992), *The Culture of Contentment*, Sinclair Stevenson, London.

Garson, B. (1988), *The Electronic Sweatshop*, Penguin, New York.

Geddes Committee (1922), *Report of the Committee on National Expenditure*, Cmd 1581, HMSO, London.

George, M. (1991), 'The high cost of helping', *Community Care*, 12.9.91, pp. 21-22.

George, M. (1992), 'Independent means', *Social Work Today*, 24.9.92, p. 14.

Gibbs, I. (1991), 'Income, capital and the cost of care in old age', *Ageing and Society*, 11 December, pp. 373-97.

Glendinning, C. (1987), *A Single Door: Social Work with the Families of Disabled Children*, Allen and Unwin, London.

Glendinning, C. (1989), 'Dependency and interdependency: the incomes of informal carers and the impact of social security', *Journal of Social Policy*, 19, 4, pp. 469-97.

Glendinning, C. (1991), 'Losing ground: social policy and disabled people in Great Britain 1980-1990', *Disability, Handicap and Society*, 6, 1, pp. 3-20.

Glendenning, C. (1992a), *The Costs of Informal Care: Looking inside the Household*, SPRU/HMSO, London.

Glendinning, C. (1992b), 'Residualism vs rights: social policy and disabled people' in Manning, N. and Page, R. op.cit, ch.6.

Glendinning, C. (1992c), 'Employment and "community care" policies for the 1990s', *Work, Employment and Society*, 6, 1, pp. 103-11.

Glendinning, C. (1992d), 'Community care and women's poverty' in Glendinning, C. and Millar, J. (eds.) *Women and Poverty in Britain: the 1990s*, Harvester/Wheatsheaf, Hemel Hempstead.

Glennerster, H. (1985), *Paying for Welfare*. Blackwell, Oxford.

Glennerster, H. (1991), 'Quasi-markets for education?', *Economic Journal*, 101, pp. 1268-276.

Glennerster, H. (1992), *Paying for Welfare: The 1990s*, Harvester Wheatsheaf, Hemel Hempstead.

Glennerster, H. and Low, W. (1990a), 'Education and the welfare state: does it add up?' in Hills, J. (ed.), op.cit, ch. 3.

Glennerster, H. and Low, W. (1990b), *Education spending projections*, Proceedings of Seminars on Medium Term Prospects for Public Expenditure, Public Finance Foundation, October.

Glennerster, H., Owens, P., and Matsaganis, M. (1992), *A Foothold for Fundholding*, King's Fund, London.

Glennerster, H., Power, A. and Travers, T. (1991), 'A new era for social policy: A new Enlightenment or a new Leviathan?' *Journal of Social Policy*, 20, 3, July, pp. 389-414.

Goldman, S. (1973), *The Developing System of Public Expenditure Management and Control*, HMSO, London.

Goldstein, H. (1991), *Assessment in Schools: An Alternative Framework*. IPPR, London.

Goldsworthy, D. (1991), *Setting up Next Steps*. HMSO, London.

Goodman, C.C. (1981a), *Natural Helping Among Older Adults*, Department of Social Work, California State University, Long Beach, California.

Goodman, C.C. (1981b), *Senior Care Action Network: Case Management Model Project Evaluation*, Department of Social Work, California State University, Long Beach, California.

Gough, I. (1979), *The Political Economy of the Welfare State*, Macmillan, London.

Graham, H (1991), 'The concept of caring in feminist research: the case of domestic service', *Sociology*, 25, 1, February, pp. 61-78.

Green, D.G. and Lucas, D. (1992), 'Private welfare in the 1990s' in Manning, N. and Page, R. (eds.) op.cit, ch. 3.

Green, H. (1988), *Informal Carers: A study carried out on behalf of the DHSS as part of the 1985 General Household Survey*, No. 15, OPCS, HMSO, London.

Greene, V.L., Lovely, M.E., Miller, M.D. and Ondrich, J.I. (1992), *Reducing Nursing Home Use Through Community Long-Term Care: An Optimization Analysis*. The Maxwell School, Syracuse University, Syracuse, New York.

Griffiths Report, (1988), *Community Care: Agenda for Action*, A report to the Secretary of State for Social Services, HMSO, London.

Hadley, J. and Langwell, K. (1991), 'Managed health care in the US: promises, evidence to date and future direction', *Health Policy*, 19, pp. 91-118.

Hadley, R. and Hatch, S. (1981), *Social Welfare and the Failure of the State*, Allen and Unwin, London.

Hall, S. (1989), *The Hard Road to Renewal*, Verso, London.

Ham, A. (1981), *Treasury Rules*, Quartet, London.

Ham, C. (1992), 'What future for the regions?' *British Medical Journal*, 305, pp. 130-131.

Ham, C. et al. (1992), 'Contract culture', *Health Studies Journal*, 102, 7 May, pp. 22-4.

Hansmann, H. (1987), 'Economic theories of non-profit organisations' in W. Powell (ed), *The Non-Profit Sector*, New Haven and London, Yale University Press.

Harding, T. (1992), *Great Expectations... and Spending on Social Services*, NISW, London.

Harrison, L. (1991), *Implementing the White Paper: Working for patients*, Studies in Decentralistion and Quasi-Markets working paper no 6, SAUS, Bristol.

Harrison, S. (1991), 'Working the markets: purchaser/provider separation in English health care', *International Journal of Health Services*, 21, 4, pp. 625-35.

'Hart' (1992), 'The Week', *British Medical Journal*, 304, p. 400.

Haycox, A. and Brand, D. (1991), *Evaluating Community Care: A Case Study of Maidstone Community Care Project*, North Western Regional Health Authority, Manchester and Social Services Inspectorate, London.

Hayden, D. (1981), *The Grand Domestic Revolution: a History of Feminist Designs for American Homes, Neighborhoods, and Cities*, MIT, Cambridge.

Healey, D. (1990), *The Time of My Life*, Penguin, Harmondsworth.

Hearn, J. (1982), 'Notes on patriarchy, professionalization and the semi-professions', *Sociology*, 16, 2, May, pp. 184-202.

Heclo, H. and Wildavsky, A. (1981), 2nd Edition, *The Private Government of Public Money*, Macmillan, London.

Henderson, J.M. and Quandt R.E. (1980), *Microeconomic Theory: A Mathematical Approach*, International Student Edition, McGraw-Hill Kogakusha Ltd., Tokyo.

Hennessy, C.H. (1989) 'Autonomy and risk: the role of client wishes in community-based long-term care', *The Gerontologist*, 29, 5, pp. 633-639.

Hennessy, P. (1989), *Whitehall*, Secker & Warburg, London.

Henwood, M. (1990a), *Community Care and Elderly People*, Family Policy Studies Centre, London.

Henwood, M. (1990b), 'Long-term care insurance: has it a future?', *Health Care UK, Policy Journals*, pp. 97-105.

Heseltine, M. (1987), *Where there's a Will*, Hutchinson, London.

Hills, J. (1987), 'What happened to spending on the welfare state?' in Walker, A. and Walker C, (eds.), op.cit., ch. 10.

Hills, J. (1988), *Changing Tax: How the Tax System Works and How to Change it*, CPAG, London.

Hills, J. (ed.) (1990), *The State of Welfare: the Welfare State in Britain from 1974*, Oxford Univerity Press, Oxford.

Hills, J. (1992), *Does Britain have a Welfare Generation?*, Welfare State Programme Discussion Paper WSP/76, LSE, London.

Hills, J. and Mullings, B. (1990), 'Housing: a decent home for all at a price within their means?' in Hills, J. (ed.), op.cit, ch. 5.

Hirschman, A. (1970), *Exit, Voice and Loyalty: Responses to Decline in Firms, Organisations and States*, Harvard University Press, Cambridge, Mass.

Hirschman, A. (1974), 'Exit, voice and loyalty: further reflections and a survey of recent contributions', *Social Science Information*, 13, pp. 7-26.

HM Treasury (1975), *Public Expenditure to 1978-79*, Cmnd 5879, HMSO, London.

HM Treasury (1976) *Public Expenditure to 1979-80*, Cmnd 6393, HMSO, London.

HM Treasury (1977) *The Government's Expenditure Plans Volume II*, Cmnd 6721-II, HMSO, London.

HM Treasury (1984) *The Next Ten Years: Public Expenditure and Taxation in to the 1990s* HMSO, London.

HM Treasury (1986), *The Management of Public Expenditure*, HMSO, London.

HM Treasury (1987), *The Government's Expenditure Plans 1987-88 to 1989-90 Volume II*, Cm 56-II, HMSO, London.

Hoggett, P. (1990), *Modernisation, Political Strategy and the Welfare State: an Organisational Perspective*, Studies in Decentralisation and Quasi-Markets working paper No. 2, SAUS, Bristol.

Hoggett, P. (1991), 'A new management in the public sector.' *Policy and Politics*, 19, 4, pp. 243-256.

Hoggett, P. and Hambleton, R. (eds.) (1987), *Decentralisation and Democracy: Localising Public Services*, SAUS Occasional Paper No. 26, SAUS, Bristol.

Hood, C. (1987), 'British administrative trends and the public choice revolution', in Lane, J.E. (ed.) *Bureaucracy and Public Choice*, Sage, London.

Horrocks, P. (l986), 'The components of a comprehensive district health service for elderly people - a personal view,' *Age and Ageing*, Vol. 15, pp. 321-342.

Horton, C and Berthoud, R (1990), *The Attendance Allowance and the Costs of Caring*, Policy Studies Institute, London.

House of Commons (1990a), Social Services Committee, Third Report, *Community Care: Funding for Local Authorities*, Session 1989-90, HC 277, HMSO, London.

House of Commons (1990b), Social Services Committee, Ninth Report, *Community Care: Social Security for Disabled People*, Session 1989-90, HC 646, HMSO, London.

House of Commons (1991a) Health Committee, First Report, *Public Expenditure on Health Services: Waiting Lists*, Session 1990-1991, HC 429-3, HMSO, London.

House of Commons (1991b), Social Security Committee, Fourth Report, *The Financing of Private Residential and Nursing Home Fees*, Vol II, Session 1990-1991, HC 421-II, HMSO, London.

House of Commons (1991c) Social Security Committee, *The Organisation and Administration of the Department of Social Security, Minutes of Evidence*, Session 1990-1991, HC 550-i, HMSO, London.

House of Commons (1991d) Treasury and Civil Security Committee, Seventh Report, *The Next Steps Initiative*, Session 1990-91, HC 496, HMSO, London.

Howe, A., Ozanne, E. and Selby-Smith, C. (eds.) (l990), *Community Care Policy and Practice: New Directions in Australia*, Monash University Press, Clayton, Victoria, Australia.

Hoyes, L. and Means, R. (1991), *Implementing the White Paper on Community Care*, Studies in Decentralisation and Quasi-Markets working paper No. 4, SAUS, Bristol.

Hoyes, L., Jeffers, S., Lart, R., Means, R. and Taylor, M. (1993), *User Empowerment and the Reform of Community Care*, SAUS, Bristol.

Hoyes, L., Means, R. and Le Grand, J. (1992), *Made to Measure? Performance Measurement and Community Care*, Occasional Paper No. 39, SAUS, Bristol.

Hudson, R. (1988), 'Labour markets and new forms of work in "old" industrial regions.' in Massey, D. and Allen, J. (eds.) *Uneven Development: Cities and Regions in Transition,* Hodder and Stoughton, London.

Hughes, D. and Dingwall, R. (1991), 'Sir Henry Maine, Joseph Stalin and the reorganisation of the National Health Service', *Journal of Social Welfare Law*, pp. 296-309.

Hulme, G. (1991), 'Expenditure on personal social services in the 1980s and 1990s', *Public Money and Management*, 11, 4, pp. 31-4.

Hunter, D., Jowell, T., Richards, H. and Westland, P. (1992), 'Stealing up on the vulnerable', *The Guardian*, June.

Hurst, J. (1991), 'Reforming health care in seven European nations', *Health Affairs*, 10, pp. 7-21.

Jack, R. (1991), 'Social Services and the Ageing Population, 1970-1990', *Social Policy and Administration*, 25, 4, pp. 284-299.

Johnson, N. (1990), *Reconstructing the Welfare State, 1980-1990*, Harvester Wheatsheaf, Hemel Hempstead.

Johnson, T. (1972), *Professions and Power*, Macmillan, London.

Jones, A. and Posnett, S. (1990), 'Giving by covenant in the UK', in Charities Aid Foundation, *Charity Trends 1990*, CAF, Tonbridge.

Judge, K. (ed.) (1980), *Pricing the Social Services*, Macmillan, London.

Judge, K. (1987), 'The British welfare state in transition', in Friedmann, R.F., Gilbert, N and Sherer, M. (eds.) *Modern Welfare States*, Wheatsheaf, Brighton.

Judge, K. and Matthews, J. (1980), *Charging for Social Care*, Allen and Unwin, London.

Kane, R.A. (1988), 'The noblest experiment of them all: learning from the national chanelling evaluation', *Health Services Research*, 23, pp. 189-198.

Kane, R.A. (1990), 'Case management: what is it anyway?' in Kane, R.A., Uiv-Wong, K. and King, C. (eds.), *Case Management: What is it Anyway?* University of Minnesota, Long-Term Care Decisions Resource Centre, Minneapolis, Minnesota.

Kane, R.L. and Illston, L.H., (1991), *Final Report on Qualitative Analysis of the Program of All-Inclusive Care for the Elderly*, (PACE), University of Minnesota School of Public Health, Minnesota.

Kane R.L., Illston, L.H. and Millar, N.A. (1992), 'Qualitative analysis of the program of all-inclusive care for the elderly (PACE), *The Gerontologist*, 32, 6, pp. 771-80.

Kanter, J. (1989), 'Clinical case management: definition, principles, components', *Hospital and Community Psychiatry*, 40, pp. 361-368.

Keith, L. (1992), 'Who cares wins? women, caring and disability', *Disability, Handicap and Society*, 7, 2, pp. 167-76.

Kestenbaum, A. (1990), *Buying Care: Choice and Control for Disabled People*, unpublished paper, Mimeo.

Kestenbaum, A. (1992), *Cash for Care*, Independent Living Fund, Nottingham.

Kiernan, K. and Wicks, M. (1990), *Family Change & Future Policy*, Family policy Studies Centre, London.

King's Fund Commission on the Future of London's Acute Health Services (1992), *London Health Care 2010*, King's Fund, London.

Klein, R. (1989), *The Politics of the NHS* (2nd edition), Longman, London.

Klein, R. and Day, P. (1991), 'Britain's health care experiment', *Health Affairs*, 10, pp. 39-59.

Klein, R. and O'Higgins, M. (eds.) (1985) *The Future of Welfare*, Blackwell, Oxford.

Knapp, M. (1989), 'Private and voluntary welfare', in McCarthy, M. (ed.), *The New Politics of Welfare*, Macmillan, London.

Knapp, M., Cambridge, P., Thomason, C., Beecham, J., Allen, C. and Darton R. (1992), *Care in the Community: Challenge and Demonstration*, Ashgate, Aldershot.

Laing, W. (1990), *Can Perestroika be Pushed Past its Limits? Empowering Elderly People in the Care Market*, Institute for Economic Affairs, London.

Laing, W. (1991a), *Empowering the Elderly*, Institute of Economic Affairs, London.

Laing, W. (1991b), *Laing's Review of Private Health Care*, Laing and Buisson, London.

Land, H. (1991), 'Time to care' in Maclean, M. and Groves, D. (eds.) op.cit, ch. 1.

Law Report (1988), 'Administration of claims for benefit complies with law', *The Independent*, 11 October 1988.

Lawson, N. (1992), *The View from No 11*, Bantam Press, London.

Layfield Committee (1976), *Local Government Finance*, Cmnd 6453. HMSO, London.

Leat, D. (1990), *For Love and Money: the Role of Payment in Encouraging the Provision of Care*, Joseph Rowntree Foundation, York.

255

Leat, D. and Gay, P. (1987), *Paying for Care*, PSI Research Report No 661, Policy Studies Institute, London.

Leat, D. with Ungerson, C. (1993), *Creating Care at the Boundaries: Issues in the Supply and Management of Domiciliary Care*, Board of Studies in Social and Public Policy, University of Kent, Canterbury.

Lee, T. (1991), *Carving Out the Cash for Schools: LMS and the New Era for schools*, Bath Social Policy Papers No. 17, University of Bath, Bath.

Le Grand, J. (1982), *The Strategy of Equality*, Allen & Unwin, London.

Le Grand, J. (1989), 'Markets, equality and welfare', in Le Grand, J. and Estrin, S. (eds.) *Market Socialism*, Oxford University Press, Oxford.

Le Grand, J. (1990), *Quasi-Markets and Social Policy*. Studies in Decentralisation and Quasi-markets, 1, SAUS, Bristol.

Le Grand, J. (1991a), *Equity and Choice: an Essay in Economics and Applied Philosophy*, Harper Collins, London.

Le Grand, J. (1991b), 'Quasi-markets and social policy', *Economic Journal*, 101, pp. 1256-267.

Le Grand, J. (1991c), 'The theory of government failure', *British Journal of Political Science*, 21, pp. 423-42.

Le Grand, J. and Bartlett, W. (eds.) (1993) *Quasi-markets and Social Policy*, Macmillan, London.

Le Grand, J., Propper, C. and Robinson, R. (1992), *The Economics of Social Problems* (3rd edition), Macmillan, London.

Le Grand, J., Winter, D. and Woolley, F. (1990) 'The National Health Service: safe in whose hands?' in Hills, J. (ed.), op cit., ch. 4.

Leibenstein, H. (1966), 'Allocative efficiency versus X efficiency', *American Economic Review*, 56, pp. 392-415.

Lewis, J. (1991), *Women and Social Action in Victorian and Edwardian England*, Edward Elgar, Aldershot.

Liddell, A. and Parston, G. (1992), 'Frozen assets', *Health Service Journal*, 102, 28 May, pp. 18-20.

Light, D. (1991), 'Observations on the NHS reforms: an American perspective', *British Medical Journal*, 303, pp. 568-70.

Likierman, A. (1988), *Public Expenditure*, Penguin, Harmondsworth.

Limb, M. (1992), 'NHS chiefs deny waiting list drive has suffered post-election breakdown', *Health Service Journal*, 102, 18 June, p. 6.

Limb, M. and Sheldon, T. (1992), 'RHAs try to mediate as contract costs soar', *Health Service Journal*, 102, 4 June, p. 4.

Lister, R. (1989), 'Social security' in McCarthy, M. (ed.) *The New Politics of Welfare*, Macmillan, pp. 104-31.

London Borough of Islington (1991), *I Know that I'm Coping if the Windows are Clean*, London Borough of Islington, mimeo.

Lowe, R. (1993), *The Welfare State in Britain since 1945*, Macmillan, London.

McConnell, C. and Taylor, M. (1988), 'Consumer action and community development', *Community Development Journal*, 23, 4, pp. 222-28.

McGlone, F. (1992), *Disability and Dependency in Old Age,* Family Policy Studies Centre, London.

McLaughlin, E (1991), *Social Security and Community Care: The case of the Invalid Care Allowance*, Department of Social Security Research Report No. 4, HMSO, London.

McLaughlin, E. (forthcoming), 'The democratic deficit: the future of British policing after 1992', *British Journal of Criminology*.

McLaughlin, E., Cochrane, A. and Clarke, J. (eds.) (forthcoming) *Managing Social Policy*, Sage, London.

Macfarlane, A. (1990), 'The right to make choices', *Community Care*, 1.11.90, pp. 11-12.

Mack, J. and Lansley, S. (1985), *Poor Britain*, Allen and Unwin, London.

Mackintosh, S., Means, R. and Leather, P. (1990), *Housing in Later Life*, SAUS Study No.4, SAUS, Bristol.

Maclean, M. and Groves, D. (eds.) (1991), *Women's Issues in Social Policy*, Routledge, London.

Mahon, A., Whitehouse, C. and Wilkin, D. (1992a), *Patient Choice and Changes to the Referral System - General Practitioners' Views*, Centre for Primary Care Research, Department of General Practice, University of Manchester, unpublished.

Mahon, A., Whitehouse, C. and Wilkin, D. (1992b), *Patient Choice and Changes to the Referral System - NHS Patients' Views*, Centre for Primary Care Research, Department of General Practice, University of Manchester, unpublished.

Malos, E (ed.) (1980), *The Politics of Housework*, Allison and Busby, London.

Manning, N. and Page, R. (eds.) (1992), *Social Policy Review 4*, SPA, Canterbury.

Marks, L. (1992), *Hospital Care at Home,* Kings Fund, London.

Martin, J., Meltzer, H. and Elliot, D. (1988), *The Prevalence of Disability Among Adults*, HMSO/OPCS, London.

Martin, J. and White, A. (1988), *The Financial Circumstances of Disabled Adults in Private Households*, HMSO/OPCS, London.

Martin, J., White, A. and Meltzer, H. (1989), *Disabled Adults: Services, Transport and Employment,* OPCS/HMSO, London.

May, A. (1992), 'Perfect purchasing', *Health Service Journal,* 102, 16 July, pp. 22-24.

Maynard, A. (1991), 'Developing the health care market', *Economic Journal,* 101, pp. 1277-1286.

Mayston, D. (1990), 'NHS resourcing: a financial and economic analysis', in Culyer, A., Maynard, A. and Posnett, J. (eds.) *Competition in Healthcare: Reforming the NHS,* Macmillan, London.

Means, R. (1992), 'The future of community care and older people in the 1990s', *Local Government Policy Making,* 18, pp. 11-16.

Means, R. and Hoyes, L. (1992), 'Needs in the Lead', *Social Work Today* 24, 15, p. 19

Means, R. and Smith, R. (1985), *The Development of Welfare Services for Elderly People,* Croom Helm, London.

Mellett, H. (1991), 'Paying for goods that were free', *Health Service Journal,* 7 January, pp. 18-19.

Millar, B. (1991), 'Broken clock in a brand new wrapping?' *Health Service Journal,* 101 (28 Feb), p. 17.

Millard, P. (1992), 'Throughput in a department of geriatric medicine: a problem of time, space and behaviour'. *Health Trends,* 24, No. 1, pp. 20-1.

Mintzberg, H. (1983), *Structure in Fives: Designing Effective Organizations.* Englewood Cliffs, N.J., Prentice Hall.

Mishra, R. (1984), *The Welfare State in Crisis,* Wheatsheaf, Brighton.

Mishra, R., (1990), *The Welfare State in Capitalist Society,* Harvester/ Wheatsheaf, Hemel Hempstead.

Moodie, M., Mizen, N., Heron, R., and MacKay, B. (1988), *The Business of Service,* The Report of the Regional Organisation Scrutiny. DSS, London.

Moody, K. (1987), 'Reagan, the business agenda and the collapse of labor,' in Miliband, R. et al, (eds.) *The Socialist Register 1987,* Merlin, London.

Morginstin, B and Shamai, N. (1988), 'Issues in planning long-term care insurance in Israel's social security system', *Social Security: Journal of Welfare and Social Security Studies* (English Edition), 30, pp. 31-48.

Morris, J. (1991), *Pride Against Prejudice,* Women's Press, London.

Morris, L.D. (1984), 'Redundancy and patterns of household finance'. *The Sociological Review,* New Series, 32, 3, August, pp. 492-523.

Moss Kanter, R. (1990), *When Giants Learn to Dance,* Unwin, London.

Moss Kanter, R. and Summers, D. (1987), 'Doing well while doing good: dilemmas of perfromance measurement in nonprofit organizations and the need for a multiple-constituency approach.' in Powell, W.W. (ed.) *The Nonprofit Sector: A Research Handbook.* Yale University Press.

Moxley, D. (1989), *The Practice of Case Management*, Sage, California.

Munday, B. (ed.) (1989), *The Crisis in Welfare*, Harvester/Wheatsheaf, Hemel Hempstead.

NACAB (1991a), *Barriers to Benefit*, National Association of Citizens Advice Bureaux, London.

NACAB (1991b), *Organisation and Administration of DSS: an examination of recent changes*, CABx evidence to the Select Committee on Social Security, mimeo.

NAHAT, (1991), *Autumn Survey of the Financial Position of Health Authorities and Trusts*, National Association of Health Authorities and Trusts, Birmingham.

NAHAT, (1992), *The Financial Survey 1992*, National Association of Health Authorities and Trusts, Birmingham.

Newcomer, R. Harrington, C. Friedlob, A. (1990), 'Social Health Maintenance Organisations: assessing their initial experience', *Health Services Research*, 25, pp. 426-454.

Newell, A. and Symons, J.S.V. (1991), 'Macroeconomic consequences of taxation in the 1980s', *Working Paper No 113 Centre for Economic Performance*, London School of Economics, London.

Newman, J. and Clarke, J. (forthcoming), 'The managerialisation of welfare.' in McLaughlin, E., Cochrane, A. and Clarke, J. (eds.) op.cit.

NHS Management Executive. (1992), *The NHS Reforms: the First Six Months*, HMSO, London.

Niskanen, W. (1971), *Bureaucracy and Representative Government.* Aldine Atherton, Chicago.

Oakley, A. (1981), *From Here to Maternity: Becoming a Mother*, Penguin, Harmondsworth,

O'Connor, J. (1973), *The Fiscal Crisis of the State*, St Martins Press, New York.

OECD, (1988) *Aging Populations: Social Policy Implications*, OECD Paris.

Office of Fair Trading (1989), *Overindebtedness*, HMSO, London.

Office of Population Censuses and Surveys (OPCS) (1990), *General Household Survey*, HMSO, London.

Oldman, C. (1991), *Paying for Care*, Joseph Rowntree Foundation, York.

Oliver, M. (1990), *The Politics of Disablement*, Macmillan, London.

Oliver, M. and Barnes, C. (1991), 'Discrimination, disability and welfare: from needs to rights', in Bynoe, I., Oliver, M. and Barnes, C., op.cit.

Page, R. and Baldock, J. (eds.) (1993) *Social Policy Review 5: The Evolving State of Welfare*, SPA, Canterbury.

Parker, R. (1976), 'Charging for the Social Services', *Journal of Social Policy*, 5, No. 4, pp. 359-373.

Parker, G. (1987), 'Making ends meet: women, credit and debt', in Glendinning, C. and Millar, J. *Women and Poverty in Britain*, Wheatsheaf, Brighton, ch. 12.

Parker, G. (1990), *With Due Care and Attention: A Review of Research on Informal Care*, 2nd Edition, Occasional Paper No. 2, Family Policy Studies Centre, London.

Paton, C. (1992), 'Firm control', *Health Service Journal*, 102, 6 August, pp. 20-22.

Patten, C. (1991), *The Times*, 3 January.

Pearson, L.F (1988), *The Architectural and Social History of Cooperative Living*, Macmillan, London.

Pearson, M., Smith, S. and Watson, S. (1988), 'Research on medium term influences on public expenditure on education', paper presented to ESRC seminar on Public Expenditure Dec 1988, Institute for Fiscal Studies, London.

Pepper Commission Final Report (1990), *Long-Term Care Policy: Where are we Going?* Gerontology Institute, University of Massachusetts, Boston.

Petchey, R. (1987), 'Health maintenance organisations: just what the doctor ordered?' *Journal of Social Policy*, 16, 4, Oct, pp. 489-507.

Petchey, R. (1989), 'Primary health care: the way forward?' in Brenton, M and Ungerson, C. (eds.), *Social Policy Review, 1988-9*, Longman, London.

Piachaud, D. (1987), 'The growth of poverty', in Walker, A. and Walker C. (eds.), op.cit, ch. 3.

Pilling, D. (1988a), *The Case Management Project: Summary of the Evaluation Report*, Department of Systems Science, City University, London.

Pilling, D. (1988b). *The Case Management Project: Report of the Evaluation*, Department of Systems Science, City University, London.

Pinch, S. (1989), 'The restructuring thesis and the study of public services.' *Environment and Planning A*, 21, pp. 905-926.

Pinker, R. (1993), 'Social Policy and adminstration in the post-Titmuss era' in Page, R. and Baldock, J. (eds.), op.cit., ch. 4.

Piore, M.J. and Sabel, C.F. (1984), *The Second Industrial Divide*. Basic Books, New York.

Pliatzky, L. (1982), *Getting and Spending*, Blackwell, Oxford.

Pliatzky, L. (1985), *Paying and Choosing*, Blackwell, Oxford.

Pliatzky, L. (1989), *The Treasury under Mrs Thatcher*, Blackwell, Oxford.

Pollitt, C. (1988), 'Beyond the managerial model: the case for broadening performance assessment in Government and the public services.' *Financial Accountability and Management*, 2, 3, pp. 155-70.

Pond, C. (1989), 'The changing distribution of income, wealth and poverty' in Hamnett, C., McDowell, L. and Satre, P., (eds.) *The Changing Social Structure*, Open University Press, Milton Keynes.

Pope, C. (1992a), 'Trouble in store: some thoughts on the management of waiting lists', *Sociology of Health and Illness*, 13, 2, pp. 193-212.

Pope, C. (1992b), 'Cutting queues or cutting corners: waiting lists and the 1990 NHS reforms', *British Medical Journal*, 305, pp. 577-79.

Power, A. (1987), *Property Before People*, Allen and Unwin, London.

Price Waterhouse (1991), *Executive Agencies Facts and Trends*, Survey Report, Price Waterhouse, London.

Propper, C. (1992), *Quasi-markets, Contracts and Quality*, Studies in Decentralisation and Quasi-Markets working paper No. 9, SAUS, Bristol.

Propper, C. and Maynard, A. (1990), 'Whither the private health care sector?' in Culyer, A., Maynard, A. and Posnett, J. (eds.), *Competition in Health Care: Reforming the NHS*, Macmillan, London.

Quam, L. (1991), 'Post-war American health care: the many costs of market failure', in McGuire, A., Fenn, P. and Mayhew, K. (eds.), *Providing Health Care*, Oxford University Press, Oxford.

Qureshi, H., Challis, D. and Davies, B. (1989), *Helpers in Case-Managed Community Care*, Gower, Aldershot.

Qureshi, H. and Walker, A. (1989), *The Caring Relationship: Elderly People and their Families*, Macmillan, London.

Radical Statistics Health Group (1992), 'NHS reforms: the first six months, proof of progress or statistical smokescreen?' *British Medical Journal*, 304, pp. 705-9.

Raison, T. (1990), *Tories and the Welfare State*, Macmillan, London.

Rawls, J. (1972), *A Theory of Justice*, Oxford University Press, Oxford.

Rayner, G. (1998a), 'HMOs in the USA and Britain: a new prospect for health care', *Social Science and Medicine*, 27, 4, pp. 305-20.

Rayner. G. (1998b), 'Should health maintenance organisations cross the Atlantic?' *Health Care UK 1988, Policy Journals*, Hermitage, Berks.

Ridley, N. (1992), *My Style of Government: the Thatcher Years*, Fontana, London.

Robinson, R. (1991a), 'Who's playing monopoly?', *The Health Service Journal*, 28, pp. 20-22.

Robinson, R. (1991b), 'Health expenditure: recent trends and prospects for the 1990s', *Public Money and Management*, 11, 4, pp. 149-62.

Room, G. (ed.), (1991), *Towards a European Welfare State?*, SAUS, Bristol.

Rose, N. (1989), *Governing the Soul: the Shaping of the Private Self*, Routledge, London.

Rose, R. and Peters, G. (1978), *Can Government go Bankrupt?*, Macmillan, London.

Ruggie, M. (1992), 'The paradox of liberal intervention: health policy and the American state', *American Journal of Sociology*, 97, 4, pp. 919-944.

Russell, N. and Whitworth, S. (1992), *Social Security Benefits Agency National Customer Survey 1991*, Report of Findings, DSS Research Report No. 10, HMSO, London.

Rustin, M. (1989), 'The politics of post-fordism: or the trouble with "New Times".' *New Left Review*, 175, pp. 54-77.

Sabin, J. (1992), '"Mind the gap": reflections of an American health maintenance organisation doctor on the new NHS', *British Medical Journal*, 305, pp. 514-516.

Sammons, P., Kysel, F. and Mortimore, P. (1983), 'Education priority indices: a new perspective', *British Educational Research Journal*, 9, 1, pp. 27-40

Sapey, B. and Hewitt, N. (1991), 'The changing context of social work practice' in Oliver, M. (ed) *Social Work: Disabled People and Disabling Environments*, Jessica Kingsley, London.

Savas, E.S. (1982), *Privatising the Public Sector: How to shrink government*, Chatham House, New Jersey.

Sayer, A. and Walker, D. (1992), *The New Social Economy: Reworking the Division of Labour*, Blackwell, Oxford.

Schmitt, J. (1992), *The Changing Structure of Male Earnings in Britain, 1974-88*, Centre for Economic Performance Working Paper No. 223, LSE, London.

Schopflin Report, (1991), *Dépendance et solidarités. Mieux aider les personnes âgées*. Rapport de la Commission Présidée par Monsieur Pierre Schopflin. Documentation Française, Paris.

Seng, C., Lessof, L. and McKee, M. (1993), 'Who's on the fiddle?' *Health Service Journal*, 103, 7 January, pp. 16-17.

Sheldon, T. (1992a) 'Shocked Tomlinson proposes new lease of life for London FHSAs, *Health Service Journal*, 102, 4 June, p. 5.

Sheldon, T. (1992b), 'Managers call for per patient funding for GPs', *Health Service Journal*, 102, 4 June, p. 8.

Shirley, I. (1990), 'New Zealand: The advance of the new right', in Taylor, I., (ed.), op.cit., ch. 14.

Sipila, J. and Levy, S. B. (forthcoming, 1993) 'Home care allowances for the frail elderly: for and against', *Journal of Sociology and Social Welfare*.

Smith, M.G. (1960), *Government in Zazzau*, Oxford University Press, Oxford.

Social Security Advisory Committee *Annual Reports*, HMSO, London.

Stacey, M. (1981), 'The division of labour revisited or overcoming the two Adams', in Abrams, P. (et al) (eds.), *Practice and Progress: British Sociology 1950-1980*, Allen and Unwin, London.

Stark, T, (1986), *The A-Z of Wealth*, The Fabian Society, London.

Statham, D. and Harding, T. (1993), 'Key Task 3, hospital discharges'. *Community Care*, January, p. 17.

Stewart, J. (1986), *The New Management of Local Government*, Allen and Unwin, London.

Stewart, J. (1993) *The New Magistracy*, European Policy Forum, London.

Sullivan, O. (1986), 'Housing movements of the divorced and separated,' *Housing Studies*, 1, 1, January, pp. 35-48.

Taylor, I. (ed.) (1990) *The Social Effects of Free Market Policies*, Harvester/Wheatsheaf, Hemel Hempstead.

Taylor, M., Hoyes, L., Lart, R. and Means, R. (1992), *User Empowerment in Community Care: Unravelling the Issues, Studies in Decentralisation and Quasi-Markets No.11*, SAUS, Bristol.

Taylor-Gooby, P. (1991), 'Attachment to the welfare state', in Jowell, R, Brook, L. and Taylor, B. (eds.), *British Social Attitudes, the 8th Report*. SCPR/Dartmouth, Aldershot.

Taylor-Gooby, P., and Papadakis, E. (1985), 'Who wants the welfare state?', *New Society*, 19/7.

Taylor-Gooby, P. and Smith, T.W. (1989), in *British Social Attitudes: Special International Report*. SCPR/ Gower, London.

Thain, C and Wright, M. (1992a), 'Planning and controlling public expenditure in the UK, Part I: the Treasury's public expenditure survey.' *Public Administration*, 70, 1, Spring, pp. 3-24.

Thain, C and Wright, M. (1992b) 'Planning and controlling public expenditure in the UK, Part II: the effects and effectiveness of the survey.' *Public Administration*, 70, 2, Summer, pp. 193-224.

Thomas, C. (forthcoming), 'Deconstructing concepts of care', *Sociology*.

Thompson, P., Lavery, M. and Curtice, J. (1990), *Short Changed by Disability*, Disability Income Group, London

Thornton, P. (1989), *Creating a Break: Home Care Relief for Elderly People and their Supporters*, Age Concern Institute of Gerontology, London.

Tinker, A. (1984), *Staying at Home: Helping Elderly People*, Department of Environment, HMSO, London.

Titmuss, R.M. (1958), *Essays on the Welfare State*, Allen and Unwin, London.

Titmuss, R.M. (1968), *Commitment to Welfare*, Allen and Unwin, London.

Titmuss, R.M. (1970), *The Gift Relationship: From Human Blood to Social Policy*, Allen and Unwin, London.

Titmuss, R. (1974), *Social Policy: an Introduction*, Allen and Unwin, London.

Tomlinson, Sir B. (1992), *Report of the Inquiry on London's Health Services, Medical Education and Research,* HMSO, London.

Townsend, P. (1964), *The Last Refuge*, Routledge and Kegan Paul, London.

Townsend, P. (1976), *Sociology and Social Policy*, Penguin, Harmondsworth.

Townsend, P. (1979), *Poverty in the UK*, Penguin, Harmondsworth.

Townsend, P. (1991), *Meaningful Statistics on Poverty 1991*, Statistical Monitoring Unit, University of Bristol, Bristol.

Trinder, C. (1990), *Pay and Public Expenditure,* proceedings of seminars on medium term prospects for public expenditure, Public Finance Foundation, London.

Tunnard, J. (1973), 'Marriage breakdown and the loss of the owner occupied home', *Roof*, 1, No. 2.

Twigg, J. and Atkin, K. (1991), *Evaluating Support to Informal Carers*, Final Report, Pt 2, Social Policy Research Unit/DHSS, 7.91, University of York.

Ungerson, C. (1987), *Policy is Personal: Sex, Gender and Informal Care*, Tavistock, London.

Ungerson, C. (1990), 'The language of care; crossing the boundaries' in Ungerson, C. (ed.), op.cit.

Ungerson, C. (ed.) (1990), *Gender and Caring: Work And Welfare in Britain and Scandinavia*, Harvester/Wheatsheaf, Hemel Hempstead.

Van de Ven, W. (1991), 'Perestrojka in the Dutch health care system', *European Economic Review*, 35, pp. 430-40.

Vladeck, B. (1979), *Unloving Care*, DC Health, Lexington, Massachusetts.

Waerness, K. (1990), 'Informal and formal care in old age', in Ungerson, C. (ed) (1990), op.cit.

Wagner, G. (1988), *Residential Care: A Positive Choice*, HMSO/NISW. London.

Walker, A. (1982), *Social Planning*, Blackwell, Oxford.

Walker, A. (1990a), 'The benefits of old age' in McEwen, E. (ed.) *Age: The Unrecognised Discrimination*, Age Concer, London.

Walker, A. (1990b) 'The economic "burden" of ageing and the prospect of intergenerational conflict', *Ageing and Society*, 10, 4, pp. 377-96.

Walker, A. (1990c), 'The strategy of inequality: poverty and income distribution in Britain 1978-89', in Taylor, I., (ed.) op.cit, ch. 2.

Walker, A. (1990d), *One Generation on: The Rising Tide of Child Poverty, 1965-1990*, CPAG, London.

Walker, A. and Walker, C. (1987), *The Growing Divide. A Social Audit 1979-1987*, CPAG, London.

Walker, A. and Walker, C. (1991), 'Disability and financial need - the failure of the social security system' in Dalley, G. (ed), op.cit, 20-56.

Walker, R. (1988), 'The financial resources of the elderly: paying your way in old age', in Baldwin, S., Parker, G. and Walker, R., (eds.) *Social Security and Community Care*, Avebury, Aldershot.

Wass, D. (1984), *Government and the Governed*, Routledge and Kegan Paul, London.

Webb, A. and Wistow, G. (1986), *Planning, Need and Scarcity: Essays on the Personal Social Services*, Allen and Unwin, London.

Weiner, J., Illston, L. and Hanley, R. (1992), *Sharing the Burden: Strategies to Promote Private Long-term Care Insurance*, Forthcoming.

Weiner, J. with Ferris, D. (1990), *GP Budget-Holding in the UK: Lessons From America*, Research Report 7, King's Fund, London.

Wilding, P. (1992), 'The public sector in the 1980s', in Manning, N. and Page, R. (eds.) op.cit, ch. 2.

Williams, A. (1988), 'The importance of quality of life in policy decisions' in Walker, S.R. and Rosser, R.M. *Quality of Life: Assessment and Application*, MTP Press.

Williams, F. (1992), 'Somewhere over the rainbow: universalism and diversity in Social Policy.' in Manning, N. and Page, R. (eds.) op.cit, ch. 11.

Williamson, O. (1975), *Markets and Hierarchies: Analysis and Antitrust Implications*, Free Press, New York.

Williamson, O. (1985), *The Economic Institutions of Capitalism*, Free Press, New York.

Wilson, G. (1991), 'Money and Independence in Old Age', paper presented to British Society of Gerontology Annual Conference, Manchester.

Wood, R. (1991), 'Care of disabled people' in Dalley, G. (ed) op.cit., pp. 199-202.

Woolhandler, S. and Himmelstein, D. (1991), 'The deteriorating administrative efficiency of the US health care system', *The New England Journal of Medicine*, 324(18), pp. 1253-1257.

Working for Patients, (1989a) Cm 555, HMSO, London.

Working for patients, (1989b), Working Papers 1-8, HMSO, London.

Yordi, C. (1990), 'Case Management in the social health maintenance organisation demonstrations', *Health Care Financing Review*, pp. 83-87.

Young, H. and Sloman, A. (1984), *'But, Chancellor'*, BBC Publications, London.

Zawadski, R.T. and Eng, C. (1988), 'Case management in capitated long-term care', *Health-Care Financing Review*, Annual Supplement, pp. 75-81.

Zook, C.J. and Moore, F.D. (1980), 'High cost users of medical care', *New England Journal of Medicine*, 302, pp. 996-1002.